Order this book online at www.trafford.com
or email orders@trafford.com

Most Trafford titles are also available at major online book retailers.

Printed in the United States of America.

ISBN: 978-1-4269-9487-6 (sc)
ISBN: 978-1-4269-9488-3 (e)

Library of Congress Control Number: 2011916236

Trafford rev. 09/26/2011

 www.trafford.com

North America & international
toll-free: 1 888 232 4444 (USA & Canada)
phone: 250 383 6864 ♦ fax: 812 355 4082

AN INTREPID TRAVELLER

Book 1

Breaking China with the Idiots Abroad

BY

MARK JACKSON

List of Chapters

List of Poems

"For all the people who worked on and with my tours in China. Thank you for the chance you gave me, the friendship and the amazing life changing experiences".

Chapter 1.

ENTER THE DRAGON

"One small step for man, one giant leap for mankind"

Neil Armstrong (Astronaut), as he set his left boot on the surface of the moon at 2:56 UTC July 21, 1969

Well, I almost didn't make it here. The girl at Heathrow was not going to let me into China because I didn't have a return flight out of the country, and that is a requirement of entering. I don't suppose it helped that I didn't look like the type of person that China would welcome with open arms. I'd tried to dye my hair a dark brown the previous night, but it hadn't really worked. The thing is; I'd been supporting a two feet high red Mohican haircut when I'd been offered the job only 5 weeks earlier. Ok. I'd not shaved the sides of my head since then, but a month's growth still made for a very odd mullet and short sides with an alternative comb-over sweeping the Mohawk from front to back. The colour was also a problem. Years of bleaching and hair abuse meant that the new dye just wouldn't take. So my hair now had an un-natural red sheen to it. As a last minute placation to the customs officials, I'd taken out all my piercings, thinking that I could put them back in once arriving in Beijing. Out went the 15 ear-rings, nose and the eye-brow. I left the ones that were lower down still in. I was counting on not getting a body search. I have been close enough to body searches to know that I don't want to get any closer. I'd unwittingly set up my old flat mate "Jack" with one a couple of years earlier and since then had been on my guard against him returning me the complement. But that is a story for later.

I said goodbye to Lindsay at the airport. Her and Mike had agreed to look after my flat whilst I was away for 18 months, then I cleared customs and got on the plane. Where was I going and what was I doing? I had just been offered a job as a Tour Leader in China. I'd spent most of the last 15 years working at Universities, running their bars, then retail and catering outlets. This was going to be a far cry from the world I was used to. How had I got this job? Well, those long summer breaks that University staff have, had allowed me to travel. I've backpacked my way around most of the globe, including a 5 week stint in China 5 years earlier. For some reason, the company I'd applied to thought this was enough to bring me over there for Leader Training. We would then spend the best part of the next 18 months taking passengers on trips around China. Over the last 5 weeks I'd tried to learn Mandarin from a CD and do some research into the country. Whilst at the same time, I had been saying goodbye to friends and family, sorting out my finances and literally, putting my house in order for what I hoped to be an 18 month contract away in China. This was not ideal preparation. The bank manager didn't understand what I was telling him and refused to extend my Halifax ATM cash card beyond the November deadline. They also wouldn't send me a credit card, as they needed to update my address, which took too long to process. I left for China with around $1000 in cash and around the same amount in a bank account that I didn't know if I could access. If Lindsay and Mike didn't come up with the rent on time, or if there were any unforeseen bills, I'd be stuffed and on the other side of the world.

I had always been interested in travel. Born a week before the first moon landing, my dad said that he watched it on the black and white T.V. with me sat on his knee, wondering what an amazing future my generation would have. At school, I was fascinated with geography books, maps, places that sounded like they were from an alien planet that conjured up the imagination. The Trans-Siberian Railway could have been a moon voyage. What I had read about different civilizations and cultures just wanted me to see them for myself. Spending the 1980's in the North of England made me question my own society, I had to experience something different. I had traveled, I had read, I had philosophised on what I knew, then, I traveled to China in 2002. This visit to China had left me in awe of the country. Of the forty or so countries I'd previously visited, China was the only one that I hadn't been able to understand. Heck, I hadn't been able to communicate or feed myself, let alone get my head around a culture of 5000 years which is just so completely different and un-westernized. The world at the beginning of the 21st Century was changing. China was moving to center stage, like being in New York in the 1920's or London in the 1880's; I was going to Beijing and Shanghai, in an age unlike any other in living memory. I had tried to gather as much information as possible about China, it is a country constantly in the news and that is the reason why I wanted to go there. What I had seen five years earlier had only scratched the surface. China was "happening" and I had the opportunity to be part of it. I listen to BBC Radio Five Live, the news channel had been full of reports about the protesters or "petitioners" at the Communist Party Annual Conference in Beijing and the way they were being treated, i.e., badly. I had a lot of concerns about going to China; I wasn't really prepared for it at all.

We left England, flying over the coast and above the clouds. I thought that they looked like whipped ice cream or a white version of the sands at Morecambe Bay. At low tide, it reveals the ripple effect that the receding waves have made on the sand. I listened to my CD of Mandarin lessons. I was actually on a flight with the Russian Women's football team, but any ideas of joining the mile high club with them would have been painful. Memories of the 1980 Olympics came flooding back, with the Soviet athletes having to undergo gender tests, let alone drug tests. Then, at Moscow, we landed in a blizzard. The passengers applauded the pilot for getting us down safely. In the airport transfer, the staff tried to get me to board a different flight, but I have a rudimentary command of the Russian language, which surprised the officials enough for them to lay off me. Already, I had a story to tell, it inspired me to jot a few lines down. I write a lot, mainly bad rhyming poetry, inspired from the days when I wanted to be a rock singer. I never quite made the grade there, but played a few gigs in my 20's around the dives of London. I still write though.

1. Racing the Blue Sky,
    14/03/07 (Plane from London to Beijing)

I'm off to the blue sky to follow my dream
Island clouds below like a 'Yes' album scene
A plane zips a line of cocaine in between
And I'm flying with the Russian women's' football team

Land-fall, cloud-fall, the kingdom falls away
To the blue of the sea and the endless high
Beyond my imagination, beyond the horizon
we're racing the blue sky, racing the blue sky

All these old words that I wrote, I said
From that old country, I've got to look ahead
As a bridge spans the islands, that look like punctuations
We're racing the blue sky, racing the blue sky

This new language on C.D. Walkman
And well known phrases that I learned in Russian
Three hours to go, then we hit Moscow
Racing the blue sky, racing the blue sky

Far above Europe
I watch the setting sun
As I fly into Asia
And the land of the Dragon
The tide has gone out over all those clouds.............

2. Moscow Transfer, 14/03/07 (Plane from Moscow to Beijing)

It's snowing
So, the red light on the wing
Reflects from the sleet
As if sheet-lightning
Creating a silhouette
Of the wing, like a shark
Death in the deep
Death in the dark

On and off flickers the vision
Glimpses of the predator
Replaced by blood red
Light from the other
Cock-pit light that flashes
First shark, then blood red
First shark, then blood red

Then shark, then blood red

Then shark, then blood red
Then shark, and blood red
'Til the wheels make touchdown
And the passengers applaud

The Controller says 'vosim'
What does that mean?
That means 'eight'
So, that's my gate
Then some official tells me
that I should be
In another queue
So, that's what I do
'Til my nerves get worse
And I re-join the first
Confused over time
But in the Beijing line
Then another official
Approaches me still
But this must be the right gate
God, I hope I'm not late

In my seat, the flight information
says we are going to Bucharest
So, I'm back pointing at my ticket again
Oh, I'd sooner rest than be distressed.

At Beijing, we landed in smog, a recurring theme in China. I asked around at the bus information desk at the airport and got pointed at a random bus, so got on. No one was speaking much English so I got out my Chinese / English dictionary to compare the Chinese characters on the notice boards with those for "train station". I had decided that if I was going to do this job as a Tour Leader, then I would have to start from the very beginning by getting myself from the airport to my hotel the way I would be expected to. No easy way out, no transfers, no taxi's, no English. If you have traveled just about anywhere else in the world, you will be greeted by English speaking taxi or tour bus at the airport. Not in China, hardly anybody speaks English, the random signage in English is never followed up by another one, so getting real information is nearly impossible and tourism is in its' infancy. You are ok if you are on one of those package deals, but otherwise it's the Lonely Planet or Rough Guide, which however helpful they are in other countries, are not much more than background reading and an overview of this vast and alien country, unconquered by western tourists.

This is where I witnessed my first of many accidents. Driving in China, certainly on anything more powerful or destructive than a bicycle, seems to still be a bit of a novelty. The drivers still weave in and out of the traffic, taking no notice of which side of the road they have to be on, presumably, just like they did in the days when they all went off to work in their thousands on identikit bicycles in identikit Mao-suits. The problem is that these days they are in cars, buses, lorries and all thinking they are the first in line to wherever they are going. The only place I've found worse was India. Here, once the driver passed an accident (and there were many), he would take his hands off the wheel to pray for the victims. God, whichever one it was, would be taking care of our safety as well. At least in godless China, there was no praying.

I found the City Central Youth Hostel relatively easy, I'd been in the area before, 5 years previously. That time I had arrived on the Trans-Siberian/Trans Mongolian railway. I'd exited the station, Rough Guide in hand and headed in the direction of where the CITS tourism building was on the map. This was my first impression of Beijing. What a surprisingly modern city it was with high rise building and a shopping arcade that wouldn't be out of place in any European city. I stopped at the road; it was an eight lane carriageway. I hadn't expected that. My experience of traveling had led me to think that a third world country such as China would not have any of these things. I was trying to figure out the scale of things, looking at my map, looking in the direction of the CITS building and assessing how to get across the road when I saw a couple of men with handcarts. They were so out of place surrounded but this modern city. I took my map over and asked them what was the best way to get to the CITS building, they didn't understand a word. One took my map, turned it up-side-down and around. He had obviously never seen a map before. All they did was gesture towards the hand cart; they wanted me to put my ruck-sac in there. I felt pretty safe, but all of a sudden I realised what a completely foreign country I was in. On the surface, it could be a modern European Capital, but these people were as unsophisticated as any peasant farmer. Not even a word of English, I was surprised, no idea what I wanted, as if they had never seen a traveler before, very surprised. At the CITS I talked to the girl behind the desk. Once again, she did not understand and had to find someone who spoke some English. This was the main tourism bureau for Beijing, I was astounded. They managed to book a hotel for me close by and gave me directions. I followed them, looking for the hotel, I can't remember what the name was, but I do remember that the building in the location that I had been given had no English signage, I asked somebody, but they didn't understand. I went back to the CITS and they confirmed that the hotel did not have an English sign, or anybody that spoke English, but they were expecting me, a foreigner. That was it. I was the sole foreigner. This was a very different country. I felt like I had set foot on another planet. This was one very big step into the unknown. This was a giant leap for me.

This time, on arrival from the bus at the train station, some "helpful" people tried to carry my bags for me, or put them in hand carts at the cost of 20 Yuan. Yes, welcome to the third world again, hassled from the moment I got off the bus. Anyway, having the body mass of somewhere between one and a half to three Chinese makes it all the more easy to swing my bag around as I put it on my shoulder, and 'unfortunately', take three of them out with one strike. They didn't bother me after that. Over the next day I met the managers of the company that I would be working for and the other 22 trainees, from all countries, all ages, all backgrounds. Our manager from the international Head Office in Australia was Hannah and she made a good impression. Her second in command in Beijing was Cathy. She had failed to reply to many of my emails before my arrival, concerning visas, the contract and just about anything else of importance. It felt like we were going to get more of the same. We met Julia, who ran the operations in Russia, Bruce "Bear" who was the "Senior Leader" in China. Li who worked in the office, who was the only Chinese girl amongst all these Australians whilst there were two other managers who had come over from Australia for the training.

Training was to start with 1 week in a classroom in the City Central Youth Hostel. Somehow, I had placed myself at the front end of the large rectangle of tables and once the managers and staff had introduced themselves, it was my turn. The first thing I said was that I was not Australian, but British, getting a few "ummms" and one "hurray" as I finished. In our training group, there were quite a lot of Aussies, including Steve, who sat next to me on the first morning and offered me a cracker with Vegemite. "Do you know what it is?" he said. I was about to go into a Rolf Harris impression, but thought better of it, I don't think they got "Cartoon Time" in Oz. Steve was around my age and with a back-ground in picture framing. He liked a drink. As we went around the table introducing ourselves I met Philip, who was still only 20 but he had just spent a year at university in China. Sheila, was on her third stint as a leader and told stories of working in Vietnam and Europe which engendered instant respect and fear at what we were about to let ourselves in for. Yes, we would often be out there with nothing but a faxed copy or rough notes telling you where you were and where you were going, often having no English speaking contacts, often in the middle of a flood or some such other natural disaster with a group of fee paying, terrified passengers who were praying that you knew what was going on.

There was a British girl, Jane who instantly latched on saying that we should stick together, as we were the only Brits. There were a couple of Chinese girls that had worked at the cooking school in Yangshuo, a destination in Southern China. One was extremely pretty, called Ting Ting. She spoke with a sort of Mid Atlantic accent which all Chinese English speakers aspire to. I soon found out had been seeing a French guy and didn't drink, so my interest in her was quickly ended. The other one from the Yangshuo cooking school that was very noisy and seemed to be fun and was called Tang. The third Chinese girl was a very quiet girl, Yu, who had worked as a local guide. There was a girl from Thailand, (soon to be known as Thai-chili) who'd worked as a leader over there before falling out with her boss, so she decided to transfer to China. Pierre was French Canadian, spoke fluent Mandarin and had worked in a number of jobs during his four years in China including bar tender and actor. He had the looks and the attitude to get away with it. He was one of those people who as soon as you meet him, you know he's going to get you into trouble, but it's going to be fun while it's happening. There were two European women Beata from Hungary and Bella who couldn't decide whether she was Spanish or French. They had both spent a lot of time in Tibet and they would be running the trips there. A younger German girl, Ada, who, it seemed, had run away to China a year earlier, hung around Beijing University with her boyfriend and now needed a job here. I was sharing a room with Jay, who was from Singapore and of Chinese decent and had been working as a guide for a number of years. He said that he wanted to get back involved with his roots, so wanted to work in China

The Americans included Janie, a woman older than myself, who had worked "in corporate" selling security software. She was a high earner and a business woman who had held her own in a man's world. Jim in his mid-twenties wanted to do the active trips, rock-climbing and the like. Lyn seemed very quiet for an American and had a background in Hotels in San Diego, whereas Sarah, was just about the opposite and argued with the service that the Chinese waitress was giving at the restaurant we visited for our first group dinner, she spoke Mandarin. Gary was also very stereotypically un-American. He was naturally a quiet guy, but said that his time here had turned him almost Chinese after spending over seven years in the country. He said that when he went back to the U.S. for days he would continue drive like a mad-man and still push in the front of queues in banks and holler at the bank teller whilst she was still serving another customer. This all has to be seen to be believed, but it is part of daily life in China. Thankfully, he said, he hadn't adopted the ubiquitous spitting habit of the Chinese and didn't spend half an hour every morning hacking up and clearing his throat. Most, if not all of these people seemed more suited to the job than I did.

I think I was in a minority of six out of 23 who did not speak more than a few basic words of Chinese. This was really going to be a steep learning curve, an up-hill struggle or whatever else you want to call it. In just over a months' time I was supposed to be taking paying customers around China. There were a couple of other experienced leaders around for us to get to know and ask advice of. Pam, an Australian woman in her fifties had lead for years and now ran the cooking school in Yangshuo, a place where most of our trips would visit in Southern China. We also met Snow, another Chinese leader who also had a bar in Yangshuo. A very good contact to have. Snow was very westernised, running the bar with her long term Australian boyfriend, Scott and she was the first Chinese that I had met who had died her hair to a sort of reddish colour. I latched onto the Mongolians, Bataar (the local representative from Mongolia) and the two girl trainees with him, Bolo and Bala, who looked so nice that you'd never expect to see them living the harsh nomadic life on the plains, wrestling with horses and living in Gerrs. However, they all knew how to drink, and along with a couple of Aussies, Yanks and the Brit we celebrated St Patrick's Day with Jameson's and Mongolian Vodka. This all got very out of hand. Considering that this was supposed to be all about making new friends and working with people from countries from all around the world with all sorts of backgrounds, I managed to argue with the British Girl, Jane about her being a Tory, and then with a Turkish girl, an experienced leader who was also in training, because I'd assumed that she'd been to Britain. She liked the same punk music that I did for heaven's sake and spoke like a Green Lanes Londoner, so it was a natural assumption. However, she hadn't because (as she said, with more than a pissed off tone in her voice) countries like Britain don't let people like her in. Her name was Esmeray and was possibly the only person in China with the sides of her head shaved and dreadlocks. Pierre was as crazy as his reputation, half dancing his way around the new arrivals rather than just circulating. He was wowing people with his drinking antics so I just had to outdo him, and whilst he was talking about snorting coke, I just got a condom out and snorted that instead. It's been a party trick of mine for some years now, ever since I saw the old Punks at the Intrepid Fox in Soho doing it. I've no idea what prompted me to think that I could do it as well, but there you go, it is now one of my party tricks and it left not only Pierre, but the rest of the onlookers including the Chinese bar men completely in awe of me.

The drinking session lasted until around 6am, with Bataar from Mongolia, Steven and Philip from Australia, Jane from the U.K. Jim from the U.S. and Pierre all sticking it out about as late as I did. I was in trouble the next day (or should that be, the next hour) in class because I was still so obviously drunk. Trying to hide beneath my note file didn't subdue the alcohol stench and being last to arrive, meant that I was at the front of the classroom again. One of my new potential managers, Bruce "Bear", mentioned that drinking was one thing that the company was watching a lot. Bruce and I just didn't hit it off; unfortunately, Bruce was supposed to be the leader acting as my trainer on my training trip at the end of the week. He was the sort of person who'd introduce himself as "Running the Vietnam and South China trips" i.e. some sort of management position, when actually, he just been leading the trips, the same as anyone else and had only just been promoted to Senior

Leader. He then went on about how many "active" trips he had done. I think the fact that he was only about 5 foot tall had something to do with this. Real "small man" syndrome. I'd certainly made an impression and not a good one. When the revised training schedule came out, I had been allocated to a different trainer.

In training we were to cover a number of topics. Accounts, cultural differences, responsible travel, Chinese history, all as well as "how to run a trip" and what to expect whilst traveling and what to expect from your group. There was a lot to take in. One of the first things that we had outlined was the contract. What was expected of us, the commitment, the dos and don'ts and what would see us getting fired. As Bruce had just said, they were watching our drinking and we were told about drugs, safety and sexual misconduct. We were allowed to have a relationship with one of the passengers, as long as it did not affect the dynamics or quality of the trip for the other people. The pay rate, although low by Western standards was good enough. Some trainees started talking about tips; I'd never expected to get tipped. We were then told that we could never take a "commission", some trainees wanting to talk more about what tips and commissions they could take. One surprise was that now we had all come to China thinking we would be signing an 18 month contract, we were now told that the Company had the intention of becoming a Chinese Limited Company and that the contract might only be for one season. This changed things a lot. I could be back in the UK in October, much sooner than I had thought and looking for a job. Would I have enough time to see all I wanted to see in China and learn Mandarin? The trainers began to relate stories of their leading days. Hannah, who was now the "big boss" had gotten a paraplegic on her first ever trip. She was with a career, but still, it's a big surprise and a tough country to get around. Others told stories of difficult passengers. Many people just can't adapt to China. They are expecting it to be like the tourist destinations that they have previously visited, catering for western tastes. But China doesn't cater for western tastes and tourism here is in its infancy. We were told that we could also just get people who were just plain stupid or demanding. Passengers would ask you what rivers were called or the village that you had just passed through or how high mountains were or what the weather would be like on the other side of China in 3 weeks' time. All of these are questions that you couldn't possibly, reasonably, be expected to know, unless the moron in your group thinks that you should know the answer to everything. Then there was the story of the passenger who was on the Essence of China trip, a trip that I would be trained on and then do my first solo trip on. Whilst staying at the monastery on Emei Mountain the monks would get up around 5am to pray. The passenger had asked the leader to tell the monks to be quiet. The leader had not done this, so, the passenger complained and put it in their feedback.

There was a lot of reading to get through and the tour company was building up a database of all things Chinese. This included subject such as Chinese emperors and dynasties and famous historical figures. This started with the semi mythological Yellow Emperor from the 5th Century B.C. Recorded Chinese history started with the first Dynasty (Xia) around 2200BC, on through the Spring and Autumn period, defined by the birth of Confucius and the spread of Taoism, on to the unification of China under Qin Shi Huang who also built the Great Wall and the Terracotta Warriors. There was the Han Dynasty, the Three Kingdoms, the Tang Dynasty with its high point of Chinese expansionism and culture and on to the invasion of Genghis Khan and his Mongolian Yuan dynasty. Then the Ming dynasty and finally the Qing dynasty who invaded from Manchuria to the North East. There was the 1911 revolution of Dr. Sun Yat Sen, the Second World War and the rise of Chairman Mao and the Communists who took power in 1949. There were information sheets on the religions, Buddhism, Confucianism, Taoism and what you might expect to find in each of the temples. A lot of this was all new to me as I could hardly tell you anything about the three religions apart from who founded them. I found out that Taoism had grown out of folk myths and superstitions which had been brought together by one Laozi, who identified "the way". An ordered universe where Ying and Yang were in balance. These, he taught, had been divided over time into an ever more complex universe and our goal was to try to balance ying and yang again. These philosophies he purportedly wrote down as he left China, riding on a black bull, heading west to find new things. Confucius was a thinker and philosopher who wrote about the relationships needed for an ordered society. His writings also covered the arts and medicine, but it was his ordered society that gained most favor with the Emperors, of successive dynasties and became the foundation for Chinese education, the examination process to become government officials and with it even Chinese thinking. Buddhism in China is a more recent introduction, coming from India via the tea trading routs around 2000 years ago. China follows the Mahayana school, or great vehicle and has incorporated other localised aspects such as Matriyama the fat "Buddha of the future" and Guan Yin, the "goddess of mercy".

There were city information sheets that gave background information and suggestions on where to take groups and where to eat. There was the Chinese calendar, with its twelve animals representing the twelve year cycle. There were the traditional festivals, of which there are many from Chinese New Year or Spring Festival, to Mid-Autumn festival with associated articles on moon cakes through to minor festivals, weddings, funerals and the coffin cleaning festival with all the associated ancestor worship that underpins all Chinese "religion". There was a paper on Chinese medicine, acupuncture and on balancing the bodies ying and yang and the five elements, which also led back to Daoism. In the Chinese calendar, depending upon which year and which 12 year cycle you were born in; you were not only an animal, but one of the five elements with influence on this animal. These elements are fire, water, air, metal and wood. Somehow, all this was starting to hang together and I could see the relationships forming between the subjects and why things were as they were in Chinese culture. I still had so much more to learn.

As an introduction to our training, we had to write an essay on a topic given to us by the managers and mine was on the Long March. I had been given this topic a month before arriving in China and as it was politics and something that I knew a little about already, I had produced a reasonable article. This I read out in front of the class. Others had produced far more interesting pieces using slides and power-point presentations. One was on Chinese weddings, which Jay had a video of from his Chinese relatives back in Singapore. Ada had an interesting piece on "smoking in China" which told us that China produced and consumed more tobacco than anywhere else in the world, over 80% of men smoked and spent over 60% of their disposable income on it. As part of the training week we also had to do an exercise with some of us acting as "leaders". On our exercise, one leader was organising bicycles to get us to the Temple of Heaven. This is a short ride, but I have already mentioned the Beijing traffic. It was also bitterly cold and it sleeted. What's more, I had not been on a bicycle in over twenty years and though "you never forget how to ride a bike", this was one hell of a re-introduction to it, amidst the chaotic swirl of the Beijing traffic and freezing sleet. When I had applied to be a tour leader, I had skipped the fact that I would have to ride bikes, or even go on a hike. The information had said that I should be able to do a 10km hike with a day pack of 5kg, but I can't remember if I had done anything like a hike in years. Most of my exercise in my twenties had been drug induced dancing in clubs. By my thirties it had amounted to the occasional shift working in the bar or the stockrooms so by the time I had tried to do a hike around Lake Baikal, on a trip, five years earlier, it was obvious that the body had seen better days. That had been my last attempt at anything strenuous. I had yet another "uphill struggle" on my hands, literally.

This was my first real experience of getting around and dealing with things in China. The previous couple of days had just been classroom, hostel bar and group dinner. Beijing can't fail to make an impression on you. It is a big city and a complex mix of old and new. Most of the six and eight lane boulevards were constructed in the last 15 years, there are modern blocks of shops lining them and there are people and vehicles everywhere. At the Temple of Heaven, Gary then acted as a guide. The first thing he did, was tell us of the time when the emperor would go to visit the Temple of Heaven, and all the streets would have to be emptied of their inhabitants, lest anyone see the God King. Then we moved into the massive complex of gardens and buildings. We didn't have too much time there, only an hour to wander the gardens and see the main pavilions. Historically, this was the place where the Emperor, during the Ming and Qing dynasties would pray to the God of Heaven. According to the Ancestry, The God of heaven had nine sons; each of them a dragon and one of these was the Emperor of China. All Emperors claim to descend from the God of Heaven. Some of us had guide books with us, others had printed information about the Temple and Gary showed us around, giving information, then giving us free time to explore and a place and time to meet up. This was going to be part of the job that I would soon be doing, although, we would usually have a local guide to do all the historical stuff and we were more there to help with the group.

The Temple of Heaven, as would only be worthy of a Temple of that name, is big. It has an area of about 2,700,000 square meters, built in 1420 A.D. and is enclosed by a long wall. The northern part within the wall is semicircular symbolising the heavens and the southern part is square symbolising the earth. For the same reasoning, the northern part is higher than the southern part. This design also reflects the ancient Chinese thinking 'The heaven is round and the earth is square'. In the architecture of the Temple of Heaven, the number nine is a recurring theme. The number nine is a "heavenly number" (and most other numbers have some significance given to them too). Nine steps up to The Circular Mound Altar, which is nine paving stones across by nine wide. Other important buildings include the Imperial Vault of Heaven and Hall of Prayer for Good Harvest. Also, there are some additional buildings like Three

Echo Stones and Echo Wall which are connected by a wide bridge called Sacred Way.

The Circular Altar has three layered terraces with white marble. During the Ming and Qing Dynasties (1368 A.D. - 1911 A.D.), the emperors would offer sacrifice to Heaven on the day of the Winter Solstice. This ceremony was to thank Heaven and hope everything would be good in the future. The Hall of Prayer for Good Harvest is a large tube like palace with circular roof and three layers of eaves, it is the symbol of Beijing and you will find this image on everything including the label on Beijing's' Yanjing beer. Inside the Hall are 28 huge posts. The four posts along the inner circle represent four seasons, the 12 posts along the middle circle represent the months; and 12 posts along the outer circle represent 12 Shichen. One Shichen is two hours and a whole day was divided into 12 Shichens. The roof is covered with black, yellow and green colored glaze representing the heavens, earth and everything on earth. Another important building in Temple of Heaven is Imperial Vault of Heaven. If you look at it from far away, it looks like a blue umbrella with gold head. The Vermilion Steps Bridge connects the Hall of Prayer for Good Harvest and the Imperial Vault of Heaven. The emperors in the past believed that they could go to heaven through this Bridge, nowadays, it is just a nice stroll for the thousands of visitors and not a one way ticket to paradise.

"Three Echo Stones" are outside of the gate of the Imperial Vault of Heaven. If you speak, or clap, facing the Vault while standing on the first stone, you will hear one echo; standing on the second and then the third stone, you will hear two and three echoes. Or somebody can hear you whisper if you stand on the East rout and somebody is listening on the west. St Paul's Cathedral has a whispering gallery built along the same principles.

We returned to the hotel and Tang from Yangshuo took over. She was supposed to organise lunch and take us to the Summer Palace. Bruce was acting as "assessor" and playing the role of a "difficult passenger", a job he did so well that he had a confused Tang in tears. Tang had taken us to a basic dumpling and noodle place by the station to eat. It was probably not the sort of place that you would choose to take your group with so many other options. It was more like a local fast food joint than anything else. Bruce played his part well. First he had said that he didn't like the food. Then he said that he was unwell and needed to go to a pharmacist. Tang was being ever attentive to her friend, not really understanding why he was asking for a burger when he surely knew that this was a local place without western food. Then she was telling him that he knew where the pharmacist was, as it was near our office. As Bruce changed personalities, trying to tell her that he didn't know because he'd never been to Beijing before, it all became too much for Tang, who then took him to the pharmacy, leaving us in the cafe. Tang had known him for over a year and couldn't understand why he was being so mean to her. Something else must have gone on in the intervening twenty minutes, as Tang came back visibly upset. This had slowed the whole day down and we were now running late. This degenerated badly and it gave very little time at the Summer Palace for Lyn to do her thing. It took a 30 minute subway journey and then taxi's to get to the Summer Palace. Lyn had handed us some information about the Summer Palace, it is a magnificent place.

Constructed in the Jin Dynasty (1115-1234), during the succeeding reign of feudal emperors; it was extended continuously. By the time of the Qing Dynasty (1644-1911), it had become a luxurious royal garden providing royal families with rest and entertainment. Like most of the gardens of Beijing, it could not elude the rampages of the Anglo-French allied force and was destroyed by fire. In 1888, Empress Dowager Cixi embezzled navy funds to reconstruct it for her own benefit, changing its name to Summer Palace. She spent most of her later years there, dealing with state affairs and entertaining. In 1900, it suffered again, being ransacked by the Eight-Power Allied

Force, a sort of "slap down" from the British, French and other European powers for the Chinese wanting to stop the opium trade in their country, have lands retuned to them and for the Qing government not being able to control rebellions against these occupying powers. If you ever managed to watch "55 days in Peking" that famous 1950's film where we get a German Ambassador to say that "God must be an Englishman" to David Niven you are along the right lines of history, but on the wrong side of the conflict. After the success of the 1911 Revolution, that deposed Henri Pu Yi, the "Last Emperor" of China, (which was also the title of another great film, in every aspect), it was opened to the public.

Composed mainly of Longevity Hill and Kunming Lake, The Summer Palace occupies an area of 294 hectares three quarters of which is water. Centered on the Tower of Buddhist Incense, the Summer Palace consists of over 3,000 structures including pavilions, towers, bridges, and covered walkways called corridors along with manmade hills, imitations of a Chinese water town and the beautifully designed Seventeen-Arch Bridge,

Once again, running very late, we only had enough time to walk through to Long Gallery, an artistic gem of a covered walkway, painted throughout. Then along the side of the lake to the Marble Boat, which, as the story goes, is a boat carved out of marble. Only a power mad Empress would dream this up and have it commissioned. As I mentioned earlier, it is a legacy of the funds that should have been spent on the Imperial Navy. The consequences of this were that the British fleet sank the Chinese fleet during the first opium war and ended up with Hong Kong as a prize. Amidst all this, a roller-coaster of new things happening, I looked up at the sunset in the pink; construction dust polluted sky and thought I was in the most wonderful place. About to live a dream in this fantasy of a world, constructed as beautifully as the Empress Dowager Cixi had constructed this amazing Summer Palace.

3. A New Page in a New Diary, 16/03/07 (Beijing)

A new page in a new diary
A new leaf, a new head
Like wiping the spots from memory
And too many stains from my bed
Women seem to do it so well
Another bad memory you lock away
But how many daemons can you fit in one hell?
How long before they break through the gate?

A new page in a new diary
And new opportunities
But there's no denying it
I'm still me
I know who I am
And who loves me
So I can write the first line
And be who I want to be

4. Red Letters in Tian An Men Square, 16/03/07 (Beijing)

The vastness of this space
Created when ten thousand people were swept away
Trapped between high noon and concrete
There is no escape, there is no shade
In this very un-natural space
This artificially created place
Designed for ego and showcase
A tomb, a portrait, an obelisk

I have that eerie sense of knowing I'm being watched
But by a thousand eyes that play act at being relaxed
Watching red letters in Tian An Men Square
Injustices on paper, held by petitioners

I am approached by a too young soldier
Who wants to see my camera

Because somewhere off in the corner
There's a scuffle with a petitioner

I hear a shout, and look around
Another person thrown to the ground
And as the crowds disperse
I see on the ground, in Tian An Men Square
Red letters, in blood on the stone
Crying for help, from anyone

So I watch, as they watch and walk on bye
They won't get involved and they won't try
Cos they're being sold a western lifestyle
But it will never give them self-control
As more factories produce more pollution
Infecting farms, rivers, the whole population
Hunting animals to the point of extinction
To provide placebos for witch doctor medicines
And women forced to have abortions
Whilst they lock up the lawyer who ask the question
Moving villages as plough-land turns to a lake
Yet another Aswan, yet another damn mistake
Whilst sending rockets to knock out satellites
Turning guns on your neighbours to show your might
Or slowly supplanting an entire nation
Modern China squeezing out the ancient traditions
Too often by force, the argument is won
Too often at the point of a gun
So, what chance is there for the petitioner
What chance is there for the world out there?

5. Living the Dream, 24 & 25 /03/07 (Beijing)

Maybe today I will go
To my Summer Gardens
Spring blossoms have replaced the snow
In my Summer Gardens
I can walk along the lake shores

Who could ask for anything more
Than my Summer Garden?

Maybe I shall build a palace
By the lake side
Have a marble ferryboat in-place
That I can ride
To my enchanted island across the water
Am I not as chosen as God's daughter
And in this dream I reside

Today I will build a temple
Upon a mountain
A new view from my private hill
Another tree lined fountain
A seventeen arched bridge across the lake
But only I can go there, my own private dreamscape
My own private heaven

I am living the dream
I stroll through the garden
As much as the Empress Queen
Created her earthly heaven
I am here, without regret
Even the rose tinted sunset
Is just the setting of the scene

Maybe I will go
To the Summer Palace once more
Or leap Tiger Gorge
Or walk the great wall
Or stroll around the Forbidden City
Or make peace with the Terracotta Army
Live the dream, live it all

Like the Empress
I am living the dream
And China unfolds
Like a map in front of me
And I can do what my heart desires
Do what I wish with my empire
And live the dreams I dream.

One other thing had occurred to me whilst I had been in Beijing. Where were all the birds? In England, in springtime, the skies would be filled with birds in flight and birdsong. On a trip to India, years earlier, I'd marveled at the trees outside my Delhi hotel being filled with birds and watched them circle into the morning sky. Beijing had no birds, even in the park which was the Summer Palace, I could see no birds. It was a couple of months later when I got an answer as to where all the birds were. The Chinese had eaten them. After the wars, the bombings then the re-construction. After the famines, the farm collectivization, consolidations and now with the massive building projects, much of the wildlife of China had been destroyed or eaten. There is a saying that the Chinese will eat anything on four legs apart from a chair and a table. This is true and I remember from my first visit being offered "Dragon and Tiger" soup, which actually contained cat and snake. The natural habitats of the wildlife had been under the plough in some areas for over 4000 years, man had changed the environment to suit his own need and animals and birds had either been brought into domestication, had been eaten, or had been killed off.

My turn as leader came that evening; however, I'd not been given any information as what to do. I found Bruce in the office and asked him. His reply was "Oh, didn't I tell you? You're supposed to lead the group to Hutong Pizza in Hou Hai". "Where the hell is that then?" I asked, well it was my job to find out, and we were supposed to be leaving in only 20 minutes, Bruce had not bothered to tell me that one either. I knew he had it in for me; he wasn't "acting" the difficult customer now.

I had a map; I am good at reading maps and reckon I can find my way about almost anywhere as long as the map is good. I've long had a fascination for cartography, reproducing maps of my home town as an adolescent and planning where to put new roads or industry or parks and better housing to make my home town of Blackburn a better place to live. Blackburn in the 1980's was in dire need of planning and investment, I later went on to complete an Urban Planning degree and post grad, but neither I nor Blackburn benefited from it. Somehow, to the amazement of myself, and most of the group, I not only got us all to Hutong Pizza, but pointed out a couple of local landmarks, the Drum and Bell towers and the historical lakes, which were constructed as waterways for trade during the Yuan Dynasty. We were there 20 minutes before any of the other groups. All those years of finding my way around foreign cities by way of a map and an innate sense of direction had actually "lead" to something useful. That night we had a party, again, which included an auction and a lot more drinking. I was sensible enough not to drink around the clock for once, taking a taxi home with some of the early birds, nondrinkers and a couple of the managers, which proved to be a very sensible option.

I was a bit surprised that we had chosen Hutong Pizza as a venue for a leader's night out. As a travel company, we are supposed to go local and get a real feel for the country, its' people, the culture and of course, the cuisine. Chinese food back home is not the same as Chinese food in China. What we get is some version of Cantonese cooking, brought over in the last century and changed beyond recognition to suit western tastes. There is no chicken fried rice, no prawn balls in sweet and sour, no beef in black bean sauce, no lemon chicken and no individual portions. The Chinese mentality is of one of sharing and so we have the Chinese Banquet. If, for example, a group of five of you is sitting around a table, you will normally order five or six dishes. These will be placed in the centre of the table, often, in the better restaurants, on a lazy-Suzy and you then share, moving the food you want from central plates to your own bowl and then eating. In the villages, you don't have a bowl; it just goes directly from central plate to mouth. It is bad manners to pass the dishes around from person to person; this is seen as being greedy. But don't worry if some of your food ends up on the table, or the floor. At the end of a Chinese meal, the floor around the table often resembles the bottom of a parrot cage and the Chinese will be shouting at each other, toasting each other with "gan bei" and chain smoking. Not what we are used to at home as civilised dining, but that is perfectly normal here in China.

Some more food and table etiquette, just to confuse you even more. Rice is a filler. If you want rice with your meal, you must ask for it over and over again, otherwise it will arrive towards the end of the meal. The people cooking for you feel that they are insulting you by not giving you enough when you ask for rice, it's one of those many cultural differences and we just don't get it. Try ordering just vegetables for a vegetarian group and you have other problems. Once again, the host will believe that he is insulting you by only giving you vegetables. This is seen as peasants' food, so they will add a little meat. This maybe a chicken stock sauce to your green vegetables or pork shavings on your fried egg with tomato dish. Don't expect tea to be served. If you ask for tea, you may be given a menu of expensive, quality teas. The Chinese mainly drink hot water and this is poured into a glass or even a flimsy plastic cup. I've never gotten over, that in a country called "China", there is little in the way of a china cup and instead, you have to negotiate burning figures and hot liquids. These days, there is a lot more beer around and you can get it in any restaurant, but don't expect it to be cold. The Chinese drink hot drinks as it is beneficial to their ying and yang where as cold drinks bring the body out of balance. Once again, the sharing thing comes into play and if you order a couple of bottles of beer, don't be surprised that they are poured out into everybody's glass who is sitting at the table, weather they have ordered or not. Just to finish off, finishing off is all over by eight or at the latest nine o clock. There is no late sitting, no waiting around and dinner usually takes less than three quarters of an hour.

I was relatively new to all this and made my first mistake, one lunch time eating with some of the other leaders, when we all decided to order 1 dish each. "My" beef dish arrived first and I tucked in, only later realising that it was for sharing. On another afternoon, I decided to try my hand at ordering. I'd been practicing my Mandarin and knew at some point I would have to give it a go, soon I would have to feed a group of paying customers. I went to the dumpling and noodle place that I'd been to with Tang on the training day, I knew the menu characters and had been practicing my pronunciation, so I ordered a beef soup and some dumplings. Dumplings or "jiaozi" are a sort of ravioli and very un-dumpling like to a man from the north of England, but that is what we call them. The waitress, who obviously speaks no English and there is no English menu to go by, was a little concerned with what I had ordered, but went away and my food soon arrived. A bowl of soup, enough to feed 3 people and a plate of 40 dumplings. Eating on your own is not normal in China, all portions are for sharing. It also took a while to get them to understand that I wanted a "coke". You would reckon that everywhere in the world, people would understand what a "coke" was, but not here. It is "ke le".

The rest of the week went well, having a couple of nights out. We went off to the bar areas of Sanlitun and Hou Hai. Five years earlier, the Sanlitun area was the main bar area. It was close to the University and Embassy area and there were a lot of westerners that frequented the place. It was a place where East met West and you could actually have a discussion about the issues in China and not just get the party line. In China, nobody discusses the three 'T''s (Taiwan, Tibet, Tian An Men Square) openly, and most know little about their countries checkered history, human rights abuses, environmental atrocities, the reality of the 1 child policy etc. The thing is that with the bars and lure of western money, the protection rackets soon got involved, then the prostitution and drugs, so in true Chinese style, they demolished all the bars. Just like that, complain all you want to, it won't get you anywhere, the government has made a decision and your favourite watering hole no longer exists. Imagine that back home, there would be an outcry; the government would be ousted within a week. Then imagine the Chinese government tanks and what they are capable of trundling down Camden High Street. This is a very different country. To their credit, they then created a new bar area in Hou Hai, around a series of lakes. This looks far prettier than the Sanlitun Street, but oh so obviously manufactured.

The area around Hou Hai Lake used to be a hutong area and part of it still is. It is in what used to be called the Royal city, the area immediately surrounding the Forbidden City and the Imperial palace. This is an area where court officials, military people, foreign ambassadors and some merchants and traders used to live. The hutongs were first created after Genghis Khan captured and burned Beijing in 1215. They comprise of a house built around a courtyard. These are located along the alleyways that are the "hutongs". There were over 5000 hutongs in the 1950's, but now, with New Chinas' modernisation, many have been demolished. When I was last here, there was a campaign by the foreigners, mainly Embassy staff, to save the hutongs as a unique part of Chinas' heritage. The government has since decided not to clear away all the hutongs, as was the original plan. Around Hou Hai, the courtyard houses have been refurbished into restaurants and bars, overlooking the lake, all sparkling with neon. It looks pretty, like a Christmas tree dressed by children would. All fairy lights and gaudy baubles

Sanlitun has now had a revival, but both it and the Hou Hai areas are now full of bars with what I could only compare to Blackpool Guest House cabaret acts playing in them. For those of you who have not experienced one of these atrocities in the name of entertainment, there will be either a solo 'artist' or 2 piece band, trying to perform middle of the road pop songs, very badly. There is no escape. On coming to China, I'm hardly here to find a Chinese version of Camden. However, I have looked and found that all references to the Beijing underground Punk movement have been deleted from the websites since December 2005

This gives me an opportunity to tell you about the internet. Firstly, to get access to the internet, you will usually have to produce your passport, for the Chinese, it's their I.D. card. From a practical point of view, everything from the in house instructions, tariff, password and screen desk top are in Chinese, so even getting onto the thing is difficult. Once you've negotiated the array of pop-ups and remembered which Chinese characters get you onto a site, you regularly find that it is unavailable, has been under repair or simply doesn't exist when you knew it did the day before. Getting onto Hotmail, MySpace etc. has been a chore and even if I get on I find that I can't retrieve messages or send items. Then, there is the environment. Internet cafes are where the youth of China spend a lot of free time, smoking, drinking, and sleeping. It's a place to really get under the skin of the people as you sit in a smoke choked dark ware-house of a place with up to 300 other users, clearing their throats and spitting, occasionally yelling out as they kill another droid or what-have-you on their computer. Because the Chinese only use the internet for games (it's a bit pointless as anything else) the keyboards aren't replaced when the letter keys are broken/worn away and the space bar is broken due to it being used as a shooting tool. This causes all sorts of problems for sending emails, as, not being a touch-typist, I can't remember where the keys are, and as the space bar doesn't work, all the words run into one. So, when you think that my emails don't make sense, now you know why.

6. The Chinese Internet, 23/03/07 (Beijing)

In the Chinese internet
You never really know what you're going to get
A keyboard with no letters on it
Surrounded by the throat-clearing, guttural, pre-spit
And cigarette smog
The bloke in the next cubical is sleeping like a log

On either side they bash the keyboard in each personal fight
And that's why all the words join up when I try to write
My email may as well be Pinyin

For all the time it's takin' and all the sense I'm makin'

Then again, half the stuff I send
Just bounces back, even though it's to a friend
Maybe his address in random letters and numbers
Is some horrible expletive in Chinese characters
And I can't find out about punk in Beijing
Since Christmas 05,there hasn't been anything
As if they converted to safe happy pop
Because the government said it had to stop
And I won't even mention the 'three T's'
Well, then again, the keyboard has no keys.

We had one last big night out on the Friday before being told whether we had passed training or not. We went to the Black Sun Bar and true to ourselves; most of us ended up out to the wee hours and were in quite a state the following day. We all had times to meet the management and find out whether we had passed our training or not. Mine wasn't too early in the morning and after years of doing this sort of thing I was functioning well enough to receive the congratulations from Hannah, my new boss, who gave me a company credit card and welcomed me aboard. I'd done it. That was a "wow" and a sigh of relief all rolled into one. I'd got too much riding on this. Going back to England would have been particularly difficult. I'd been trying not to think about it. No job and no prospects, with a mortgage to pay. I couldn't face it. It turned out that a couple of my new friends were not quite so lucky. Jane and Steven never got out of bed in time for them to receive their passing out and so were put on probation for the following six months. I never found out exactly what that meant, although they didn't receive the company credit card, but they were being watched. Things slowly came to light that I was too.

I suppose this is where I can go back to the beginning of this story and tell you more about who I am and also tell you about Jack and the body search. Jack and I had been sharing a flat for many years, playing practical jokes on each other and any other unwitting flat members. For example, one Christmas we re-wrapped an Australian flat mates Christmas presents that had been sent from home. Replacing his gifts with some of our own including old underpants, telephone directories, empty cans of Guinness; you get the idea. As he opened his presents on Christmas morning, being videoed by his girlfriend, he was slowly traumatized as he began to believe that his parents were sending the gifts as a sign of disownment. I don't think I'd ever laughed so much. Anyway, in much the same vein, Jack was off to visit an ex-girlfriend in Japan. The night before he left, I came home, suitably drunk, wrote something in the inside cover of his Lonely Planet guide to Tokyo, went to bed and thought nothing more of it. When Jack returned from his trip abroad, he was uncharacteristically quiet. Things had not gone as well as they could have done with his ex, so I left it at that, not wanting to pry too much. Then, one evening, his currant girlfriend came to talk to me and told me what had happened. It turns out that she had secreted a going away present in his hand-luggage. It was a soft toy in the shape of a rabbit. When Jack had got to the airport, he'd been asked if he'd packed his own bag and whether he had anything to declare. Unwittingly, he'd got on the wrong side of the customs man (Jack did this a lot) and he'd been asked to open his bag. Out popped the rabbit. Jack says "What the fuck....I've never seen it before in my life". The search continues until they find the Lonely Planet. And this is the killer. When I was drunk, I had written, on the inside cover "I have drugs up my arse". Well, when I heard this, I just could not contain myself and although Jack never elaborated upon the ordeal, there it is. For years afterwards, every time I left for the airport, I was on my guard. Re-checking everything, especially when it came to light that Jack was in the process of manufacturing an Al-Qaeda membership card for me, complete with my photograph with a super-imposed Muslim style beard. That could have been quite nasty. So, would you have me as a tour leader on your trip to China?

Chapter 2

THE ESSENCE OF CHINA

Twenty years from now you will be more disappointed by the things that you didn't do than by the ones you did do. So throw off the bowlines. Sail away from the safe harbor. Catch the trade winds in your sails. Explore. Dream. Discover.

Mark Twain (1835-1910) U.S. humorist, writer, and lecturer.

I started my training trip on 23rd March. Duan Chen (Eugenie is her English name) had been selected as my trainer. She was a 23 year old Chinese girl with attitude. She had a reputation for being tough. She was a Beijing girl who had been working for two seasons with the company. She had a "bob" style haircut and her choice of clothes looked a bit alternative or boyish, I couldn't decide which. I was also being co-trained with American Janie, who I knew liked a beer, so things were going to be ok. In the Friday afternoon after I had received my confirmation as a leader, Eugenie had called us to her room to go through the itinerary of the trip. I tried to strike up a conversation about Eugenie's name, as, it is quite unusual. I said that in the U.K. we had a princess with the same name, but the correct pronunciation was more like "eur jenny". She looked daggers at me. She said that when she was at school, she had chosen the name, as it was one of her Korean pop idols, but his name was Eugene, so she had to change it to the female version, Eugenie. I tried again, "the correct pronunciation is....." She cut me off straight, "It's Eugenie". I had been told and I had been put in my place.

It was the first time that I had looked at the Essence of China trip. Three weeks, three big cities, a hike up a mountain to monasteries and a three day boat cruise along the Three Gorges, before we got to Yangshuo and ending in Hong Kong. Eugenie set herself as a hard mistress and I was not ready for this. I could have done with a few days to prepare, I was tired, but Eugenie was not giving any slack and we were straight into the training trip. As would be the case with the start of every tour, we had our group meeting at 6pm, in the lobby of the Harmony hotel. Here we were introduced to the group of twelve that were coming on our Essence of China trip, three weeks from Beijing to Hong Kong. The group was quite diverse, all ages, Brits, Aussies, Americans, Canadians and a young German couple. Eugenie did the introductory meeting and talked about the itinerary, what to expect in the way of accommodation, transport then food as it would be group meals. She talked about safety and security, bad Beijing taxi drivers, not really realising that there are probably more dangers for us in our home cities. She finished, by inviting us all for "duck dinner". However, in her Beijing accent, a couple of the group said "dog dinner?" and there was a lot of face pulling until we had to clarify the mistake as "Beijing duck, Peking duck".

We had the first group dinner in the restaurant at the Harmony Hotel. I was sat next to Annie, who was in her 70's and her son, Adrian in his 40's who I spotted immediately as being gay. The others in the group were Joe, in his 20's from America, who I would be sharing with. Steve and Sarah were English "gap year" students on a round the world trip, next stops, Thailand and Australia. There was a young American couple, Jake and Jill and an Australian lady in her 50's. Another couple in the group, Mike and Michelle, were older Brits on a round the world trip, they did not arrive until after 10pm. We were all tired; especially me after such a busy day, but Eugenie would not let us knock off. We had to meet Mike and Michelle, go through the group meeting again with them, then, entre their details on the computer. Both Eugenie and Janie had laptops. Eugenie couldn't believe that I didn't carry a laptop, whilst I was surprised that her, being Chinese, had one. It had her and Janie off to a bosom buddy start, as they both chatted about how good their laptops were. I, on the other hand, said that one of the reasons for me to take this job was to get away from the office, not carry one around with me. This didn't get me into Eugenie's gang or good books, I was already an outsider and not wanting a laptop was a heinous crime. Eugenie was as tough as her reputation and we finished our day around midnight. No chance of a beer

According to the next schedule, this was also going to be the trip I would repeat as my first trip as a 'Leader'. In many ways this was excellent as it was very similar to the trip I undertook in 2002. I was going to visit places I was familiar with along with a couple that would be completely new to me. It was also going to make things easier for convincing the passengers that I wasn't the novice that I actually was. I am a prolific note taker and started to take notes on everything that Eugenie would point out throughout the training trip. Eugenie had also been asked to help me with my Chinese language. Janie and I were two of the novices in this field and I don't think Janie knew more than "Ni hao". At least I had been listening to my language C.D. and had a couple of phrases that I could trot out. What I really needed was to get to know useful things for my trips and get the pronunciation correct, so, from the very beginning I got things like food ordering as a practice lesson. Eugenie said that she would go through bookings, accounts, and the trip notes with us and on the first afternoon had us writing a blow by blow account of where we would be going and what we would be doing over the first week. It was all pretty organised, but also looked like a mountain of things to do that could all go wrong.

In the morning the itinerary had us going to the Great Wall at Jin Shan Ling, (Jinshanling) followed by a 10km walk along the wall to Si Ma Tai (Simatai). This was a 7am start and a 3 hour bus journey. Eugenie gave us some background info. Being a Local Beijinger who had worked as a guide for a couple of years before signing up for the Travel Company, she was a sort of standard bearer and someone that I could learn a lot from. Most of the info about the Great Wall can be easily found in the guide books and the travel company also has information on the Leaders Website. The Wall was originally a number of fortifications around cities and counties built as early as the 5th century BC. These were joined up to give better protection to the provinces from the marauding barbarians and then the first Emperor of China, Qin Shi Huang conquered the territories, he ordered the building of the Great Wall in 221BC, to defend his Middle Kingdom from the tribes to the north. Eugenie also told us a story about a man who was sent to work on the wall and when he died his body was built into it. The girl he loved then found his remains in the wall, she now has a statue dedicated to her somewhere on the coast. China is full of stories, parables, superstitions which all play a major role in cultivating the Chinese psyche. Something that doesn't make any sense at all to us is perfectly reasonable once you have read the relevant historic parable.

With such an early start, it is difficult to get the attention of the group, especially the ones who were more interested in why they could not have breakfast before we left. We leave early to avoid the rush hour crowds out of Beijing, avoid the crowds on the wall, to make sure we are not walking in the hot afternoon and to get us back to Beijing in good time to have a night out at the theatre or bar area. We pass the modern high rises on the eight lane airport express way out of the city, then slowly move into the countryside. I've got to mention the little device that all drivers in China seem to own. It is an annoying contraption, placed on the dash-board, which talks to you. Every time you get too close to the vehicle in front, or go over a bump, it calls out a warning. This is constant on our three hour journey as the driver tries to disappear up the exhaust pipe of every car that we follow. Driving in China is one mad rush, honking the horn continuously as you go. The horn honking is to tell the car in front that you are coming, it is not aggressive, but as a westerner, it all sounds the same and adds to the impression of chaos. We are on highway all the way to the Great Wall, there is a lot of construction everywhere you look. Then after a hundred or so kilometers, the construction becomes fields, rows of planted trees, and finally, the hills where the Great Wall lies like a long Chinese dragon defending the lands of the Middle Kingdom

At around 10am we took the spur road to the car park at Jin Shan Ling. There is a kiosk here where Eugenie paid the entrance fee. Now, we have our first "Chinese" experience. The option of a toilet stop. Everybody filed into the building, then quickly filed out again. Many were visibly disgusted. "It is just a hole", they exclaimed, then another couple of them returned, "and there is no toilet paper". Lesson number one: Most toilets in China are squat and they don't provide toilet paper. So, we started the 15 minute walk along the pathway and slow, steep climb up to the Wall. I may have said to people before. The

Great Wall of China is more of a great broken staircase than a wall and not so easy to negotiate. Also, for those people who were not thinking clearly about the Great Wall of China, it was built as a defensive fortification across the hilltops that divide China from Mongolia. The purpose was to stop the barbarians from crossing into the civilised world. So, it straddles the hills, climbing and descending with the terrain. It is definitely not flat. You have to ascend a staircase and steep pathway for twenty minutes just to get on to it.

Once you enter through the gate house and up the steep staircase to get on top of the Wall, you are hit by the most magnificent scenery. The mountains extend into the distance with valleys in between and the wall, un-clicks and coils around and over the peaks. You can count tower beyond tower as the wall marches on into the distant horizon. With every group and every time I go here, this is a real highlight because you get away from the touristy areas. Our itinerary is to hike a 10km section between the villages of Jin Shan Ling and Si Ma Tai. This is a real China experience and when you leave the local Beijing tourists behind who only hang around the start or end points, you are really on your own. Well, almost. There are some local farmer women who are quite persistent in trying to sell you T shirts, or postcards, or books. There are a couple of people who also bring drinks onto the wall to sell and it is a bit of a surprise when you reach one of the towers to find a miniature shop set up inside. Somebody had even carted a refrigerator up to this tower. Even so, the scenery is as magnificent as any in the world.

Some of the passengers find it all a bit of a struggle. It is a tough climb and four of the older ones in our group returned to the car park and the waiting bus. Eugenie had pre-arranged this with the driver, to wait for 1 hour in the car park for anyone who did not want to do the difficult 10km hike. The bus would then drive them to the finishing point of the hike, Si Ma Tai, where we would meet up later. There was no such option for Janie or I, we had to do the hike, and we would be leading our own group here in little more than a month. The wall itself is also in a state of disrepair between the two towns because the local government is in dispute over who should pay the repair bills. So as the wall deteriorates, some of us have to go down the rubble slopes on our arses. A couple of the group were close to tears, but that was what I found out later to be a regular experience. There are so many people on these trips that simply don't know what they have signed up for. Four out of this group did not do the full walk, that's ok, older people, having a chance to see this wonder of the world don't need to climb on it for five hours, but it's the other ones that really get to me. They complain that it is too steep, too hot, there are no safety rails and they might fall off it. Now, I always think of the Chinese soldiers, a couple of thousand years ago, in full armor, having to run from tower to tower and defend against the Mongol hordes. I don't think they had issues about safety rails.

Just before the end of the hike, we cross a bridge. This is a narrow plank bridge that crosses a 100m gorge and is suspended around 50m from the river below. The bridge sways in the breeze and you see fear in the eyes of the group as they approach it. It is the only way across, there is no going back. When we came up to the last climb, you cannot see the exit and some of the group actually said that they didn't want to go any further. Well, without a magic wand or a helicopter, we were not going to be able to get them off the wall, so I'm not sure what they expected us to do. The reward though, that is, in the end, they all said it was worth it and a highlight of the trip. It is something that I think I will never get bored of seeing.

When I was here five years ago I had a very different experience of "The Wall". Then, I had decided to take a local bus to The Great Wall at Badaling. This was a defining moment in my learning about China. I got on at the Beijing Zhan bus station, to find a bus full of locals having a day out. The nearest thing I can liken it to was the charabancs of the pre 1980's, when working class families would all get on an organised bus together and go to Blackpool (or wherever) stopping at a couple of other attractions on the way. I wasn't quite prepared for this. Neither was I prepared for the constant karaoke on a smoke filled bus, locals shouting (the Chinese voice is permanently set a couple of decibels above the pain threshold for us Westerners), three generations of the same family, all on a day out. The bus stopped at a jade factory and shop, then some tourist attraction, I can't remember what, but I remember getting quite concerned as the day went on and then we stopped at a water-slide theme park. I thought I'd got on the wrong bus and wasn't going to the wall at all. In fact, was I ever going to get back to Beijing because I had no idea where I was. When I got to the wall, it was a crush. A good proportion of China had also decided to go to the wall the same day that I did and that's a hell of a lot of people.

As part of our trip, in the evenings, Eugenie would offer to take the group out to dinner. This always got a unanimous turnout, if for no other reason that nobody knew how to order food without Eugenie. This was something that I needed to get right in the three weeks before I started my own trip. There are also the options of going to see a show. The three recommended shows are the Beijing Acrobats, the Kung Fu Show and the Peking Opera. Our group decided they wanted to see the Kung Fu Show. We got there from the hotel by taxi. It's not far to the theatre and Eugenie had instructed the drivers, so there should have been no problems, but nothing is straight forward. We couldn't all leave at the same time from the hotel, or arrive and park directly outside the theatre, which also meant losing one of the cars. Then running around the front of the theatre, me phoning Eugenie and her calling Janie to see if we could see the four in the group that had got lost. This was another quick lesson in the perils of being a tour leader. Expect the unexpected and taxis are no exception here. If Eugenie couldn't get this right, how we were supposed to communicate with taxi drivers when we couldn't speak Chinese? It was going to make us look pretty stupid and already I was worried about my first trip, still one month away. The show was like a West

End or Broadway theatre production. For those in the group expecting a Kung Fu demonstration, there was disappointment. As a show, it was very well done and there was a drop down screen that had the dialogue in English, so following the story wasn't a problem. We decided to walk back to the hotel and had a quick beer in the City Centre Hostel on the way. There were still a couple of leaders in town and I was now on good terms with the bar staff there.

On the next day of the trip, the groups have an "included activity", visiting Tian An Men square and Forbidden City. We had Eugenie acting as our guide, but when we have to do this on our own, we have a pool of local guides to choose from, all who work regularly with the Travel Company, all who know the route and the costings and all who have their favourite tour leaders who they go with. Eugenie's advice was "book early, otherwise you will not get one". At eight o'clock after checking out of the hotel and leaving our bags in day rooms, we set off for Tian An Men Square and the Forbidden City. I don't like Tian An Men Square very much. Too big, exposed, a few concrete structures including Mao's Mausoleum, the Hall of the People and a few statues. People always ask where the tanks were and although the guides may know something about the 1989 protest in the square, they can't say anything about it, or will try to cover it up. Many guides only know about the taking over of Tian An Men square from the foreign tour groups that they bring through the square, there is no official account of the uprising. The horrifying thing is, the atrocities are still going on and if people protest too much, the tanks that were there in 1989 will soon come back. As Eugenie talked us through the sights, men would wander up and listen to what she was saying. I never thought anything of it at the time, but in hindsight, they were not curious individuals wanting to take a closer look at the foreigners with our pale faces and lanky bodies. They are men, invariably in their forties and fifties, just wandering around the square and once you see them for what they are, it seems very odd. They are not tourists, they just don't fit the profile, they are the undercover police. Other people are trying to sell postcards and books or a "Mao Watch". This has a picture of the revered Chairman Mao on the clock face and his arm is the second hand, waving in time to the seconds. Very comical and you can haggle the sellers down to around 10 Yuan for one. You have to haggle in China.

On leaving Tian An Men square, you are faced by the Tian An Men gate. The large red wall come observation platform that has Chairman Mao's portrait on it and is also the entrance to the complex containing the Forbidden City. There are always masses of people here. This brings into focus the other great Chinese trait of not being able to queue. Whether this is for a bus, or in a supermarket, people will push in front of you, then their family will pile goods on top of the original shopping. "Queuing" at the bank or cashpoint it is quite concerning when you have taken out the equivalent of a month's wages in front of these people, as they push in front and chat to the bank cashier. Again, at any information desk, usually you will end up speaking to some random person who happens to be chatting to the girl on the counter but can speak a little English. If not, then you've no chance of being served. Or, what I'm getting on to, is Tourist Attractions. Over the last decade or so, China has taken tourism to heart, even creating its own new tourist attractions where there weren't any before. In places like the Forbidden City, the crowds go wild. Thousands upon thousands of people, all pushing like it's the Hillsborough tragedy, trampling all underfoot to get a photo of the re-constructed (very little is original) Temple of Supreme Harmony, or Temple of Complete Harmony or Temple of Preserving Harmony, (the middle one was built as a resting place between the other two, just in case the Emperor got tired of being carried from one to the other). Needless to say, the temples were only harmonious in name when surrounded by the baying crowds.

I like the Forbidden City. It is a place that you have to visit many times in order to get a real feel for the size and intricacy of the place. I visited in 2002 and could remember some of what Eugenie was now telling us, but it has such a long and complex history and there are many story's to be told. For example, there are supposed to be 9999 and a half rooms, only one half less than there are in Heaven. There aren't really that many, but it is a palace in the grandest scale. It is built according to the principals of Feng Shui, another aspect of Taoist philosophy, concerning the flow of "qi", so there is a dominating hill to the north of the structure and manmade rivers crossing the south of the complex. It is the largest palace in the world and mostly re-built after surviving wars and revolutions over its six hundred year history.

After exiting the Forbidden City, our itinerary takes us to Beijing Huiling. This is a short walk into a hutong area and a converted courtyard house. On the whole, Beijing is a very modern city. Broad boulevards lined with large modern buildings, be they office blocks, retail centres or government buildings. The original housing in the city is being bought up and demolished. Much of it is over 300 years old, and is of a "flat-house" type in a Hutong. Beijing Huiling is a charity supported by our travel company. It is a scheme for people with mental disability or learning difficulties. It all seemed to be a haphazard arrangement when we arrived. We sat in a room by the courtyard as Eugenie went to organise food.

I, like many other people who visit Huiling, are a bit unsure about what we are doing there. Two or three disabled people come in to look at us. Curious about why the foreigners have come to their home. We are then served food by a couple of the trainees and a girl is there to sell us drinks, if we want any. This all seemed very awkward and Eugenie was arguing with one of the staff about how much vegetarian food we would get and why it wasn't ready. This just made us feel more awkward. When the food arrived, then arrived again and again there were enough dumplings to feed 30 of us. We ended up taking away four boxes of these, out of our sense of western embarrassment for putting the charity through so much trouble. We moved on to a classroom, through the curious trainees, some of who were trying to communicate, but there was much more in the way than just the language barrier. In the classroom, one of the staff introduced one of the trainees, via Eugenie's translation, as somebody who was good at calligraphy. We were to have a lesson in how to paint Chinese word, or "character". This worked pretty well, going step by step, how to paint a character for good luck. Then, there were booklets handed out for us to practice painting the character representing our own astrological sign, mine being "the rooster".

The last part of our visit to Huiling was a performance. We sat on chairs in the courtyard and watched the trainees sing and dance. This didn't sit at all well with me. I thought that we had moved on from having disabled people as entertainment for tourist's years earlier, well, not in China. The performance had little merit. We were encouraged to get up and dance with the trainees for the last song and then play hacky sack. It was good to see these guys enjoying themselves, but there was definitely something not quite right with the activity.

Whilst there, we met Emma. She was going to be our Hutong Guide. Another 23 year old who was guiding as she was studying at university. I talked to Emma on the walk through the hutongs. We were to visit a hutong house on the tour and she described the area and what was happening to it. They are mainly a 3 or five room building in the north of an enclosed courtyard, facing south. This is used as the main family house. There are other buildings, or rooms on the East and West side of the courtyard for other family members (useful before the 1 child policy, but we won't go there quite yet). Due to the market pressures on land, this is prime site development. The inhabitants can no-longer afford to live there and are also quite glad to leave for the new developments on the edge of the city. They replace the small rooms and communal toilet for double glazing, central heating, modern indoor bathrooms, in spacious apartments. Now what does that remind you of? yes, it's Britain in the 1950's and 60's all over again. The same mistakes being played out, with the same people trying to get white collar jobs to pay for high rise accommodation. Whether it all turns out the way it did in Britain, who can say. At the end of the tour, we were in Hou Hai. A few of us had a drink there and I left the boxes of dumplings, carried from Beijing Huiling, on the table, we would not be eating them. As we walked off, to my amazement, the waitress ran after us, possibly 200 meters, with the boxes of dumplings. They were obviously just left overs to any westerner, but to her, she treated the food as if we had left some valuable jewelry behind.

In order to travel from city to city in China, we usually take trains. Train stations in China are a hassle. There are far too many people and even though most of the stations are newly built, they just don't have the capacity for the traveling Chinese population. We are always advised to get to the stations one hour ahead of departure time. This is good advice, as the roads on the way to the stations are congested and if there is ever an accident, the traffic is not allowed to move until the police can investigate and apportion blame. Even one hour ahead of departure time, the waiting rooms are crowded to the point that all we can do is make a pile of our backpacks and stand around them. The looks on the faces of the group when they can't have a seat. Well, some people just shouldn't be traveling.

We are always the centre of attention, local people coming up and staring at the foreigners. Some will want photographs of us. Then, as we sit on our bags in the vast hall of the train station waiting room, with half an hour to go, the Chinese will all be standing and pushing towards the platform gate. We all have seats or beds on the train, but that doesn't seem to make a difference, they all have to be pushing to be the first on. I learned to hang back with our group. No point in standing for 30 minutes with you backpack on, getting more and more irate with the jostling locals. We just walk onto the train when we are good and ready and have to put up with them once we're maneuvering our bags into the cabins. For some reason, the local people don't seem to be able to read the train tickets, so they will no doubt be in your cabin when you arrive. It is perfectly ok for people to sit on the bottom bunk in the cabins, it's a sort of communal space, but you usually hope that they have the correct cabin and are not inviting all their family members into yours. The trains are surprisingly comfortable, modern rolling stock only a few years old often carpeted and spotlessly cleaned by the ever present attendants in their white gloves. The only real down side is if you draw the short straw and get a snoring, throat clearing Chinese in your cabin. But these things are still not good enough for some people. The odd perfectionist in the group will always complain about something.

There is the constant radio broadcast, which we westerners will turn off, then the Chinese will turn back on again. Its loud music and announcements about the railway and the cities that we visit are all in Chinese. It becomes an un-necessary noise, especially when it starts up as a "wake up call" at six a.m. in an almost "Hi-de-hi, hello campers" but without any of the laughs. The squat toilet, on the train is a sort of evil assault course. At the beginning of the journey, it is spotless, but by the morning, it is covered in everything that the human body can throw at it. This is one place where there should be a sign saying "gentleman may prefer to squat" as the compartment is often drenched in urine. The swaying motion of the train isn't of much help to relaxing your bowel movement, even if you can manage to squat. There is a rail to hold on to as you sway your butt above the hole that opens onto the tracks below, but at some point, you will have to go "one handed" when it comes to wiping. By the way, you did remember to bring your own toilet paper, didn't you? For many of us westerners, there is the issue of the beds not being long enough or there is not enough room to store all that shopping you bought in Beijing. As I will say over and over again, some people just shouldn't be travelling in China.

So, on to Xi'an, an amazing city with a history of over 3000 years. It was the Capital of China for 13 dynasties and had a population of over 1 million around the time that Londinium was being established by the Romans. We were picked up by our private bus from close to the train station around 8:45am and checked into the City Hotel. Eugenie wasn't happy because the hotel had been changed without her knowing it and she was shouting down the phone at the local operator, Ren Ming. This seems to happen a lot and it hit home to me that my lack of Mandarin would have had me completely at a loss if it was my group. The rest of the group was happy with a marvelous location, right in the heart of the city. Eugenie then took us for an orientation walk. It is a city that I spent a few days in on my last trip in 2002 and it all started to piece itself together again. The hotel was located just off South Street and from here you can see the Bell Tower, the Ming Dynasty construction that is the geographical heart of the city. Then we walk south to the South Gate, along South Street, a four lane carriage way with wide pavements and hotels and restaurants on either side. Another thoroughly modern city centre. It is also a walled city. The original wall used to enclose the city including the Big Goose Pagoda, a medi-evil 7 story skyscraper that stands 8Km from the centre of the City. The present wall was built in the Ming dynasty and reconstructed again only a few years ago to complete a 14km circuit of the inner city that you can get on top of and cycle around. For the lazy, there is the option of hiring a golf buggy to do the circuit. The highlight of coming to Xi'an is to see the Terracotta Warriors but there are so many other places around Xi'an that are worthy of a mention. The museums are world class, the two pagodas are structures of monumental architecture set in grounds that would rate as the top attractions in any other city. There is also the Muslim Quarter and the Great Mosque, which are such a contrast to the other more typical Chinese areas.

Xi'an has one of my favourite buildings in one of my favourite areas in China. The Great Mosque, in the Muslim Quarter, not unlike the souks of Moroccan Fez, with stalls and cafes selling everything as long as it isn't a pig. There are birds in cages hanging from the lamp posts along "Muslim Street" and a sense that you are in a completely different country from China. The

Mosque itself is hidden in the back alleys of the Muslim Quarter, where you have to push past all the stall holders and shoppers. It is quite a shopper's paradise here. On entering the Mosque, you see that it is more like a series of gardens, and was first established nearly 1000 years ago. When we Europeans were fighting the Muslims across Spain, Austria, and invading Jerusalem, in our East, the Muslims had also expanded across India and into China. It was they who kept the Silk Road open for Marco Polo in his fabled travels. Inside the Mosque, you just have to see all the Chinese dressed as Muslims coming to prey in a temple that mixes Chinese Dragons and Arabic script. There are Middle Eastern arches and an eight sided pagoda as a minaret and three steals with the opening verses of the Koran in Chinese, Arabic and Tibetan. Truly a wonderful building, all in a peaceful garden-courtyard setting.

On my training trip to Xi'an I ran into some other people from training and had a good couple of nights out with them and our passengers. Pierre, Snow and Jane were there. Pierre taught me the dice game, that has kept me in good stead with the passengers ever since and I visited my first ever Chinese nightclub with him. On the next night, out with my group, I ended up singing Karaoke on Bar Street. Bar St. is a manufactured street with attempts of western style bars along it. Bar St. is a bit of a disappointment, there is just no atmosphere there at all. Many of the bars will have a bad covers duo playing so loudly that you just have to vacate the premises in order to have a conversation. As you walk down the street, you get a limp accosting of "welcome to my bar" and nobody seems to go into the places unless, like us, you manage to get a cheap beer deal. The nightclubs are a real contrast, packed full of the young and upwardly mobile. It reminded me a lot of growing up in Blackburn in the 1980's with lads sitting on the bar stools, drinking with the bar man until they fall off. I went to the toilet and saw my first projectile vomiting since my days working at the Students' Union. These people do shot after shot, cheering "Gan bei!" as they go. China has a big drinking culture now. They are more than happy to get us westerners involved in the rounds of shots too, very accommodating and generous. The drink of choice is usually whiskey, but this is mixed with sprite or maybe peach tea and served in a carafe. You get a side order of fruit to go with this and do round of shots after round of shots, often playing the dice game as a means of having to knock another round back. The dice game is all about gambling on what dice you, or the other people may have, a game of chance and luck more than skill and judgment. The Chinese love it.

Eugenie invited me out to meet Snow again, the leader who has the bar in Yangshuo, who was also running a trip through Xi'an. We went for hot pot. This was my first experience of this style of meal and is more a Sichuan specialty and usually very spicy. The meal consists of a pot of broth, usually chicken based, but it could be fish or veg. Then you order a selection of side plates, beef, taro, meatballs, whatever, and as the pot boils, you place the side dishes into the pot and cook your food. A real theatre of a meal. The service here was also attentive and first class. The sort of thing that you would struggle to get outside of a top restaurant back home, all for the price of a Big Mac and fries.

Jim was our local guide in Xi'an and we had a private bus for the 45 minute journey to the Terracotta Warriors in which he gave us a different insight to the city and its people. Eugenie said that he had a standard spiel that he gave on almost every trip and that he would be our regular guide. We also went to meet Ren Ming. He was the Local Operator. He arranged the hotels, transport, local guides and the train tickets to the next destination. He was a quite important man in Xi'an and as he sat behind his oversized wooden desk in his office, surrounded by pretty secretaries, you got the sense that he knew it. Eugenie didn't like him. She said that you could not trust him and that his service was not so good. There was a bit of the Beijing girl coming through here

I should mention the Terracotta Warriors and more importantly, the First Emperor "Qin", who united the Chinese in 221 BC.

This was no mean feat, being the size of Europe and over 5 million people at the time. He also unified the legal system, the currency, weights and measures, instigated the building of the Great Wall and gave China the written language that it still uses today. This is only equaled by the likes of Alexander the Great, Julius Caesar, Genghis Khan and very few others. When He died, he built a tomb, only part of which has been excavated, revealing the four pits of the Terracotta Warriors. He also has his mausoleum in a pyramid the size of the Great Pyramids in Egypt that still has to be dug. The warriors themselves are also very impressive, I would be visiting them again in 3 weeks' time and would be referring to the extensive notes that I had taken.

We took an overnight train again arriving around 5:30 am in Chengdu. I had never been there before and we were met by Chicory, our local guide here and once again I was bowled over by the friendliness and helpfulness of the Chinese. Chicory had been a leader for our travel company a couple of years earlier and had returned to Chengdu, her home town, to set up a tour business and look after her ageing father. I was surprised by her choice of hotel, as was Eugenie, but for completely different reasons. Once again, the hotel was not the one on the itinerary, so she made a stink about that. I was surprised because the bathrooms were made of glass, so you could see in on whatever your room mate was doing. I suppose this is ok for the liberated married couples, but I was sharing with a bloke that I'd only just met and I don't think he wanted to voyeur on me any more than I did on him. It turns out that the glass bathroom is a bit of a theme in Sichuan province. Chicory gave us some background information about Chengdu then took us to the Panda Reserve. It's a sort of breeding centre come zoo. I wasn't too sure about this, but after getting the info, it's so obvious that Pandas are going to become extinct naturally if we don't intervene. The big question concerning the conservation is about how, exactly we do this and the Chinese Government has to be influenced to get things right. The reality of the place makes you want to question what they are actually doing. For Y1000 you can have your photo taken holding a baby panda. No Pandas have been sent back into the wild, and never will be.

Chicory was giving the group a lot of information. I decided that I would tell her "The panda story". I had been told this story five years earlier when I had first visited China. It is all about how the pandas got their distinctive black and white markings, as according to legend, all pandas were originally white.

"Many, many years ago, in the Kingdom of Sichuan, there lived a king and his daughter, the princess. The king was getting old and knew that one day he would have to hand over the kingdom to the princess. He had worked hard throughout his reign, had done everything he could for his people and his daughter, but now he realised that he had spoiled his daughter too much. He watched as she would go shopping, buying frivolous gifts for herself, spending all day at the hair dressers and not caring about her people. So, the king decided to act. He told the Princess, that she could no longer spend her days shopping or going to the Hairdressers and would have to concentrate more on governing. The princess hated this. They argued and argued over the following months. The King saying that the Princess was not fit to govern and the Princess saying the King was an unfit father. In the end, the King said to the Princess, "If you believe that I am an unfit father, you can go and live with the pandas and see how bad an unfit father I really am".

Now, everyone knows that the pandas are lazy, sleeping all day and they don't breed frequently and they are not successful parents. When the princess arrived at the pandas, they were overjoyed to have a real princess visit them. They ate and ate their favourite bamboo and then slept. The next day, it was the same, so pleased that the princess was there, that they ate the bamboo until they fell asleep again. By this time, the princess was getting hungry. She could not wake the pandas, so she went off into jungle to look for food. Unfortunately, she did not look where she was going and fell into a deep hole. The pandas were so concerned with their eating and sleeping, that they forgot about the princess, until one day, they found her, at the bottom of the deep hole, she was dead.

The pandas were so upset when they found her. They climbed into the deep muddy hole and tried to wake the princess, but they couldn't. So they all began to cry, rubbing their eyes as they did so. Then they cried and rubbed their heads. Then they cried and hugged their sides. The mud that the princess had died in was rubbed around their eyes as they cried, onto their heads and around their waist as they hugged themselves and the mud would not come off. Since then, all pandas have had these black markings."

After the Pandas, we went for a meal in a Buddhist temple. The Wenshu Temple is the largest in Chengdu, in extensive grounds with numerous gardens and pavilions. It also has a vegetarian restaurant attached and does the most fabulous fake meat dishes. We walked back through the City, looking at the massive statue of Mao in the City Tian Fu Square, looking over his people. Chengdu was another modern city and although it has a history of 2500 years, very little of it is in evidence. Then we walked south, to the Tibetan area. It is not a very big place, from what I saw and is populated by some robe wearing monks, a few people in Tibetan traditional costume and beggars. Not the best of introductions to the place. Close to here we took a look at the Jin Li Street, which is a reconstruction of the old town, turned into a shopping street. It is very nice to look at, but oh, so obviously fake. Chinese tourists took our photographs as we took photographs of them in their fake medi-evil street scene. We also went to the Cultural show here. This, in my opinion is the best cultural show in China. There are seven different performances including, puppetry, shadow play, a musical section, a short costume play. There is a hilarious comedy sketch, where a husband is being berated by his wife for spending too much time playing mahjong with his friends. The husband then has to perform a series of tasks, ever more complex, in order to convince his wife not to throw him out of the house. The grand finale of the show is "changing faces". The performers wear traditional masks, each with bright colours depicting gods, demons or characters from the Sichuan Opera. Somehow, they change these masks, right in front of your eyes, with no obvious means of swapping one mask for another. Their hands are empty; they make a gesture in front of their face and the mask changes. To top it all, there is fire breathing and masks that disappear to reveal the performers true face, then re-appear again. Chicory said that the "changing faces" was a trade secret and though we all tried to guess how they did it. No one could get the correct answer.

Chengdu is another very modern, well ordered city. Before my trip had started, I had been in touch with my old friend Lu Dai, who I worked with at The Rocket, for some tips on where to go out in her home town as she had always been a very outgoing girl in London. Lu, a 26 year old, had recently got married, which was a surprise to me and everybody else who knew her. She had married another Chinese who she hardly knew and was now pregnant. This just didn't seem like the girl I knew, with the enviable mix of good social life and exciting career prospects. She hadn't lived in Chengdu for around five years and didn't know anything about the local scene and before arriving in the city, I had not been prepared for it to be so un-westernised. Modern, it was, without a doubt, but as I was quickly realising, there was a difference between modernisation and imitating the west. The Chinese were doing all this their own way. On the surface, it may look like a western city, but in reality it was something quite different. Maybe, I should have known better and I was learning fast that even cities of over five million people may not have anything that we could call a pub. Unfortunately, China hasn't evolved a decent bar scene in the provinces. There was a rumor of an Irish Bar on the Third Ring Road and there were some restaurants and small bars around Jin Li Street and the Tibetan quarter with monks if you like that sort of scene. Personally, I prefer beer, and monks and beer don't go together.

The next morning we were on our way again, Emei Shan via Le Shan. (Shan translates as "mountain" in Chinese). After a 2 1/2 hour drive, we get to a river, with the largest stone carved Buddha in the world carved into the river cliff. The previous two largest carved stone Buddha's in the world were destroyed by the Afghan Taliban a couple of decades earlier. We walk the 300 or so stone steps, past carvings and statues, to come out at a terrace, on a level with Buddha's ear. He is big. Totally 72m in height. On this hill are extensive monasteries and temples. The whole area is a holy place of great significance to Buddhists. A short drive from here is Emei Shan, another sacred Buddhist mountain, with more monasteries and temples. I slept on the way there and woke in what appeared to be a wilderness wonderland in the mountains, with a medi evil temple. Part of the itinerary is to stay in two monasteries on two different mountains over the three days. The monasteries are very impressive buildings with Buddha's, incense, painted carvings. Monks come and go, tending gardens, praying. In the first monastery we met Patrick, our local operator who never stopped trying to help us, running around, bringing breakfast, taking laundry, buying bus tickets and explaining the itinerary to us. We also met our local guide for the mountain. We had a choice of George or Nathan. Once again, Eugenie was not happy. She told me that George was possibly the worst guide that she had taken, anywhere in China. What's more, she had also told this to George and he was not happy about guiding her or the group. So we got Nathan, who according to Eugenie was only marginally better.

On the first night on Emei Shan we stay in Baoguo Monastery. This is a large working temple and the home to over 40 monks. As you enter through the main gate, there is a large open courtyard with an incense burner of maybe 5 feet in length. Pilgrims, tourists and monks are moving around the place, preying, lighting incense sticks and going into the main hall where the statue of Buddha sits. Behind this building are other prayer halls and accommodation for the monks and at the back of this there is the accommodation for guests and another prayer hall with its seven Buddha's. Baoguo Monastery is a very important spiritual place. The accommodation was better than I expected. A year earlier, the monks realised that they were on to a good thing with the western tour groups coming and staying four times a week, so they re-decorated the rooms and now they even have T.V.'s. However, the re-decoration had not yet got as far as the shower block and they were possibly the worst looking showers I had seen since my stay in a Bangkok drug den in the early 1990s. Two small cubicles next to the temples' boiler, they had never been cleaned and were covered in years of dirt and lime-scale. It made me wonder how I would actually end up cleaner coming out than going in. Needless to say, there was a certain amount of resistance to showering from the group. When people book this trip, one of the highlights is the stay in the monasteries. It doesn't take too much intuition to get an impression of what sort of standards a monastery on a mountain in rural China will have, but some of the group were completely unprepared.

It was around this time that the peculiarities of the people in the group started to come out. There was the young American couple, Jake and Jill, married in their early twenties and church goers. They had found the trip difficult in the big cities. Now they were in rural China, they were completely out of their depth. We hadn't noticed, but they had not eaten very much at the group meals. What they had then done, is find a KFC or MacDonald's, filling up there on western style junk food. Jill had asked at one point whether there was Dairy Queen in China. I didn't even know if there was Dairy Queen in England, whatever it was. The reason why they said they had come to China was that they wanted to take outward bound church groups into the Appalachian Mountains back home. They thought they needed to travel more in order to get recognition when they set up their own company and also wanted to know how other companies operated. This all seemed fine on the surface, but they just didn't like the backpacking or the interaction with locals and just could not understand why the service standards that they wanted just couldn't be catered for. Jill was taking a lot of photographs as were a couple of others in the group. There was talk of exchanging the photos at the end of the trip. However, it turns out that Jill was planning to publish a book of her photographs. The rest of the group had quite a few comments to make about this. She wasn't enjoying her time in the country and didn't get involved or know much about where they were, however she thought that she could publish a book on China off the back of a group tour. It didn't seem quite right and she wouldn't share any of her photographs. This did not endear her to the rest of the group.

One other peculiarity came to light around now. Earlier in the trip, they had asked Eugenie if they could maybe visit an orphanage. Around Emei Shan, there was the possibility of going to a school. These are the sort of activities that a Responsible Travel Company loves to get involved with. Eugenie had apologised that, so far, she had been unable to set up the orphanage visit. There was more to this than what we first thought. The Americans had decided that they wanted to go to an orphanage to "adopt" a Chinese baby. The thinking behind this was that they could "rescue" a Chinese baby from this Godless and backward country and take her to the U.S. where she would have a much better life. When Eugenie realised this, she was astounded. That people would take Chinese children away and brainwash them into a culture that was totally alien to her identity. Eugenie was proud of her country and this was the biggest insult anyone could give her.

For the hike into the mountain, we were given "monkey sticks". These are dual purpose walking sticks. The dual purpose being to frighten, but not beat off the monkeys, that inhabit the mountain, when they attack you for food. We weren't too sure about this, but the guide, Nathan, was more than too willing to demonstrate how the monkey would come for the food you carried and how you should beat him. I think at this point a few in our party had decided not to tip Nathan. In the morning, we were wakened at 4:30 by the monks being called to prayer, then one hour of chanting. This novelty soon wore off for me. I had been warned about this, as in one of the complaints sheets from the previous year, a passenger had reprimanded the tour leader (this could be me) for not telling the monks to chant so early in the morning.

We walked into Baoguo village and took a bus that raced up the switchback road to the place where we alighted and began to walk. As we went up the mountain it was obvious what was the root cause of the monkey/monkey-stick problem. There were stalls that sold all sorts of souvenirs and stuff en-route, including food. There were signs all the way up saying not to feed the monkeys, look after the environment and the like. Most very badly phrased and spelled, wonderful examples of "Chinglish", I needed to take photographs, I wanted people back home to really see how hilarious they were. However, the signs were quite correctly written in Chinese, so there was no excuse for the Chinese to throw plastic bags of food at the monkeys, encouraging them to come for more (we reap what we sow). Then there were the butterflies in cases on sale whilst at the same time there was a noticeable lack of flying butterflies. You get a cable car for the last leg of the journey to the summit. This runs from some concrete monstrosity of a building. I was beginning to wonder about this supposedly "sacred mountain environmental park" thing. On the top is a temple complex. In the swirling clouds it was quite atmospheric, with all the incense sticks and chanting. There is also 72m high Golden 10 faced Buddha, and we got tantalising views of this, as the weather and incense clouds moved, then drew in again, very impressive. There were tourists and pilgrims at the site, performing rituals at the three temples on the top of the mountain. A strange mixture of the spiritual world meeting the modern one.

On the way back down, on our way to our second monastery homestay at Hung Chun Ping, one of our tour group, Joe was determined to do the long hike back down the mountain rather than take the bus. Neither Eugenie or I was up for this, so we sent him off with a note asking the way to the monastery where we were staying (in Chinese). What we also put on the note was "beat me with my monkey stick". He arrived at the monastery seven hours later and never could understand the reception he'd had from the locals on route.

On the walk we passed some of the most amazing scenery. Over a swing bridge across a lake, through a farm, along another lake to a pavilion with two stone bridges spanning two streams and joining under the stone octagonal Chinese pavilion. It ticked all the boxes of what you want to see when you come to the Chinese countryside. I got chatting to Eugenie. She had first come to Emei Shan as a child. We stopped at the "Elephant and Tiger meeting" Pavilion, a beautiful Chinese gazebo at the confluence of two streams. She said that she remembered this place from her childhood. Her father had suffered from cancer and they had visited Emei on holiday when he got the all clear. Eugenie is from a wealthy middle class background. Her father worked as a government physician. In China, in the old system before the opening up to market forces, the place where a person worked would provide such things as accommodation and health care. The better the workplace, the better the accommodation and insurance cover. Eugenie's father, as a government worker had 95% cover for his medical bills. Without this he would have died. Eugenie thought that the old system was better than the new, where people have to cover the cost of their accommodation, medical bills, and other services largely by themselves. The older generation still have some of these benefits if they worked for one of the better government industries, but fewer and fewer young people have cover unless they can find a way of providing for it themselves.

Beyond the Elephant and Tiger meeting pavilion was another pavilion, then a large temple. Next we took the path along a river gorge, then crossed the river on the stepping stones, back onto the riverbank path and across stone bridges and into the monkey area. Here the wooden platforms and swing bridges are defended by Tibetan Macaques. The last part of the hike is a 1300 step climb, straight up and a real test for the older ones in the group. Then, we reach our second monastery.

On this hike to the second monastery, Hung Chun Ping, I had the role of acting as sweep. At the back of the group with me was Mike. He was 66 years old, ex IBM employee with a slight heart condition and the beginnings of Alzheimer's'. He kept me on my toes with countless questions and interesting stories. He was there in the first meeting that I.B.M. had about the internet. He told me that the professional view of the company was that the internet would never work and to demonstrate this, the representative from the head office in the U.S. had thrown the keyboard from one end of the room to the other saying that this was the only way that information would be transferred. It was only now in the trip that I realised how much he was repeating himself. He had asked on a number of occasions, where we were going to next and what would we see and do there. Then the next day, he might ask the same questions again and sometimes even ask why we were going to a particular place. Being new to all this, I just chatted away to him, answering the questions as best I could. Only later, realising that he didn't have a clue where he was or what he was doing there. It was also a struggle getting him up Mount Emei, but I think we spent so much time laughing about miss-counting the steps that we made it before we knew it.

Hung Chung Ping Monastery is even more of a highlight than Baoguo, where we had stayed the night before. This place feels older, dark stained creaking floorboards. There were empty courtyards. We had smaller basic rooms but with four poster style Chinese beds covered in netting to fend off the mosquitoes. A real sense of atmosphere. The sense that you are somewhere off the beaten track is heightened as there were only the monks there as we arrived and we were told the showers were communal, so we would be sharing them with the monks. The girls do have a separate block. Then the toilets, communal again, door less squats with what must be the most fantastic view from any toilet. As you sit, you can look out over the hillside that you have just clambered up, the rainforest and the mountainside. It's just little bit off putting with the monks wondering by.

Just down from the monastery is another gem. Hard Wok Cafe. It is perched on the side of the hillside. It is just two long tables under cover and a kitchen through the back of a shack. Betty and Harry are the smiling proprietors and they can't do enough to make you welcome. The biggest surprise is the menu. As our tour groups have been coming here for a few years, they have developed a few western dishes, so, to our amazement, amongst the usual Chinese banquet fayre, was a plate of chips. There was also a freezer with cold beer and for the morning, a menu was produced with a selection of pancakes. Considering this was the most rural we had been, far from any city or westernisation and half way up a mountain at the end of a four hour hike, we were amazed. There was another tour group there from The Adventure Company and the leader was Ollie, a Chinese man who enjoyed a few drinks with me and our guide, Nathan and some of our group.

In the morning, it was back down the mountain, through the monkey areas again with them hungry for breakfast and stalking around us, ready to grab any visible bags or bottles. The monkey police, locals who are employed to protect us with monkey sticks from the hungry primates, were out in force. Some with catapults aimed at the monkeys. It became pretty obvious to me, that to keep yourself in a job as a Monkey Policeman, you need aggressive monkeys and food. The monkey sticks and catapults were all heading to the same end. At the pavilion, we split the group into those wanting to do a long walk back or a bus ride. Eugenie was getting the bus, so Janie and I had to take the long walk.

Emei Shan on first inspection was a fantastically beautiful place, but, scratch the surface and there is a lot of environmental management that just isn't right. It turns out that about 20 years ago, Deng Xiao Ping visited the place and said "turn your rice into gold" and thus tourism was born in China. Since then, the farmers have had their rice terraces compulsory purchased and they now have a permit to sell souvenirs to tourists (reminds me of the old Native American saying, that you cannot eat money). The monkey police and the sedan chair porters all used to be farmers as were the many people carrying the 50kg blocks that were constructing the pathways that we were walking along. All are in the name of improvement, progress, modernization. There are now fake wooden handrails (made from a sort of concrete) and fake stone carvings (made from fibreglass mounted on breeze-block). At the top of the mountain, the 72m tall 10 faced Buddha, which people from all over China come to prey at as Emi Shan is on one of the 4 sacred mountains was only completed in July 2006.

When we got back to Baoguo, Eugenie had changed the accommodation to a hotel. Some of the group couldn't stand a third night in a monastery.

7. Yellow City, 02/04/07 (Chengdu)

What was it that Jimmy
And his girlfriend sang about 'Yellow City'?
Asking if it would make her pretty
All about that first ride in a taxi
And wondering where that journey
Would lead them both, and if they
Had made the right decisions to be
Starting a new life in the Yellow City

I just kept humming 'Yellow City'
And thinking, what will become of me?
And as Mao was quoted by Geddy Lee
'To arrive is not the soul point of the journey'
I have written poetry
And travelled a thousand miles already
Living in my own wondrous story

8. Enlightenment, 02-04/04/07 (Emei Shan)

Up amongst the clouds again
At the top of the sacred mountain
This vast expanse of white I'm surrounded by
Becoming part of it, almost floating away
But what I really wanted to see
Was the cloud-tops, with only blue sky above me
So, I turn around and watch the courtyard unfold
As the buildings and people appear and dissolve
Mixed in with the chanting and incense sticks
The golden ten faced tower is revealed for only a glimpse
This is some sort of connection
This other world, halfway to heaven
And I wish I could get some enlightenment
Of what this all means on the sacred mount

A monk says a prayer for a woman
I can see the outline of her mobile phone
In the back pocket of her jeans
And I have to question what this means
The statues and oh so obvious fables
The incense, the gong, the chanting rituals
What place has religion, what is this religion
That has survived so much and for so long
And again I need enlightenment
About the Buddha, and what it all meant

And then I feel, as I observe
I'm imposing on someone else's private world
The incense sticks that I light and leave
Cheapens the prayer of one who believes
And I'm walking on someone else's sacred ground
Desecrating without knowing, religion, heaven, comes
crashing down
And again I feel so ignorant
And again I want enlightenment

So full of questions, humbled and unsure
I head back down the mountain in the cable car
And I remark at the breeze blocks and concrete construction
Once again getting the urge to be enlightened
About how this could be on the sacred mountain
I begin my descent and peruse the question
As I see the information signs on the trail
Whilst there are butterfly's in cases on sale
And a man throws a plastic bag to a monkey
To photograph it eating junk food cos it's funny
And again I look for enlightenment
About what's being done to the environment

Two parallel plastic blue lines
Twist through the distance through rocks and vines
Then, I notice the fake wooden hand rails
Made of plastic surrounding metal cables
And the larger than life figures carved in rock
Is actually fibreglass, mounted on breeze block
Man is definitely making himself known
Amongst the sacred mountains' blood and bones

I descend the staircase to the temple pavilion
Workers carry stones on their backs in the opposite direction
All these improvements for tourism
Another environmental achievement
Then we are met by a monkey troupe
And an army of stewards in blue suits
Each wielding a stick to protect you
From the thieving monkey as you try to pass through
These beggars, these thieves, these addicts
That we have created and shown tricks
Then I see the man with the catapult sling
Shoot at the mother that is nursing
Well, monkey see, monkey do
I hope monkey learns to shoot back at you

Then another monastery trapped in time
Where walking in feels like trespass of a kind
An I think about my impact on this shrine
Then compare it to those much bigger crimes
farmers removed from their terrace plantations
That they have lived from for generations
In order to beautify for increased tourism
Now they have a permit to sell souvenirs to them
This processed environment that you see
Which is losing its reason to be
From rural community
To theme-park employee
From sacred shrine
To Disney-time

And I really am looking for enlightenment
As I see the Chinese, quite content
As I'm offered yet another cigarette
And a luke-warm beer that I haven't finished yet
We watch the T.V. game show
Then the adverts of what we can buy tomorrow
Has the search for enlightenment
Been replaced by cheap entertainment?
And a manmade religion
On a manmade mountain
In a manmade China, turning modern
Where everything is under construction

9. Dairy Queen, 08/04/07 (Yangshuo)

Life must be sweet
When you're as pretty as an ice cream cone
Walking down the street
With your laptop and your mobile phone
But you can't stand the heat
And you want to go back home
'Cos there's nothing to eat

Stupid stick things, is there no spoon?

Dairy Queen, Dairy Queen, Dairy Queen, Dairy Queen
Dairy Queen, Dairy Queen, Dairy Queen, Dairy Queen

You went to Tiananmen,
And MacDonald's by the square
You photographed them
Why do these people stare?
You went to Xi'an
No Dairy Queen out there
Why can't this place be more like, um
America?

Dairy Queen, Dairy Queen, Dairy Queen, Dairy Queen
Dairy Queen, Dairy Queen, Dairy Queen, Dairy Queen

Back packing
Aint my thing
I want to go to the disco
And party
Look at me
I'm wearing all my designer clothes

This place sucks
Just old rocks
Boring stuff that's not even clean
These beggars
Postcard sellers
Why are they always bothering?

Dairy Queen, Dairy Queen, Dairy Queen, Dairy Queen,
Dairy Queen, Dairy Queen, Dairy Queen, Dairy Queen,

It's not my scene, said the Dairy Queen
It's not my scene, said the Dairy Queen.

The following morning we had a 10 hour bus ride to Chongqing. This is a city of 33 million souls and one of the most soul less places on earth. It has a checkered history, stretching back over 2000 years and was the short lived capital of Kuomintang (or Guomindang, or Nationalist Party Government) China during the Second World War. In the last decade or so, money has been pumped into this strategically placed port city on the Yangtze and construction has covered the numerous hills. New skyscrapers raise the skyline into the perpetual smog. We arrived earlier than planned; the 10 hour bus journey from Emei had only taken around 8 hours, so Eugenie suggested lunch at Pizza Hut. Chongqing has all the modern, western franchises, but as ever, it is a mistake to believe you are anywhere else but in China. Eugenie got annoyed with the waitress because she could not speak English. She told her that if she worked in a western Restaurant, with a menu in English, then she should learn the language. She then argued about the drinks re-fills. This was all typical Eugenie, but we hadn't witnessed it quite like this before. After lunch, we had some free time to wander around the city and go shopping in the massive Carrefour shopping centre there for supplies for our boat trip before meeting our local guide.

The only good thing to say about Chongqing, is that Amy comes from there. She was the local guide and would spend the next three days on the Yangtze River boat with us. On the way to this part of the trip, Eugenie had mentioned Amy as a pretty girl. I thought nothing more of it. When we met Amy, she seemed a bit shy to talk to us. She was pretty, but not in a stereotypical way, with a fuller mouth than is common with Chinese girls and a fringe covering her high forehead. Eugenie was trying to get her to take us to dinner, but Amy wanted to go out with her friends instead. She wouldn't see them for a while and there was some sort of party going on that evening. There was a compromise, where Amy took us to the Trade Winds Restaurant and I ordered food with her, practicing my new Mandarin skills. Eugenie had gone elsewhere; she had told me that it was the local guide's job to look after the group, not the role of the leader. She had issues with Amy, just as she had with just about everybody else we had met so far. We got though the dinner ordering, my first real attempt at doing this with a group and something that I needed to practice to get right. Once I had rattled off our favourite dishes, with a couple of forced changes, with Amy laughing at my difficulties, I sat down with great relief, then Amy left.

On this Yangtze boat trip, we had far better accommodation than my previous time when I was the only white face on a stinking ferry. That time, the heat was 40 degrees and sweating bodies filled up all available space. The toilets were overflowing 20mins after leaving port and I was sharing 10 to a cabin with chain-smoking, throat clearing, spitting and constantly yelling Chinese. The only really unpleasant thing on my second trip was the karaoke lounge, or rather the Chinese tourists who would insist on singing at the tops of their voices in there until midnight, drinking as they sang and keeping the rest of us from a much needed night's sleep. The other tour group leader, Ollie, was on the same boat and he was an enthusiastic participant in the karaoke, much to the angst of his group who mostly wanted a quiet night and a game of "who am I?" This is a game where the tourists were pretending to be historical characters and all very pseudo-intellectual and very dry. Eugenie wrote up an itinerary for the following three days and took to her bed. We only saw her for the essential meals and my Chinese lessons, as she had said; "It is the guides' job to guide on the boat". There are a number of excursions that you can do as part of the boat trip. It docks at certain ports, we get off with Amy and have a guided look around. I'd been asked by head office to check out these excursions, so I did every one of them.

The first was the Ghost City. According to the Chinese, when a person dies, their soul comes to this place to be judged. It is a complex of temples, built on a hillside and looked over by the immense statue of the Taoist Jade Emperor built into the hillside. This place is a must for all Goths. Temples dedicated to different demons with gruesome frescoes. There are statues depicting all the different sorts of torture you can receive in hell. Thoroughly enjoyable. On the other side of the valley from the old stuff, they've built a theme park in true Chinese tourism style with a Ghost Bazaar (street selling tack) and a Ghost House, a bit like you'd find on a local fair ground on a Bank Holiday Sunday.

I got chatting to Amy, who had worked as a local guide for the last year or so, taking trips down the Yangtze, then returning to Chongqing before doing the trip again. She told me that the previous group had been very unhappy with the boat and she and the leader and trainee Tang had cleaned the toilets before the group agreed to stay on the boat. I wondered how they would have survived on my boat five years earlier. I wondered what sort of expectations these people had, after all, this is a trip with an adventure tour company, not a luxury cruise. I was pleased to find out that Amy would drink a beer, although she knew Eugenie would not be pleased if she found out. Some of the group and Ollie's' group who were also on board had a few drinks. I told Amy the panda story, which had her rubbing her eyes and laughing, we were getting along so well. In the afternoon, she taught the group how to play mahjong, the Chinese game that looks like dominoes, but plays more like rummy.

Other Excursions include the Largest Waterfall in Asia, The White Emperor City (a must for all you who have read "The Romance of the 3 Kingdoms"... what, you haven't?) and the village of the poet Qu Yuan, where you can try dragon boat racing. Somewhere in the midst of all this, and I didn't find out the whole story until my second trip, Eugenie had a go at Amy and left her crying. It turns out she had been spending too much time with me! Well, I'd only been in the country for 3 weeks and already I had girls fighting over me. What is a bloke to do?

The trip continued, but a little more subdued apart from my co-trainee, Janie, who really came into her own on the Three Little Gorges Tour. There was a lot of scenery to look at, so I plugged myself into my Walkman and listened to the Mandarin lessons. Amy seemed very pleased that I was trying to learn the language. We watched on as our group found beer. So much so that they drank the boat dry. As we were leaving the boat, Janie, along with some of the more drunk members of our group, decided that the exit from the deck was a stage. Once up there, she shouted out at the top of her voice "Ni hao!" Back came the reply from the waiting Chinese "Ni hao!". So she did it again in true "can you hear me Long-beach Arena?" style. "Ni hao!" It was a real rock-star moment, with the Chinese crowd in her hand. I think it was still the only word she'd learned in Chinese, but that was all it took.

The boats last stopover was at the village of Zi Gui in the Xi lin Gorge. This is the home town of Chinas most famous poet Qu Yuan. He was a minister in the government of the state of Chu, during the Warring States Period, around 300 BC. He was a champion of political loyalty and truth, eager to maintain the Chu state's power. Qu Yuan advocated a policy of alliance with the other kingdoms of the period against the hegemonic Qin state, which threatened to dominate them all. Legend has it that the Chu king fell under the influence of other corrupt, jealous ministers who slandered Qu Yuan and banished him. In exile, he continued to write literature expressing fervent love for his state and his deepest concerns for its future.

According to legend, his anxiety brought him to an increasingly troubled state of health; In 278 BC, learning of the capture of his country's capital, he is said to have waded into the Miluo River, carrying a large rock and performed ritual suicide. The villagers carried their dumplings and boats to the middle of the river and desperately tried to save him, but were unsuccessful. In order to keep fish and evil spirits away from his body, they beat drums and splashed the water with their paddles. They threw rice into the water as a food offering to Qu Yuan and to distract the fish away from his body. The act of racing to search for his body in boats gradually became the cultural tradition of dragon boat racing, which is held on the anniversary of his death every year. Today, people still eat "*zingzi*" dumplings and participate in dragon boat races to commemorate Qu Yuan's sacrifice on the fifth day of the fifth month of the Chinese calendar

At Zi Gui, we could visit the temple dedicated to Qu Yuan and take part in a dragon boat race. There were enough westerners on the boat to form a team, so that is what we did. Ollie told us that the westerners always won the dragon boat race because the Chinese were not used to exercise or competition and that all we needed to do was get ahead in the race and the Chinese boat would give up. Excellent coaching, as we pulled ahead in the first few minutes and true to Tour Leader Ollie's advice, the Chinese gave up and we romped home.

At the end of the three days on the boat, it is customary to tip the guide. We have a tipping kitty with a prescribed amount for each guide, then it is up to the group if they wish to contribute further. The idea is that you only tip for good service, and usually, the service is good and the group will contribute. Eugenie took Janie and I into her cabin and asked what we thought about tipping Amy. We both said that Amy had been a good guide and deserved a tip, Eugenie didn't agree. I don't think she put the full amount of the tipping kitty into the tip envelope. What put Eugenie's back up, is that I, then Janie, took out our own money and put this into the envelope. Then the envelope was passed around the rest of the group. As we left Amy, saying goodbye and thankyou at the dock, I went over and said that we had something for her. Eugenie was reluctant, but also thanked Amy and handed her the tip envelope. This was strained, but I knew that I had done the right thing. It goes completely against Chinese culture to question or disagree with your teacher or boss and that was the role that Eugenie had. As we left, Amy texted me, thanking me for the tip, it was much more than what she expected, or got the last time from Eugenie and she said that I would be a good leader, then she texted again, saying that I WAS a good leader. I knew that I had made a friend and I was going to come this way again in only three weeks' time. Eugenie still had to have the parting shot though. She asked me if I liked Amy. I said, hesitantly, that I did, not wanting to be drawn into anything more than finding new friends in this new and foreign country. "Well", said Eugenie, "I am sure that if you offer her 300 or something she will go with you". I said, "what? is she that type of girl?" Eugenie replied, "what do you think?" She had taken me completely off my guard.

One thing that really brought home the changes on the Yangtze River since I had last visited in the last five years was of the suspended bridge "Dragon Bridge". It used to span the Three Little Gorges from a height of 80 m above the river and was now at water level. All the houses, market, farmland and a few ancient monuments were now under water. We also took a look at the Dam that is responsible for this. This is a three hour tour that has all the nerds asking technical questions and all the girls wanting to get out of there as soon as possible. I could go into one here about group dynamics, but instead I'll leave the juicer stories for later. Anyway, the dam is another environmental catastrophe in the making but on a scale that is breathtaking. With all the industry now churning out all the waste upriver, this is going to turn into the world's largest blocked drain.

We had a tour of the Three Gorges dam with our guide Emily, where I bumped into Sheila, on her training trip with Suzy Li, an experienced Chinese leader, then spend the night in a town called Yichang. I had a night in Yichang five years previously which had turned into me being stuck there for two days. After getting off the boat, I'd gone to the train station asking for the next passage to Guangzhou, and was told (sort of, because I knew next to no Chinese then) that the next train was in two days' time. There was nothing in Yichang for foreigners then, not even a hotel that foreigners could register in (apart from the big Star Rated that was completely out of my budget). I had obviously looked desperate and someone had taken pity on me, putting me in a small basic hotel which acted as my base for two days as I tried to occupy my time and find food to eat. My second impressions of Yichang were no better. These days the only difference is that with the Dam came workers and a lot of security and army and with them came brothel after brothel, after brothel. Prostitution is rife throughout China, but this place is the pits.

The next couple of days were traveling. In the morning we move on, via a bus and on to an overnight train with our destination being Guilin for a couple of days in Yangshuo. I had managed to make it to Guilin in 2002, but hadn't taken the short journey down to Yangshuo. My Rough Guide at the time had quoted an astronomical fee for taking the river cruise down the Li River and I had decided that my time and money would be better spent on the Yangtze Three Gorges. We arrived early in the morning. The train station was bustling, like all train station exits in China, dozens of people pushing against the barricades, as if they have come to a festival and you are top of the bill. Eugenie led us through with touts trying to persuade her to go to their bus or their hotel. There are a lot of people crying out "Yangshuo, Yangshuo", that was where we were going. There are public busses in the train station car park, Eugenie knew where she was heading and soon we were on the bus, filling up with the locals and a random western backpacker who had gone it alone in China. As all the seats filled, more plastic stools appeared and people sat in the aisle on them. We packed as many people on the bus as we could. It is an hour and a half journey from Guilin Train Station to Lisa's Hotel in Yangshuo and it was raining, so Eugenie took us to a bar which did a breakfast at 7:30am as we waited for the hotel rooms to be readied. M.C. Blues provided us with the first western food and orange juice in three weeks. It also served Oreo Milkshakes, which had the Americans salivating whilst I had never heard of Oreos before arriving in China.

We walked around town with the cafes and shops just opening up. This is a backpacker's paradise, unlike anywhere else that I had seen in China and would not have been out of place in Thailand. The whole of the main street, West Street, has converted the village houses into souvenir shops, T-shirt shops, cultural gifts and cafes. These, such as Café China advertise shepherd's pie, blueberry cheesecake and cold beer. I found out that Yangshuo was "discovered" amongst the limestone karsts about 12 years previously and the traveling backpacking community liked it so much that they never moved on. There are now dozens of bars and cafes in the town catering for Western and Chinese tourists alike. I met Snow here again in her Bar 98 and was also introduced to Monkey Jane at her bar. The two are sort of rivals for western drinkers, but in the best possible way.

In the afternoon, we took the Li River Cruise. Our local guide was George Chan. He was in his mid-twenties and was in business with his brother in law, Richard. We all got on the boat which easily catered for the 14 of us and set off, George explaining the scenery, the limestone karsts, many with names. It is a truly beautiful place. The hills rising steeply out of the riverbank, just like in one of those traditional Chinese paintings. These places actually exist, with the wisps of cloud circling the lofty peaks; only a dragon is missing to complete the picture. We stopped at a village and George explained about rice cultivation, the farmers growing a mixture of crops and raising chickens, pigs and sometimes other livestock and fishing in the river. It all seemed like a self-sustainable paradise. The village, he said was old and the people were poor, but they had all the things that they needed, they just wanted nicer, bigger houses than the traditional baked mud brick ones. They wanted cars rather than the 3 wheeled vehicles that had the multipurpose of being able to hook the engine up to drive farm machinery. They wanted T.V.'s, then everything else that they saw advertised on T.V. We all thought George was a pretty cool guy. He wasn't married either, which in a rural area is surprising, he was good looking, a part owner of a business and was building his own house on his own land in this most beautiful part of China. He was quite a catch really, so I asked Eugenie what she thought. I was surprised by her response. "He is a peasant" is all that she said.

That evening we ate on a terrace overlooking the town and watched the sun go down over the karsts. Then it was off to Bar 98 for drinks but not until Eugenie had me typing up a trip booking and going through some accounts on her lap top with her. I had hardly done any "paperwork" since the start of the trip. Both Eugenie and Janie had lap tops, so they were spending time together going through the systems and background reading. I had got my Chinese lessons from Eugenie, but didn't know anything much about the paperwork side of things. Trying to learn this, in a bar, when all I could think about was having a beer, was not the best place. Eugenie, like most Chinese girls, does not drink. Luckily, she goes to bed early too, leaving me in the bar for the rest of the night. I got a taste for Yangshuo and the westernised bars that I had been missing over the last month.

Part of the itinerary here includes a bike ride to Moon Hill, through the rice paddies and terraces. Moon hill is a karst with a hole through it. George Chan was our guide again. For two hours, with a hangover, I followed at the back of the group, down country roads, along the bumpy stone paths between the rice paddies, looking at the farmers working in the fields, the ox ploughing, the three wheel carts driven passing by. This was the real experience of being in China again. Being a part of the wonderful scenery. I didn't actually climb moon hill, though people say that the view from the top (800 steps up) is amazing, it just seemed too much like hard work and Eugenie agreed with me. She doesn't like the hiking, like most of the other Chinese, she can't see why she should do hard work if she doesn't have to. Hard work is for peasants. I reckoned that Moon Hill would be there the next time I came through, and the next, so there was no hurry in going up it. George took us to a local house, where an old lady lived and he cooked lunch there. We found out that the old lady had no family, so, was happy that the group would eat at her house and pay her for the use of her Kitchen. It was one of those feel good moments that you get when you know that you are not just a tourist, but helping to improve the lives of the people that you meet.

On the way back to the town, I rode side by side with Eugenie and she put her arm on mine, then her hand in mine as we rode. I'm not sure what it meant, I think it was just a Eugenie thing, but it was nice.

I managed to meet Monkey Jane at her roof top bar with fantastic views of the town in the karsts. Ting Ting was in town, along with Ada, they were both training together with Nigel an experienced leader from Australia who at 6 feet 6 inches towered above everybody else that I had seen in China. In the evening we went to the Cooking School, which involved a visit to the Yangshuo Market then a ride out to a beautiful setting in Chao Long village amongst the paddy fields and karsts. We met Pam there, who I had seen in Beijing during training. We cooked five dishes, this was the only time I have had to cook myself a meal all month. I thought to myself "When I get home I intend to be dazzling the ladies with my new found Oriental culinary skills". Yangshuo has a load of other activities to get involved with, but on this trip, there just wasn't the time to do any more and to be honest, I was just wanting to relax and soak up the atmosphere for a while. I was completing my training, I was in a rural idyll with home comforts and I had the adventure of my own trip, starting in just a few days' time. I was on the cusp of the greatest chapter of my life.

10. Moon Hill, 11/04/07 (H.K.) 28/04/07 (Yichang)

Maybe I would take you to the moon and back
Instead of waiting at the foot of Moon Hill
Was there more happening as we rode along the track
Hand in hand as we ride side by side on bicycles
You were the one who has taught me so much
The one who taught me how to say 'you are beautiful'
But we both have to move on, so one last touch
And you become just another no-name girl

Riding back home from Moon Hill
Arm in arm on a bicycle
Like two young lovers, what a thrill
And the world was beautiful

Riding back from Moon Hill
Arm in arm on a bicycle
Like two young lovers what a thrill
Neen shir piao liang

11. The Last Day of the Holiday, 11/04/07 (HK. West Hotel)

The last day of the holiday
The last blink of the trip
And I....am coming down
Thoughts for my diary
I try to make them fit
As I revisit Kowloon town

I have a story to write
A personal message
As I think of everyone
In this afterglow of light
My mind plays the footage
Am I missing being home?

Just worried about so many things
What's going on, what am I missing
What will I go back to
No job, my house, and who?

I have got to check up on so many things
Now I've signed up my life, left my old one behind
And I'm worried again about money coming
And surviving the unknown, wondering what I'll find
Part of me is already here forever

But for that, there's no grantee
Will I find my true calling, true life, true lover
Or will it all bypass me?

Just worried about so many things
What's going on, what am I missing
What will I go back to
No job, my house, and who?

But then again, I always think
Of London as my home
And a night out in Camden
With my friends for a drink
Find a girl on her own
And then she'll be the one

So, this trip is over
But, it's the start of another

And London is still there
And I wanted this adventure.

The last leg of the trip was off to Hong Kong. It's a city I still haven't fallen in love with. I think it's because the first time I went there I was knackered after a two month trip on the Trans-Siberian Railway and then on through China and I was just ready to go home. Hong Kong reminds me a lot of home, the hustle and bustle of London, modern, westerners and a mixture of cultures. It just doesn't have the alternative edge that would make it enough like home for me to like it. Just like home, it pissed it down with rain, just like the first time I was there. Eugenie had suggested that we could go to Disney World Hong Kong. I definitely wasn't one of the things on my list to do. The Chinese have a love affair with Disney and try as I might to tell Eugenie that it was a horrible corporation, she said that Mickey Mouse was her favourite and wasn't it all cute and good fun at Disneyland? This obsession with all things cute, including Mickey and Minnie Mouse has led to a lot of Chinese girls actually dressing like their idol. Don't be surprised if a life size Minnie walks across the street, complete with party dress, bows and ribbons. The only things missing are the ears. I've got to compare this with the dress sense of the Chinese men. Most will be wearing a stripy T shirt tucked into their trousers, which are always pulled up above the waist. From their belt, keys will be jangling; this is some sort of status symbol. Then, as they walk along in some sort of stagger as if they are trying to make themselves larger, spitting and hollering down their mobile phones as they go, they will lift their T-shirts to reveal their belly. The girls pointed this out that it could be quite nice, to see some of the athletically built boys, but the belly exposure was not limited to the good looking and lithe, but the fatter men were even more determined to walk along with their bellies out. Being fat is good in China, it is status once again and proves wealth.

We had a last night dinner on Knutsford Terrace, a nice area of bars and restaurants. We had a drink in the American Bar. Eugenie does not drink, but a few of the group convinced her that a daiquiri was nonalcoholic. Within a couple of sips she knew that they were lying. Some of the group had to leave early the next day, so they began to drift off. Considering that we had all spent three weeks with each other, I thought that we had all got along very well and got to know each other very well. It was a bit of a surprise when Eugenie whispered to me, "is Adrian a gay?" She had never met one before, or didn't think she had and was so surprised that he was just like a "normal person", he was even travelling with his mum. The group also had given me a farewell and good luck card. Lots of messages thanking me for playing my part and encouraging me, saying that I would be a good Tour Leader. One in particular from Mike caught my attention more than the others. It said "thanks to the man at the back, I would not have made it without you.... you will bring something to the Travel Company that they never even knew that they didn't have". At last, maybe I had found my niche and was on the wandering road of a fantastic new life.

Chapter 3.

FLYING BY THE SEAT OF MY PANTS

"Every one thousand mile march must start with a first step"

Mao Tse Tung, quoting Lao Tzu
(ancient Chinese philosopher)

I didn't get very much time in Hong Kong. I was supposed to be starting my first solo trip on the day that I finished my training trip. This was to become a regular workload, covering half of the country to start a new job on the same day or even run two trips at the same time. Fortunately, to do the latter, you would have to be in the same city, finishing and starting a trip. As I crossed the border and my China mobile phone became active, I received a call from Li in the office in Beijing. Two of my passengers had turned up and there was no accommodation for them. How soon could I get back and sort it out, oh and there was no accommodation for me either, should we try to put us all in the Youth Hostel? This was the admin assistant, Li asking me what to do, and I hadn't even started my first trip yet, let alone got to the correct city.

Once in Beijing I managed to book two of the couples in the group into the City Centre Youth hostel. They said that the hostel was ok, but I could see that Henrietta and Henry, forty something's from New Zealand and Graham and Geraldine, retirees from Australia's Gold Coast were not happy about the "hostel" tag. I quickly found out that people from the "Gold Coast" thought themselves a step above the average Australian and therefore, the average human being. People retiring to the Gold Coast have "made it" and are quite happy to tell you as much, whilst you look on, horrified as they tell you about playing golf, fine wines and how wonderful everything is there. I had to tell them that they would struggle to find decent wine in China, then had to tell them that the traveller's cheques they had brought and the U.S. dollars were of little use to them and they should get them changed as quickly as possible. The trip notes had mentioned bringing travellers' cheques and U.S. dollars, they had decided that there would be no ATM's in China, of which there are many, but travellers' cheques are unknown outside of the major hotels and the Bank of China branches in the tourist areas. They also assumed that I would be showing them around, as a personal guide for the afternoon. I had to tell them that the trip didn't start until we had the six o'clock group meeting and I needed to prepare before then.

I then had a couple of hours spare for preparation, and to do my first set of accounts. I was totally unfamiliar with the computer system. I'm not good with them at the best of times and I couldn't figure out where information was kept on our website, or how to upload or download information. There were a couple of other new leaders in the office, similarly struggling and a couple of managers hanging around. I asked Cathy, the Manager and then Bruce, the Senior Leader for help. The response I got was not really what I expected. I can't remember Cathy giving me any information beyond, "it's on the website". Bruce, however, said "don't you know?" then laughed condescendingly, and asked if my trainer had not shown me what to do. She had, but there was a lot to take in. I needed a bit of help. Then, suddenly, it was lunch time, and out filed Cathy, Bruce and the admin assistant, leaving us to negotiate the broken computers and unfathomable website as they ate cake. They were definitely, "out to lunch"

The start of this, my first solo trip as a Tour Leader was always going to be tricky. At my first group meeting I met the eight passengers, who had parted with their savings for a trip around China and explained that I was new, (but not exactly how new). There were the 2 older couples in their 60's, Graham and Geraldine who I had already met and Geraldine was still looking miserable. We were joined by Gerry and Georgina, also from Australia. Henry and Henrietta were the couple in their 40's and then Alison walked in, 20 years old, blond, looked at the group and said "is this it?" She was not expecting a trip with her grandparents. She had just had the time of her life on a trip around South East Asia with a group all her own age. Luckily for her, there was another girl in her 20's who arrived late. I went through the meeting as best I could, though there were a few random questions thrown in that I was not able to specifically answer. My preparation had been to go to a restaurant behind the Harmony Hotel and pre-order the dishes, a trick that many of the western leaders do. However, I had just found out that having two vegetarians and one glutose intolerant on the trip would not make things easy for me as my language skills just couldn't deal with food on that level if questions are asked. The meal was well received. Then we went on to the City Central Youth hostel. It was quickly becoming a home away from home and the bar had been nick-named the "living room, or lounge". So, here I was and it was really happening. I was running my first trip. I had a mixture of passengers to deal with, all countries and all ages. Some were going to be more difficult than others.

On the trip to the Great Wall, I gave out some information gained from the database of information on the Travel companys website and the two Guide books that I always carry with me. I gave them some history, how it had been built as a defense wall, but also worked well as a customs point, a trading entrepot, and also a highway from East to West. The towers were used as signal towers. Many historians have said that the wall was a failure as a barrier, but it had many more functions and was only breached on a few occasions in its 2250 year history. Over successive dynasties, it had been built and re-built. During the Tang dynasty it had been far inside the expanded borders of the empire, thus served no use as a defense wall and had fallen into disrepair. Similarly, under the Yuan dynasty, which breached the wall in order to conquer China from Mongolia, the wall lost its primary function. Genghis Khan had said "A wall is only as strong as the people defending it" a dig at the weakness of the Chinese. Then during the Ming, the wall was reconstructed again. The Qing dynasty, the last in China, also invaded through the wall from Manchuria and as the threat of attack began to come more from the sea, with the European powers, the wall fell into disrepair again. I talked about its comparative size (it's as long as going from New York to Los Angeles) that it was between 5m and 15m wide and 15m and 25m high. That you could not see it from the Moon, as the myth goes. The only thing that is manmade that you can see from the moon is Staten Island Dump, not the nicest legacy from our human civilization. I thought I was giving them all the information that they could ever wish for. I was wrong.

I was getting questions about the trees in the fields, our height above sea level, the Olympic village and whether I could understand the radio in Chinese. I was already out of my depth and I'm not a convincing liar. I had talked to the group about the 10km hike on the wall at some length, so thought that the wall would be a relatively easy walk for us, even for the older ones, as long as we took our time. I briefed the group about the options for returning to the bus early but they were all ready to do the hike, saying how fit they were and we set off at quite a pace. I could see that Geraldine found it very difficult, but was being determined to carry on with the rest of the group. Once again, I had people who had no idea that The Wall was a steep climb; they had assumed that it was flat. We had walked too far, when Geraldine talked about heading back. It became quite an ordeal, with me having to hold her hand on the steep down slopes. It was at this point that Geraldine said that she did not want to walk Emei Shan and could I change the itinerary for her. Already I was getting unsolvable problems on day one. At the end of the five hour walk I couldn't find the driver at Simatai car park, so I had to ring the Local Operator, Xiao Feng, in order to get him to pick us up whilst the group were all asking me where he was. Far too many questions, wanting so many answers. Once back in Beijing, I suggested dinner and the main response I got was "do we have to walk far?" they were not adventurous people.

The following morning I organised how to send the group to the Summer Palace, getting the hostel reception to write the Chinese characters for them and showing them how to get there on a map. Their lack of adventurousness was there again, thinking that I would go with them. I had done little in the way of preparation, just thrown into this trip, still having to confirm the hotels, guides and transport for the next three weeks. I had to go through the concept of the tour companys travel styles and of "free time" for them to go off exploring. Otherwise, they were not going to get the most out of the holiday, I was going to have a hard time managing their expectations.

That evening, the group had decided to go to the Kung Fu show. I thought that this would be easy enough for me to organise as Eugenie had done it only three weeks previously. The local operator, Xiao Feng had quoted me Y180 per person, per ticket, so I decided that I would take the group to the theatre myself and buy the tickets for Y100. We went to the taxi rank and got quoted Y80 for the Y10 journey. We walked on and the same happened at the next taxi, another quoted Y100 and another just laughed at us. There is no requirement for them to take us or use the meter if they don't want to. Drivers in China, including taxi drivers, are some of the most obnoxious and arrogant people you will ever meet. We walked towards Chong Wen Men, still a half hour walk away from the theatre, but with more chance of getting a taxi. Time was getting short, the group getting irate with me, not happy with the walk, the wait, the lack of organisation on my part, but we got three taxis to the Theatre. Once there, once we had gathered ourselves together, I headed to the theatre ticket office and they refused to sell me tickets. Unbelievable, how could I face the group now? I got on the phone to Eugenie and she asked me why I had not got the tickets through the Local Operator. She then explained that, as she had been a local guide, with a license, she could get show tickets, I couldn't. I was in a ridiculous position with the group wondering what was happening. About to admit defeat and deal with the consequences of a very pissed off group, I was spotted by Melody Wang. She was the other Local Operator in Beijing and she asked me what I was doing. I came clean and she took pity on me, saving my bacon by buying the group tickets for me at only Y100 per person. I left the group at the entrance to the theatre, relieved and with much to think about. I walked back to the City Centre Youth hostel and the bar for a couple of drinks.

I had not got the local guide that I had wanted for the tour of Tian An Men square and the Forbidden City. Being a new leader, I was not very far up the pecking order, so I got Karen. She needed a lot of prompting and I got little in the way of new or interesting information. Not that the group were over interested in the details of the largest palace in the world. The questions that I got from the group were concerned with why the children that we saw, at toddler age, all wore pants with a split in the crotch. It was obviously for easy toilet and the kids just went wherever they felt comfortable. "Don't they have nappies?" Well, nappies are expensive and not ecologically sound, so they don't use them. The next questions were also about toilets, asking how the Chinese wiped their arse, or if in fact they even wiped their arse, as my group had not found any toilet paper in the toilets. Our guide just said "we always bring our paper with us, you know you will visit the toilet, so why don't you?" So much for our cultural experience.

We went onto Beijing Huiling charity afterwards and there was the similar lack of organisation as before. I managed to jolly it along, but it was difficult and I was so pleased when Emma turned up for our hutong tour. She was able to fill in the gaps at Huiling and then talk us through the next part of the tour, going to a different courtyard house and explaining the local area to the group as we went. I noticed how she dealt with the rickshaw drivers. These were all men over forty years old and she was a 23 year old girl. In traditional society, a girl would never tell an older man what to do, certainly not order them about, but here, she was telling the rickshaw pullers to hurry up, get organised and was bossing them about. If this would have been in any other circumstances, it would be extremely disrespectful, but the men knew what was expected of them and grudgingly did what she asked.

We finished the tour in Hou Hai again. I had researched the area and knew that it was part of the Royal City, traditionally home to government officials, military officers and merchants. Emma had pointed out the door stops of the military officers houses, shaped like stone war drums. She had pointed out the plinths above the doors and explained that the more plinths you have, (2, 3, or 4) the higher status you were. She talked about the high steps at the bottom of the door, to "keep the ghost out" and also part of the Feng Shui folk lore, "to keep the money in".

She was quite a fun guide too, very chatty with the group. The lakes around Hou Hai were originally part of the canal system, bringing goods to and from Beijing. Emma had another story for us. Many years ago, there was a Chinese Emperor who was fighting many wars with the surrounding countries. He had used up his war chest and needed money, so he went to all the merchants in Beijing and seized what he could from them. The richest merchant in Beijing had held out, so the Emperor arrested him and threw him in jail. The rich merchant was tortured, until he finally told the Emperor where he had stashed his wealth. He told the guards that he had buried his treasure chest in the Hou Hai area, which at the time was just fields. The guards then went out, armed with spades and started to dig. As they did not know the exact location of the treasure, they dug and dug, creating a vast hole, that filled with water and is now Hou Hai Lake. The treasure, some say, is still buried, somewhere beneath the lake.

We decide to have a beer before heading back to the hotel. This is where I was asked, for the first of so many times by the Australians about the beer. I'd said that the Chinese drink it warm, to which the Australians would say, "well, that's ok for you, because you drink beer warm in England". This puzzled me the first time, as, running bars for nearly twenty years, cellar temperatures always had to be below six degrees and all lagers went through remote coolers. Evidently, the myth in Australia is that we Brits drink warm beer. A pint of bitter isn't necessarily served ice cold, it isn't supposed to be and I think that in the pre cellar cooling days of the 1960's, we served at cellar temperature, but the Aussies think we drink warm beer. When our bottles arrived, they were cold, so I expected happy customers, but no. "It's far too big, I only want a small one" they cried. The beer bottle size in China for a Tsing Tao is around 600ml, or a pint. Not unusual for me or any other Brit, but the Aussies were crying off.

We got back to the hotels around 5pm. On arrival, we found the rooms locked because I had not yet paid the bill. I had no idea at which point I was supposed to do that, we had booked "day rooms". I then had to run around, trying to find cash, as the Hostel did not accept credit card and could not exchange dollars for Yuan. I finally had to take my own money out of the cash point to settle the bill. I got a call from the local operator, Xiao Feng saying that I had booked the bus to the train station at 7:30, when I should have booked it at 7pm. I couldn't find everyone in the group to tell them this, so when Henrietta and Henry arrived back at 7pm, I was hurrying them along they were not at all pleased. When we got to the train station, they were not pleased about the wait, standing around our bags in the waiting hall either. Then came the drama getting on the train. I had told the group how to read their tickets, but it was quite confusing. You never know exactly what the train carriage will look like until you actually get onto the train. My group seemed to think I could predict the future.

I had rushed through an explanation of the sleeping arrangements in the compartments of the train. They could read their bed number and whether they were top or bottom. I told them how hectic it could be with all the Chinese getting on and off and looking around from compartment to compartment. It wasn't enough. The ticket allocation ended up with 8 passengers thinking they were sharing a 6 person berth. It's not easy as both the cabins and the beds were numbered and my group could not understand which was which and it had baffled them when it came to who slept where. The group were walking in and out of the cabins, dropping their bags, then moving them again, all in a tight space and getting upset with one another. Then the Chinese were pushing and shoving, backwards and forwards. They seem to have the urge to want to scout the whole carriage, peering in all of the cabins. Then they chat to all the new comers, inspecting us with over the top most curiosity and quite simply, getting under our feet. I don't intend to be insulting when I say that the Chinese have the enthusiasm of children. Children on a diet of coke, MSG covered noodles and chain smoking withdrawal. Henry the mathematician was the most displeased. He thought it not good enough and told me that it was a shambles. I had slowly been finding out a little about the people in my group. Henry worked creating unbreakable mathematical security codes for a bank in Singapore. He was the sort of person who had actually brought his work with him on his lap top to do in the quieter moments of the trip. He had certain expectations. I later found out that he not only was a hard working genius, but also, in his spare time did 100km runs. When the question came up of "how long did it take you to run 100km" he said, that it took just under 10 hours. Next came the question, "how long did the winner of the race take?" The answer, just under 10 hours. He was only the regional champion at this event. I also found out later on he'd never been to a night club, but that's a different story. Dealing with the sort of people that you don't often meet in everyday life is part of this job. Putting them in situations where they are completely at a loss and where you cannot help them is also part of the job too. The evil side of me gets a certain kind of glee when the wrong person ends up in the wrong place at the wrong time. It's a sort of a just desert. Then they look to you for your help and knowledge, unable to help themselves. When that happens, and you can help them, it gives you a feeling of worth, that you are capable of doing your job well and that you are appreciated. That night though, I didn't sleep well. I was worried about the next three weeks with the group. I knew I could not dodge any issues, I could not hide. Somehow, I would have to come back the next day, more able and capable than before.

Once again in Xi'an we stayed at the City hotel, which was not expecting us. I had to call the local operator, Ren Ming on arrival to sort this out. I took the group on the orientation walk and readied them for the tour of the Terracotta Warriors. I had Jim as a guide again. He elaborated on his previous information, telling a story about the changes in China. Years ago, if a man wanted to get married, he would have to possess 3 things. These would be a sewing machine, a bicycle and a watch. The sewing machine to mend his clothes, a bicycle to look for work and a watch in order to get there on time.

Nowadays, he said things had changed. In order to get married, a man would need an apartment, a car and 100,000 Yuan. He continued as we travelled through the ever growing city talking about the price of a new apartment being Y300,000 and far too expensive for the average person to buy. The average wages for a farmer in China are still only Y7000 or Y8000 per year. Compare this with the average wages in a city like Xi'an or Chengdu where it's Y20,000 per year. In Beijing and Shanghai it tops Y30,000 per year, but there is an ever growing middle class who can earn this sort of salary in just 1 month. The differences between the earnings of the rich and the average is striking. Jim continued with his complaint. We found out that he had previously worked as a teacher in a university, but it was better pay being a guide.

There is a vast lack of understanding about the West. This is something that I was hearing over and over in conversation. Jim said that it was so hard for the people to buy a house. In the old days, a farmer would just build it, or it would be provided as part of a workers benefits. People could not afford to buy a house, as we did in the west and would have to go to the bank. The bank would then lend money, but you would have to pay them interest, maybe as high as 3 or 4%. Jim was one of the many people who assumed that all westerners owned their own homes. When the tour groups would come through, everybody would say "we own our own home", without mentioning the most important part, that they were paying off a mortgage for 25 years in order to buy their homes. When I talked to him later about this, saying that nobody could afford to buy a house outright in the West, that we all had mortgages and at a much higher interest rate than the Chinese, he didn't believe me. He mentioned people who he had previously talked to on the trips who owned mansions and saw this as typical, not the exception. He couldn't see that we were both in a similar position. He said that westerners earned far more than Chinese, so buying a house was easier. Trying to compare the prices of houses in the West got me nowhere. It just proved how rich we really were. So I talked about taxation and how so much of our wages go back to the government or on daily expenditure, everything for us being more expensive. Jim replied, saying that a car in China was even more expensive to buy than in the West and it is true, an imported model along with designer and luxury goods are as expensive or even more so than in the West. But he was missing my point. I was trying to talk about an average person's cost of living.

We got on to talking about tax. The Western economies and the Chinese are very different. To give a better understanding, we have to look at the historical context, where the Communist Party, technically owned everything. In the last 20 or so years, it has sold of chunks of business and industry to some favoured individuals, but for this example, we have to look at China as one large single workplace. This workplace also provides accommodation for its workers and services such as health care and education. The way that it does this is by paying a low wage, keeping the profit from selling what the workers produce and turning it into housing, roads, a better welfare system. With this sort of society, there is no need for taxation. In China, income taxation, for a large part of the population is a new thing. Different provinces set different rates, but in Beijing, the tax earning threshold was recently set at Y1,600 per month. Below this amount, you don't pay any tax. So, about 90% of the population, or, put it another way, only about 12% of Chinese people pay income tax. Once you earn this princely sum, you pay 2% tax. There is a progressive taxation system with higher earners paying 5% and the super-rich paying even more. Jim was complaining about having to pay the government so much tax and having to pay interest to the bank for his mortgage. He didn't know how lucky he was.

Once we got to the Terracotta Warriors Museum, we began a tour of nearly three hours. Jim first took us to the cinema, where we get the background information to the first Emperor of China, Qin Shi Huang and his Terracotta Warriors. He ascended the throne of the Qin state at the age of 13 in 221 BC when he killed his prime minister. He then went on to conquer the neighbouring six kingdoms to create the empire of China. He thought himself a god, ruling with an iron fist, subduing his people. He also started to build his mausoleum, filling it with a Terracotta Army. When the emperor died, prematurely, there were uprisings and peasant revolts against his son and heir. This culminated in the plundering and burning of the mausoleum. Then the site was forgotten about for 2200 years until a farmer, who was digging a well, found the first terracotta warrior in 1974. The mausoleum itself is a pyramid, of the scale of the Great Pyramids in Egypt, a couple of kilometers from the site of the excavated Terracotta Warriors. I visited the place on my first ever trip to Xi'an. The pyramid was a grass covered hill and easily mistaken for one. By the hill was a small exhibition theatre, showing what was believed to be inside the mausoleum. The Emperor was buried in a scale model of the known world, with rivers of mercury representing the Yangtze, the Yellow river and the seas around China. Above this, the sun, moon and stars revolved in a false sky. Our tours don't visit the mausoleum and it will be a few years before the government agree to excavate it.

From the Cinema, we walk on to "Pit One". Here there is a scale model of the whole site and you can see that the Terracotta Warriors are just a small part of it. Then we walk into the large, aircraft hangar of a hall, the size of a football pitch, where over 8000 of the 9000 the Terracotta Warriors discovered so far are restored. The Warriors were placed there to protect the tomb from the east, where all the conquered states lay. The pit is solidly built with rammed earth walls and ground layers as hard as concrete. Pit One, 230 meters long, contains the main army. It has 11 corridors, most of which are over 3 meters wide, and paved with small bricks with a wooden ceiling supported by large beams and posts. This design was also used for the tombs of noblemen and would have resembled palace hallways. The wooden ceilings were covered with reed mats and layers of clay for waterproofing, and then mounded with more soil making them, when built, about 2 to 3 meters higher than ground level. Pit Two has cavalry and infantry units as well as war chariots and is thought to represent a military guard. Pit Three is the command post, with high ranking officers and a war chariot. Pit Four is empty, seemingly left unfinished by its builders. Jim said that the excavations were still going on in Pits Five, Six, Seven and soon more.

In the evening, I took the group for a meal in the Muslim Quarter. As with all the cities that I was visiting, I would have to find time, sometime in the afternoon to go to a restaurant and try to pre order the food. It is the only way I could organize a meal as any requirements or questions from the group just could not be catered for. We went to a restaurant, Number 52, Muslim Street. It has an unfathomable name to both Chinese and Western tourists alike, hence all the buildings on Muslim Street have a large numbered plaque. I had decided not to venture to the street stalls because they were just a bit too daunting for many of the passengers. On my training trip, Eugenie had refused to eat in the Muslim Quarter, saying that it was just too dirty. Here, it's kebabs, breads and a real feel of the Middle East. None of the group wanted to go out for a drink, but I had a walk through Bar Street, realising that it is the most disappointing Bar Street I know and completely manufactured for the few tourists that go there. I got talking to a couple of American English teachers, who mentioned a bar called Music Man, that supposedly played live music. That night, I went in search for it and found it in the Amusement Park, outside the city wall, when it was just about to close at 1am.

The next day was a free day. Most of this was spent getting the paper work up to date, meeting Ren Ming for payment and tickets. That evening I took the group for hot pot, but Henry was feeling ill and soon after, Alison also started feeling ill. This happens a lot with the groups and there is little that you can do. It is just the change in environment, different food etc., but they will usually tell you that they have food poisoning or some terrible disease. Then I was back on Bar Street again, on my own, until I was joined by an English teacher. He was a strange bloke, but I went along with him and his friends to a couple of night clubs where they all got extremely pissed and ended up dancing on the platform behind the bar. This is usually reserved for the clubs' employed dancers, but this bloke didn't care and it all looked bad and was only going to get worse. It reminded me of the Alan Partridge "lap dance" sequence. I didn't stay too late.

12. Missing Something, 19/04/07 (Xi'an) 22/04/07 (Emei Shan)

It's an odd sort of feeling
Though there's little I'm missing
I'm missing some birthdays
So, I feel I have to say
How much I'd like to be there
And how much I care
When I'm composing letters
To send out in the ether

But I do wonder how my emails are received
And wonder how people are thinking of me
And there are people I try to contact every day
But the Great Wall of China seems to get in the way
So, a quick look on MySpace and a reply to some friends
'A month in China' didn't do it justice in the end
And though I smiled at those whose replies were sent
There is that odd feeling of missing those who didn't

I've met some good people, up mountains, on boats
Exchanging stories, philosophies, our thoughts
But there was always going to be something missing
Compared to the people that I've known for so long

So into the internet place
I click on MySpace
To take me back home
Some sort of discussion
Who's in the inbox

For the China de-tox?
I need this connection
To what's happening in Britain

But I get a questionnaire
'What toilet paper do you prefer?'
The 'yes' and 'no' show
That's not worth an answer
I thought T.V. was bland.
Now, I'm living in a land
That has clipped what we can know
Oh, knowledge, my friends
And the chance to write something
That might change anything
That internet that I hate so
'Cos it's all packed full of nothing
Some more trite questions
About life in two dimensions
Pulling the strings in a puppet show
When we could have revolutions

So, in a bar, on my own
With a bottle of Tsingtao
Dice with the barmen
And a non-conversation
Just going through the motions
'Til a mixed table beckons

I've met 'the son of Alan Partridge'
But far more out on a limb than Norfolk
In a club, like, when Ibiza was all the rage
Then everyone came home and relived the joke
It's 'Peppers' in the eighties all over
The boom and bang of the continental holiday
Places on a bootleg D.V.D. cover
Places that would always be so far away

I'm missing something
So, I keep clutching
In a bar, on the internet
I am waiting
I'm missing something
Thought I don't need anything
And I'm not lonely yet
But, I'm missing something.

We had another train journey to Chengdu, with the group getting mixed up with the compartments and sleeping arrangements again. Most took it in good humor, but not Henry and he was constantly asking what time the train would arrive. Chicory met us again at 5:30 am and we dropped our bags off at the hotel and then off to the Pandas before 7:30 am. Tired and grumpy passengers. Chicory does an astounding job under the circumstances, keeping them all informed and chatting to them. Her spiel on the bus starts off with the background history of Chengdu. It's a city with over 3000 years of history. The meaning of Chengdu is "becoming a city, or capital" and that is what it was, the capital city of the Shu kingdom (the kingdom of the "Three Kingdoms" fame). It was the first place to have a field irrigation system. Over the centuries, it has been a city famous for its brocade, its hibiscus trees, paper making was invented here and the first paper money used, primarily, due to its position on the Tea Horse trade route. Tea and Chengdu are synonymous. It is famous for its Tea Houses. Here, the locals will sit, play mahjong, chat, have massage or even ear cleaning for the best part of the day, over a re-filling pot of tea. The tea is one half of the dining culture of Chengdu. The other half being Sichuan Hot pot.

The climate in Chengdu favours the eating of spicy hot pot and drinking tea, to warm and invigorate in the winter and to sweat and cool down in the summer. Sichuan province is noted for its more leisurely pace of life, its spicy, beautiful women and its "soft ear" men. Chicory said there was a saying, comparing Beijing with Chengdu. In Beijing, you get up early, go to work, change your job before lunchtime, skip lunch, have no time to go shopping and get home tired. In Chengdu, you get up late, go to the Tea House, chat with friends, go shopping and are home early and feel much better about life. She said that in Chengdu, the spicy girls will tell the men what to do and it is common for them to grab their husbands by the ear and twist it, so giving him a soft ear. The women in Sichuan are beautiful; the climate is often cloudy and cooler than in other parts of Southern China and the girls have a clearer complexion, aided by the tea drinking and the spicy hot pot. The men, however, are small as they have not enough sun-shine to grow tall and strong. Giving us "spicy girls and soft ear men".

Before too long, we were at the Panda Research Centre. One thing that was another cultural eye opener this time was the reaction westerners can get. Over the previous weeks, there had been a lot of occasions where Chinese had come up to us and wanted their photos taken with them. First one, then another, sometimes a whole group, all with the identikit "V" sign poses. A seedy part of me has often wondered what they do with the photos when they get home, but there are so many Chinese wanting photos of westerners, that they can't all be perverts. Admittedly, some people get photo requests more often than others. I get the odd group wanting me in there, but the prize is always the pretty girls. The blonder, the better, so it seems. And we had the youngest, blondest photo opportunity this side of Scandinavia in our group. At first, the kids were happy enough in the Panda Centre, screaming at the poor animals and trying to get them into their photographs. However, once Alison arrived, things changed. First one, then a dozen, then up to 40 children were trying to get a photograph with her. Next, someone handed over a pen and paper for an email address, (this is also quite common, but I've never seen it lead to anything much). Before you could say "cuddly panda", there was a crowd of "Britney" sized proportions, all clamoring for email addresses and photos. One westerner had taken all the attention away from the pandas, who were idly chewing their bamboo on the other side of the fence.

After our visit to the pandas, we went on to the Wenshu monastery again. Henry didn't eat the vegetarian banquet. The whole group just wanted to go back to the hotel after that. Whilst in Chengdu, I also did a side visit to Sam, our other Local Operator who Eugenie had introduced me to the previous month to ask about getting into Tibet. I was being given time off at the end of this trip and wanted to spend it wisely. The prospect of spending a week in Shenzhen was not appealing and as it looked like I was only going to be employed for one season in China, I wanted to see and do as much as I possibly could. This would possibly be my one and only chance of going to Tibet.

After our whirlwind day in Chengdu, we were on our way again to Le Shan to see the big carved stone Buddha and then Emei Shan. At Le Shan, our bus driver took us to a place for lunch. This had seemed a good idea at the time, but it turned into an over-priced farce, with us getting what the restaurant wanted to give us, rather than what I wanted to order. We ended up with a spicy fish dish that was inedible and at over Y40 per person, was the most expensive meal I had eaten so far in China. I decided to avoid any suggestions from bus drivers the next time I came here. The queues for the walk around the statue were almost two hours long. Once again I had disgruntled passengers, who didn't seem to understand that there were a lot of people in China and that we were going to one of the most popular tourist sites in the country.

We arrived at Emei Shan around 5pm. I spotted Patrick right away. He is one of the nicest and most helpful people that I have ever met and a godsend for me. He organised dinner for us and introduced the accommodation at the monastery and went through the itinerary. I was expecting complaints about the accommodation, the shower, the hike, but to my amazement, there were none and Geraldine had decided that she could now walk Emei Shan. The only other option was staying on her own in Baoguo Monastery. This time, I had George as a guide. It was at this point that I started to find out about Eugenie's reputation. She had openly told me that the guides in Emei Shan were not very good. She was one for complaining at a lot of things, but here she'd taken it further and was refusing to work with George. Her reputation was that of a spoilt princess from Beijing and she looked down on local people. This made a little more sense in the context of her argument with Amy on the boat, it also had me prepared for out later encounters. On the trip, I could see why George was not regarded very well. His English was basic, he had no delivery, in fact, I could almost say no personality. This came through, even in his dress sense of shoes, sensible trousers and a shirt, just like you were working in an office. We stopped at the "tourist sites" along the route, George giving a background to them on the way. This included stopping to look at the "Donald Duck tree", a tree, on a hillside, that has a passing resemblance to Donald Duck's profile. I won't talk too much about how ridiculous this is here, but George was adamant that it was not Donald Duck, but a woodpecker. As we ascended, I pointed out all the usual signs in Chinglish, the miss spellings and outrageous language and we all had a laugh. The crowds on the mountain were large and we had half hour queue for the cable car. The summit was cold, wet and Henry was not happy about us staying up there the 45 minutes as George gave us an over lengthy explanation of the site. He has all the information, it was just so badly presented and he couldn't see the group's frustration at all. At the Hung Chun Ping monastery I was welcomed with open arms by Betty and Harry, who run the Hard Wok Cafe, on only my first return. I also met Ollie again, the guide for The Adventure Company and once again, we enjoyed a drink and chat together.

We got on to talking about the differences between westerners and Chinese as usual. Once again, it was the perceptions of the Chinese that I was spending most of my time trying to re-dress. I was told, how rich we all were. There were the students holidaying around the world, where did they get the money from? How we all travelled and had such interesting lives. I was trying to tell them that the majority of people that I know, go to work early, finish late, then do nothing but watch rubbish T.V. in the evenings. I said that very few had travelled; most would spend their two week holidays in Spain. When it came to money, most could not afford to do much else. Yes, so many had modern appliances, the T.V.'s the music systems, home computers, the D.V.D.'s, two cars per household, but it was all relative. We did not own our own homes, even though we said that we did, we had mortgages. What I couldn't get across to them was that it was the very few who traveled around the world and came to countries like China. I said that we were the exception, not the norm. I gave myself as a very good example of this. At the age of 37, I had never been married and had never had kids. This was definitely not the norm. I had made a decision about the kind of life that I wanted to live. For years, I had worked in a University, a wonderful, fun environment, where I was able to do as I pleased, free from the pressures of being conventional. I had always wanted to travel and to see different countries. Other people who traveled were similarly, sacrificing things at home, careers, families, the material possessions that others chose. Very few people are in a position to have it all.

This lack of having a family or a stable job puzzled Ollie, Betty and Harry. It was possibly the first time that it had ever been explained to them the way I had explained it. So, the conversation moved on. Would I like a Chinese girlfriend? I said that this was not the reason why I had come to China. Doing a job as a leader, I couldn't see how it was possible to have a relationship. They saw some of the Western Leaders as having girlfriends and moving on, a Western thing, whereas the Chinese would be getting married. There were a lot of leaders working for the same tour company as I did, none of which was married and the Chinese had never had a satisfactory answer as to why. I put it to them, that if we were the marrying sort of people, then we would already be married, at home, in England, with a career, a house, a family. Westerners had a bad reputation with the Chinese girls, it was just a cultural difference that neither party understood. In China, if you are going out with somebody, it usually means that you will get engaged and soon end up marrying them.

To get back to Baoguo, the group split into those wanting to do the long hike, which I had done the previous trip and those wanting to get the bus. I had to take those to the bus station and get the ticket, which was a first for me and a little nerve racking. They kept asking, "how long" "what is that tree" "is it the bus station that we stopped at before?" and all the other questions that I couldn't answer on the way to the bus station. My Chinese had improved to the point that I could ask for tickets to Baoguo and then which bus and when it departed. All was going well as I led the group, who were still asking "how does he know if this is the right bus?" We waited and were joined by a group of Chinese tourists, all having a great day out and shouting and laughing. I caught sight of Henrietta, with her fingers in her ears. She hated the noise, the hustle and bustle, the constant moving. She had previously stated "why are there so many people?" as, for some reason, she was not expecting a country of 1,350,000,000 people to have crowds or noise. On one of the bus journeys, she had asked me to tell the driver not to honk his horn so much, and then later on, stated that he must only be doing this to annoy her. This was my first taste of travelling New Zealanders, who for the most part are great people, but live in a country with a lot of peace and quiet, very unlike China. She had also struggled with the "too spicy" food, which no-one else had bated an eyelid to and that was why she was not on the long hike, strange food and an upset stomach and too much noise to sleep.

Back at the Baoguo monastery, there was another Tour group. My friend from training; Yu was on her training trip with Eva, an experienced Chinese leader. Their trip was not going well. It looked like there was an attitude towards Eva. The group did not like Chinese leaders. I talked to one of them and she said that on the first night dinner, Eva had taken them to a restaurant and eaten and drank for free whilst the group was saddled with a bill for over 40 Yuan per person. They thought

Eva was ripping them off throughout the rest of the trip, taking back hander's and commissions. She was not going with them on the activities that they wanted to go on. Eva was one of the largest Chinese girls I had met. Three years of hanging around with westerners and adapting to a western diet for them had put the weight on and her nick-name was "Panda". Her group labeled her as lazy. They didn't like the trains, they didn't like the basic accommodation. A catalogue of complaints. This was so unfortunate. Many restaurants won't let a group leader or tour guide pay, it is part of the custom. This had happened to me earlier that day, where I had eaten with George at a café that he had brought us to, rather than with the group. It hadn't cost me anything, but the group had eaten much nicer food than the stuff provided free for the guides. It was not Eva's job to take them on excursions, no more than it was mine, but they had not read their trip notes and once they are complaining, they will complain about anything. Yu was having the worst introduction to life as a Leader.

The next day we had the long drive to Chongqing, so Patrick took us to dinner in Emei Town, where we had access to a supermarket and dinner in the local market. I was starting to wonder what sort of people I had in my group when they started to ask me again, what they could eat on the bus journey. I thought to myself, were they every bit as bad as Eva's group? I hoped all groups were not like this, maybe this job was going to be a lot harder than I had anticipated with so many difficult, demanding idiots. When they were asked to leave their bags in the lockers at the front of the supermarket (a very sensible means of cutting down on theft and found throughout China), they were concerned that their bags would be safe, in the security lockers. Once inside, Henry was asking me where the cheese section was in a supermarket that I had never been in before, then walking off in a huff when I couldn't give him an answer. With no real dairy production in China and around 20 per cent of people being lactose intolerant, finding a cheese section anywhere is pretty difficult. To leave the supermarket, they had to produce their receipt for the goods they had bought; once again, a security measure, but they just saw it as an inconvenience. As we met up with Patrick and his family, who had organized our dinner, they complained about the food in the street market where we ate. I thought this was a fantastic, wonderful, colourful experience which we would never would have been able to enjoy without the help of the hard working Patrick, who was now embarrassed and "losing face". Then they complained that Patrick's children were eating the 1 Yuan kebabs for free, about the lack of a western toilet and that it was raining.

The journey on the public bus from Emei to Chongqing took over ten hours and although I was pleasantly surprised with the newly built toilet stop, it wasn't of the standard that the group was hoping for. When the driver lit up a cigarette, Henrietta was in near panic and I had to ask the driver to put his cigarette out.

I met up with Amy again in Chongqing. She was waiting for us at the central bus and train station. She did an introduction to Chongqing on the way to the place where we would drop our bags. She told us that Chongqing was established over 3000 years ago. The name was devised by a local governor who called it "double happiness" as he had been given the city and crowned emperor at the same time as he had got married. She told us that this was the place where chopsticks were invented, by the boat men who needed a way to eat their food as their hands were always dirty from the river mud. Chongqing is also the home of spicy hot pot. The city is renowned as the spiciest hot pot in China. The city is built over a series of hills and has a number of nicknames including mountain city and motorcycle city. The second nick name is firstly because it is the major manufacturing place in China for motorcycles and there is a saying here too. Due to the hilly terrain, nobody rides a bicycle and instead, all the inhabitants ride motorcycles. Local people say that the only people who ride bicycles are those training for the Olympics, or the insane. We dropped our bags and went for dinner at Trade Winds again, this time, with Amy helping with the ordering.

We headed off to the Carrefour Supermarket in order to get supplies for the boat, but before too long, Amy was ringing me for us to hurry us up. She said that the driver, who was to take us from the bag store to the boat, wanted to leave. According to my timings, we had a couple of hours before the boat left, but Amy was insistent. I had a group scattered across a very large supermarket, impossible to find them all and they were the sort of people who didn't like being rushed. She told me the driver would not take us if we were late. In China, drivers rule the roost. It is not many years ago that few people had private cars and if you wanted to go from place to place, you would have to take public transport. Drivers were elevated to an important position in society. They have the title of Shi Fe, or "Master", the same as an engineer, qualified trades man or a chef. With this title has come a sense of self importance to the point of arrogance. It is difficult to meet a friendly or helpful driver. They do as little as possible. Helping with bags is not part of their job description. Whilst in the cab, they smoke, talk loudly and try to get you to go to their cousin's restaurant, at inflated prices. All this is on top of the crazy driving and the constant beeping of the horn. I would often have the group asking me to tell the driver not to smoke, not to beep the horn too loudly and not to triple over take on the bends, all with a resulting grin from the arrogant sod in the driving seat. To top it all off, the driver would always ask for a tip at the end of the journey. Drivers believe that they always deserve a tip and also believe that westerners always tip, yet another misconception between the cultures. When we got to the bag store, Amy was apologising to the driver at the same time as trying to chastise us. The driver was predictably unhelpful and arrogant.

This time, Amy also had her cousin with her who was doing a private trip. He was a couple of years older than her and in business in Chengdu, but had never been on a Yangtze River cruise. We had a beer that night and met up with Ollie and the Adventure Company tour group who were on the same boat with us again. Over the three days, first Alison, then Henrietta were ill on the boat and there was nothing that either I or Amy could do for them apart from prescribe rest and to keep taking liquids. Amy had got used to westerners getting ill, trip after trip, it was just normal. The following morning we went to the Fengdu Ghost City again and Amy told us the history. Two officials from the imperial court: Wang Fangping and Yin Changsheng, wanted to escape from the political life in the court and came to Mt. Minshan outside Fengdu City to practice Taoist teachings. Both of them later became immortals by carrying out practice aspects of Taoist "Self Cultivation". Years later, people said they had seen the ghosts of the two hermits and superstitions and stories began to arise. They became widely spread and Mt. Minshan became famous. When combined together, their surnames Yin and Wang, sound very much like "King of Hell" in Chinese, (or as Amy called it "king of the hell") hence the people began to call Fengdu the "Ghost City". According to superstitious legend "the dead come to Fengdu and the devils go to hell". Since the Tang Dynasty, forty-eight temples have been built here.

We started the walk up and Amy said that we would have to complete three tasks in order for us to enter Heaven. First of all we passed a temple guarded by statues of two monstrous figures called Hua and Hoa. One was said to be able to send a bright piercing light from his mouth and be able to see into your soul, the other was supposed to emit a stench that would turn people away from the entrance to the temple and the hill. In comedic style, Hua, the one who emitted the stench, looked like he was breaking wind. There are a group of 16 large statues, all depicting devils with different attributes, who will be sent to punish those who had lived a bad life. There is one who is depicted suckling a fawn, another who is eating a human hand another who can run fast, another is the hungry ghost, who will eat and eat but never be satisfied. The next temple had two parts to it. The building on the left is dedicated to the god of health and was actually a renowned physician of the Tang dynasty. The one on the right is dedicated to the god of wealth. Beyond these temples, the open area holds the first of the three tasks that we have to perform in order to get into heaven. In front of us are three bridges, called "nothing to be done bridge", crossing the "blood river". We have to choose which of the three bridges to cross, and then cross it in three strides.

There is a staircase from the rear of the next temple that has another test. If you are over 30, you are supposed to run up, holding your breath, in less time than it takes to count to your age. This is not one of the three tests for gaining entry to heaven, but everyone does it, all of the same. The next real test is the "Ghost Torturing Pass", Amy said, that you should walk the length of the pass, but the ghosts would try to distract you and entrap you. She said, that if a ghost touched you, you should just ignore it and walk on. As we crossed the Ghost torture pass, she crept up behind random people the group and prodded them, getting the surprised reaction that she wanted.

The "Last Glance Home Tower", is a tower where the dead soul may take a last glance back at the world they have called home before they move on to where ghosts are said to have left the mortal world and entered the world beyond. This is a place called the "Ridge of helplessness". The last point, at the top of the hill is the Tianzi Palace. Standing outside, you have to complete the third task. There is a half sphere set into the ground. The task is to be able to stand on the sphere with one foot and look into the Tianzi palace, to where there is a statue of the King of Hell; Tianzi. You are supposed to look into his eyes and read the inscription set there which reads, "God can see everything".

In the palace, you are greeted by a number of statues that have all your deeds written on a parchment and they will read this out for the king of hell to make judgment on your soul. Around the sides of the Tianzi Palace there are statues depicting hell and all the tortures that you can endure there. Adulterers had their genitals burned; liars had their tongs ripped out, people being sawn in half, crushed, impaled, every conceivable torture in graphic detail. I wonder which torture you would receive if you had committed more than one deadly sin. Maybe the devils would have to draw lots.

As we walked back down the hill, I talked to Amy who told me of her boyfriend, who worked as a car salesman. A good job, but he didn't sell many cars and he didn't seem capable of sorting anything out. She said that she spent most of her time, working, organising things and trying to sort him out, they were the same age, but she thought of him as being years younger and she was tired with having to take the lead all the time. She wasn't happy with the relationship, but her mother was putting increasing pressure on her to get married, at the age of 25, she was supposed to be engaged, but the boyfriend just wasn't measuring up. It was going to be a big decision for her to end the relationship. She wanted to work for the same Travel Company as I did, but thought she was not good enough to get a job with them, I strongly disagreed. She wanted to travel more and have an interesting life before settling down. She just wasn't ready for that at all

There was an auditorium built into the complex and I had, what could only be called a "wicked idea". How about putting on a rock concert here. Live in the kingdom of Hell. All your favourite metal bands from Marilyn Manson to Alice Cooper to Slipknot and Slayer would all love to play a gig like that. Chongqing was a gateway airport city, not too far away. Now, all I had to do was find a business partner and convince the Chinese authorities. Maybe an anti-Olympic games theme for 2008 would be pushing it, but what a concept.

In the afternoon, Amy and I taught the group mahjong and then we went up on deck as the night fell. The boat has two searchlight style lights that sweep the cliff face on the side of the gorge. As I watched, I saw Zhang Fe temple, having its lights turned on as we approached. One minute, there was total darkness, the next, it was gaudy light bulbs covering the archway and the temple buildings. Taking a look here, there are numerous market stalls, mostly selling old plates with pictures of Mao on them, miniature statues, Buddhist relics, some old magazines. There was little of interest and most stalls sold identical brick-a-brack. One nice thing is the food, it's an area which has potatoes, and for a Yuan, you can get three on a stick with some chili. The other snack is the tea egg, an egg, hard boiled in tea. There are also sprats and other small fish, but I never bothered with those. In the evening, Amy, her cousin and I had a few beers together to pass the time as, if anything; this is the only time in the trip where you can relax.

Next stop was Baidi City or the City of White Emperor, located at the entrance of Qutang Gorge and not a real city, but some temples and gates on top of Baidi Hill. Climbing over 500 steps, you can reach the top. It is the starting point of the Three Gorges and is most famous for Li Bai's great poem about the city written in the Tang Dynasty called "The Romance of the Three Kingdoms" This is a story of Arthurian proportion, recounting the days of the Three Kingdoms period, after the fall of the Han Dynasty in the 3rd Century.

Amy guided us around and gave us the background story again. White Emperor City gets its name from a well, where the local lord saw some white smoke rising. He took this as a sign that he was to be the king of the whole area. The surrounding kingdoms did not like this and war broke out, but the white Emperor City survived, to play its role later on in the Romance of the Three Kingdoms. The three Kingdoms in question were the Wei, Wu and Shu, which existed around 1700 years ago. In the city at the sites of the Yong'an Palace, Liu Bei, emperor of the state of Shu in the Three Kingdoms period, entrusted his only son to his Prime Minister Zhuge Liang who was a legendary wise man. Liu Bei was supported in his battles by his two "blood brothers" Guan Yu and Zhang Fei. The former was a most formidable general who gained notoriety over the following centuries and was often prayed to as a God of Protection. He can be seen on the doors of houses across China. In 1911, one of the last decrees of the Emperor Pu Yi was to raise

Guan Yu, along with Confucius, to be officially Gods. Around the complex are frescos depicting the story of the Romance of the Three Kingdoms, battles, intrigue, and political allegiance and backstabbing. If we had all day, we could have got the full story, but neither Amy nor the group were interested enough in it. To get the most out of White Emperor City, you have to know the legend; it is much more a place for the Chinese than the foreign tourists.

In the Temple complex, there is a museum. The Three Gorges area is famed for its hanging coffins and there are a couple preserved here. It is thought that the Three Gorges area is one of the cradles of Chinese civilisation beginning over 5000 years ago. The tribes that inhabited the area at this time used to bury their dead in coffins and somehow, they were suspended, in crevices, high up the side of the gorge. Nobody knows how they got there. There is the top down theory, where the coffins were lowered into place from the top of the gorge. The bottom up method has the coffins being carried up. There is some evidence of this with the ancient plank walkway being driven into the side of the cliff face. Others believe that the river may have been higher at some point in the past, making it easier to place the coffins in the cliff. Whatever the academics decide, there is one very intriguing aspect to the coffins in the museum. One contains two children a boy of around 14 and a girl of around 11. The girl has a nail driven into her skull. The academics don't have an answer to this either.

As you enter the Qu Yuan gorge, Amy started to give us more information. The gorge is depicted on the back of the 10 Yuan note. It is the most impressive of the gorges, with the sides rising nearly 1000m, but at a little over 3 km is also the shortest. There was a story about how it was formed. Amy pointed out the coffins in the side of the cliff. It was only recently that people had found out what the coffins actually were and until then, legends had sprung up around them. She said that in ancient times, there was a dragon persecuting the local people, so one of the ancient heroes, "Yu the Great", came to this place and forged a magic sword. With the sword, he killed the dragon and also cut through the rock to form the gorge. The coffins on the cliffside looked like the magic bellows that were used to forge the sword. Another legend, said that the coffins were a spell book, left by a magician. As we passed through the gorge, she pointed out the Goddess Peak, a natural obelisk of rock, that has its own legend.

In the Prehistoric Times, there lived many fairies in the palace of heaven, among them, a clever and beautiful one was called Yao Ji. On the traditional Mid-Autumn Festival, she invited her eleven sisters to visit the earthly world, as she felt lonely in heaven. When they arrived at the Wu Gorge, they encountered Yu the Great controlling the flood there. Moved by his spirit, Yao Ji decided to help by sending him a sealed book relating to the control of water. With the help of Yao Ji and her eleven sisters, the flood was finally overcome. Since then, Yao Ji and her sisters remained in the Three Gorges area and helped the local people to tame the water. They forgot to return to heaven and turned into twelve elegant peaks along the banks of Wu Gorge.

There is more up to date history concerning the gorge. Due to its strategic position, the only access to the west of China, many battles were fought over the control of the gorge. This started at the time of the Three Kingdoms, but the Japanese in the Second World War also fought for control of the river. Along the walls of the gorge was anti-Japanese propaganda and nationalistic poetry carved into the rock. This is always a favourite photo stop for the Chinese, who still have an anti-Japanese temperament.

The next day we stopped at the Lesser Three Gorges. This refers to the three separate valleys of the Daning River, a tributary of the Yangtze, namely "Dragon-Gate Gorge", "Misty Gorge" and "Dicui (Emerald) Gorge". Here sheer cliffs and steep mountains rise on either side. We boarded a small junk to view sharp turns, and caves full of stalactites along with the wildlife of monkeys, water birds and fish. There are a number of historical relics such as the suspended coffins, boat coffins and the remains of ancient plank walkway. Of this, there is hardly anything left. I'd seen the holes in the cliff face on my first visit, years earlier and asked what they were. It was a great archeological site, but with the flooding of the Yangtze and the three gorges, it is now under water. There is a painting of it in the White Emperor City, but that is as close as you can get to it these days.

We had Emily as our guide at the Dam again. She does a fantastic job and is obviously proud of her city Yichang, but, for the group, there was little of interest. The city of Yichang is also no more than a stopover and we ended up eating in the hotel restaurant and not venturing any further. I got one very big surprise as we got to Wuhan Train station. Considering that I was only here three weeks ago, I didn't expect the main waiting rooms to have been demolished and re-built in a different part of the station. This is the pace of change in China. The old five story building which housed the station was being demolished and a completely new building had appeared immediately by the old one in less than a month. It was still not quite ready to be opened and covered in concrete dust, but that is where we had to go. Once again having to put all our bags through the bag scanners, my group noticed that there was no-body actually watching the screens, but they were told to comply with the regulations anyway. They huffed and puffed as they put their bags on, then had to scramble with the Chinese travellers to get to their bags before they ended in a heap at the other side of the X-ray machine. Bags of oranges were spilling and fruit rolled everywhere over the dusty waiting room floor. It took me a while to find the platform queue, the group complaining again and very unhappy about the lack of seats, the construction going on and the dust. They wanted to go for lunch, especially when a man came over with a sign in English saying that we could go for lunch in his cousins restaurant, but I said that I wasn't moving, I didn't trust getting out, finding somewhere and getting back again. Without me, they decided they would also for-go lunch and wait in the building site come waiting room with the other thousand or so travellers.

Then it was Guilin again. We arrived early in the morning and I headed for the bus to Yangshuo. As we left the station, there are always a couple of people who want to take you to the Yangshuo bus, for a price, even though I know where the buses are parked. Another annoying scam. Then I have to convince the driver that I'm not paying the "guide" who walked with me to the bus, or paying more than the locals pay for a seat, or paying for the baggage to be put in the luggage hold, or tipping anyone to put it there for us. It was a Saturday morning and it looked like some of the local youth had been partying all night. There was some arguments happening, not something you often see in China. One boy was annoying another until he got a punch. Another lad vomited into his own lap whilst he sat next to a disgusted Alison. Definitely not the best introduction to Yangshuo and I'd been talking up this place as the "holiday within a holiday" destination. Most of the group came for breakfast at M.C. Blues and were suitably impressed to get western food. Then I did the orientation walk with them. I had also been asking the group what activities they wanted to do whilst in Yangshuo and had contacted Rosemary, the Local Operator, for help. It rained throughout the first day that we were there, my miserable group were left to their own devices. I made it to Bar 98 and Monkey Jane's.

The weather had cleared up in the morning. We had Meg as a bicycle guide, a pretty local girl recommended by Rosemary. I had asked for George Chan again, but he was booked out. One of the first questions that Meg was asked was "are there any wild animals around here?" I didn't think that there were, but Meg answered "Yes". So, they asked her what these wild animals were. Meg said that she could not remember what the name was in English, they were "Rrrr...Rrrr...Rrrr.." Somebody in the group cried out "Tiger?" another called out "Bear?" as Meg continued to announce "Rrr" than it came; "Rabbit". What a letdown. We took a different route than the previous time, arriving at Moon Hill. We had our Farmers Lunch there in the restaurant, which was a disappointment, as the group pointed out, it wasn't what was in the itinerary. On the way back to Yangshuo, a chain broke on one of the bikes. Meg had not taken any tools for repair with her. We were in a bit of a predicament and the only solution was that she would wait with the broken bike, whilst I took the group back into town. I had only a vague recollection of how to get back, through the rice paddies and winding roads. As soon as we hit a main road, I was driving on the wrong side of it, not used to the direction of the traffic. I made it, more through luck than anything else and once again, although I was relieved, my group were not impressed.

I organised for us to go to Monkey Jane's for a sunset Dinner, but half of the group never made it in time. It is not too difficult to gauge a sunset, try looking at the sky. It's when the big yellow ball starts to get close to the hilltops and houses. But my lot seemed to think I should have given them a specific time. I finished off with a few beers meeting a lot of Leaders in town including Snow and her boyfriend Scott. Lyn, Sarah and Ada from training were there. I also met Zef, an experienced Australian leader of four seasons and Suzy Li, for the third time. Unfortunately, also in Yangshuo there are the usual drop outs that spoil it for everyone. A number of "English teachers" (because, due to their ability to just about string a coherent sentence together and hold a U.K./U.S./ Aussie passport, they can become teachers). They just live the lifestyle, sell drugs to travellers and locals, rip just about everybody off and try to fuck anything that moves. It's the sort of thing that ruins everything for the rest of us. Otherwise, it's a holiday within a holiday. To be honest, it's a bit too easy to get sucked into the lifestyle here and I can see why the Western Leaders usually spend too much time in the bars. The following morning, most of us went to the cooking school but Henrietta was ill again, then in the afternoon I ran into Eva and Yu's group. They were still complaining about their leaders. Things had gone from bad to worse for them, as the local operator in Yichang had been unable to book enough places on the train from Wuhan to Guilin. It was the May "Golden Week" holiday period, when most of China takes a vacation and goes travelling. Not being able to get the train tickets you want at this time is a regular thing. Eva had put the group on the train and organised a local guide to pick them up from Guilin. She was flying down to meet them later. I had got my train tickets From Guilin to Shenzhen from Rosemary, but the bus to pick us up to Guilin Station was stuck in traffic and we only made it with twenty minutes to spare. Then we were on the overnight train to the border and Hong Kong

I ended my first solo trip in Hong Kong. I'd met some fantastic people and, even though there were hitches and complaints, the trip had gone as well as I could expect. Still, as I walked the group to the last night dinner at Knutsford Terrace, I could hear them complaining again, "he walks so fast, oh, not more stairs...". I was glad it was nearly over. We then had a last night out. It was a bit of an odd mixture of age ranges from twenties to sixties and I don't know Hong Kong at all so after we ate on Knutsford Terrace, just popped into what looked like the liveliest bar on the strip. As it happens, there was a promotion going on for Carlsberg in only the way that China could do a promotion. There were a couple of girls dressed up as sailors and walking around, on and off a makeshift stage. There was also Captain Cathy, who did very little and Gordon, Gay Gordon (though you can't be gay in China) with the waxed eyebrows and effeminate mannerisms. The locals were all really getting into this, screaming every time Cathy or Gordon moved. A film crew interviewed them about how great it must be to pretend to be sailors for a day or something. There was some sort of game going on where the sailors were supposed to be bathed in beer, but that was so tame it didn't really happen. Then someone was supposed to get up on stage from the audience to do something with Captain Cathy. Well, he dropped his pants. Well actually, he didn't. The bloke from the audience was a plant and was actually wearing fake arse cheeks. The crowd went wild and somebody fainted. While all this light hearted entertainment was going on for the middle classes, the rest of

Hong Kong has billboards offering massage and girls handing out sex cards. This is a crazy place.

13. A Song for a New China, 27/4/07 (Yangtze Boat),
    29/4/07 (Yichang)

I saw a boy in a "Punk's Not Dead" T-shirt today
But would he have a beer with me
Understand the irony, comedy
Of singing "So What!" by the Anti Nowhere League?

And in this East of Eastern Communist Countries
Another T-shirt for rebellion
Because it is in fashion
Whilst all around, all the western fake copies

From burger bar, to Irish pub to strip club girlie card
Rolex and a mobile phone
A lifestyle in neon
Advertised and consumed, another 'Great Leap Forward'

Girls and boys in European styles you find on the bargain rail
In the bars of Beijing
With the Karaoke singing
Or mimicking Beatles songs in a second rate cabaret

Living in alley ways, with high rise ambitions
The white collar career
To which you all aspire
A Britain in the Sixties, you'll repeat the same problems

Living the dream of New China, a new mind control
More effective than
Any five year plan
You can be everything you want to, just don't be anything at all

Temples converted to shops selling replica souvenirs
Mirrored from stall to stall
The same junk, one and all
Buddha jostles with Mao for cigarettes and warm beer

Selling that Great Wall, brick by brick to foreigners
As Chairman Mao
Takes his final bow
What was a Forbidden City, is open to all strangers

And as I look at the rats in the rat-race
This two world collision
A cultural explosion
The quick, the dead, and life at every other pace

Like the story of Mao, in his interview suit
No money for shoes
China, its boys and girls
Dressed in fine fakery, still standing in the dirt

I saw a threadbare man today trying to cross the street
Shoulder pole, loaded down
The traffic, just moved around
Tinted windows, conical hat. Alloy wheels, sandaled feet.

The group had tipped me and what more, it was a decent tip of around two thousand Yuan. I was also impressed by the card they gave me, all saying what an amazing experience they had had and Henry thanked me "for going the extra mile". Maybe I had got them all wrong, it was just that they had seemed to be disappointed with every leg of the trip. I had my usual Pechora in Chungking Mansions, then wandered Nathan Road, being hassled by Indians trying to sell me tailor made suits and "Genuine copy watches" before buying a Camera. Yes, I have taken the technological plunge again. Hopefully this one will last longer than all the other electronic devices that I have ever bought. My last digital camera lasted less than a month and when I sent it back under warranty the manufacturers said that I'd had it in strong light and some water had gotten in it. I'd been on holiday to Indonesia, what did they expect? and what was the warranty for then?

The reason why I finally bought a camera is because I was going on holiday. This seems a bit cheeky, going on a holiday when most people think that I'm on holiday already. But, so what? I hope you're all jealous. When I looked at my work schedule it showed that I had 10 days off between trips. This is a lot of free time, possibly more free time than I would get again for a long time and I just had to use the chance given to me. My next trip was starting in Hong Kong, so the sensible thing to do was to stay in the Travel Companies Apartment that was in the Hong Kong area. I say area because the company that I work for are a bit tight that and won't pay for us to stay in Hong Kong. Instead there is an apartment near the city of Shenzhen, just on the Chinese side of the border where it is cheaper. I've been through Shenzhen and thought it was horrible. It was Chinas experiment in the 1990's with capitalism and it's a high rise concrete jungle. I really didn't want to stay there. So on my way through Chengdu, I had talked to Sam. He is a local operator who books hotels and travel and he specializes in Tibet. After a few emails, he sorted me out with a deal that for under Y5000 got me to Lhasa and back with the permit included. All I had to do was take the flight to Chengdu airport and pay some bloke, in cash, then receive the rest of the itinerary and paperwork. What could be simpler? How easy is it to con the gullible? Well, life is an adventure, so I agreed to the shady deal, giving me just a couple of days at the end of my trip to do my paperwork before flying to Tibet.

Chapter 4

THE ROOF OF THE WORLD AND HIGHER

*"I hear and I forget. I see and I remember.
I do and I understand.*

**Confucius, Chinese philosopher & reformer
(551 BC - 479 BC).**

The reason why I finally bought a camera is because I was going on holiday. Most other leaders would normally stay in or around Hong Kong, depending on whether you wanted the bright lights and added expenditure or a cheaper chill out, you would opt for the Travel Company, Leaders Apartment. The apartment that our company had for the leaders was in Shekou, a suburb of the Chinese city of Shenzhen

On arriving in Shekou port, by boat from Kowloon, I was pleasantly surprised. Janie was in the apartment and gave me directions. It was a sort of holiday village, modeled on some Spanish/Portuguese resort. Cafes with tables around the town square, Pizza Hut and all the usual western fast food outlets, European style restaurants and a couple of bars. There was an actual cruise liner embedded in the concrete of the town square, with restaurants and night clubs spilling from the decks. This wasn't going to be so bad. I met up with Janie and things were looking even better later that day we were joined by Esmeray, the punky Turkish girl who I had met in the first week of training in Beijing. We had argued then, but put it all down to a misunderstanding. Then, we found out that Cathy, the manager was also supposed be staying the night. The 3 off us avoided her, having no interest in covering anything more than pleasantries with her, her husband and small child, so we went out for a drink. We started off with an outdoor barbeque that Janie had tried the night before, then found the Irish bar. Over the next couple of days I became a temporary resident here.

I had a couple of excellent nights out in the Irish Bar. It was the first actual bar that I had seen in China outside of Beijing and Yangshuo. I had quickly got the measure of Shekou as the place where the foreigners lived when their companies sent them to work in Shenzhen. The Irish bar was full of westerners, it looked the part and it had a rock band playing four nights a week. The resident band was called Mind the Gap and was fronted by a Brit; Paul, from South London. The rest of the band, all from the Philippines, were some of the best musicians that I've ever seen playing whilst still consuming bucket loads of alcohol. They had really taken the rock'n'roll lifestyle to heart. They knocked out some Green Day, then on to Chili Peppers, Pearl Jam and AC/DC. We all got into the music, singing along, drinking pint after pint in quick succession. Before too long, I was head banging with a chair for a monitor until the guitarist took pity on my pathetic comedy attempt to pretend that the stool was a "foot monitor", so with guitar in hand and still playing, stood on the chair. There are some fantastic photos knocking about and a couple of me on the microphone as well; it's just a good job that there is no sound recording. Needless to say, with my rock and roll persona, long hair and all these antics I was very popular with the locals.

I suppose this is where I tell you about how I discovered a new Chinese word. Well, after the Irish bar, I went off with the band to another bar that was open later for more drinks. It was at some point later that night that I found myself with one of the girls who had been wowed by my earlier rock star performance. One thing led to another, as far as I was concerned it was a sort of a Friday night back home and I had "pulled". So after a few too many beers I was back at her place, doing what comes natural and taking my time getting to the climax of things, if you know what I mean. I had drunk way too much and things were taking their time. Anyway, she starts saying "tongue, tongue" and indicating her neither-regions. Well, always being a considerate sort of bloke, I thought, "What the hell..." and start making a move South. The girl was almost in near panic! It was only later on that I found out that "tong" means "hurt or sore!"

14. Untitled, 05/05/07 (Shekou)

A T.V. screen, a port - hole to England
And behind me plays a rock and roll band
I could touch that green and pleasant land
Straddling the continents, beer in hand

F.A. Cup semifinal day
The English sunshine on the turf in May
Thinking of all the games I've played
Thinking of how far I am away

Watching a very English English teacher
Incompetent dancing in a white shirt
Grinning as he holds on to a mini Chinese girl
The wedding party/school disco flirt

Along with the unbelievably mutton
Trying to dance her way into a conversation
With the cutest local who was having fun
Attempting to translate Chinese into lesbian

Is this a night for inspiration
Or more observation turning to condemnation
The weird angle on prostitution
East and West, the real and television

Getting a little bitter, a little twisted and blue
Another beer to add to a frustration that cuts through
I celebrate a birthday, I think of, and miss you
With ten pints of lager and a prostitute

It was after the third of these late night Irish bar sessions that I was heading off to Tibet. I'd had good intentions to go to bed early, but as Janie says, at one point in the night I said "I'll sleep when I'm dead" and she knew there was no way I was going to have a quiet night. Oh, the foolishness of drinking too much alcohol and believing that you are still in a fit state to function. Well, I picked up my backpack from the apartment at 4 ish and got a taxi to the airport. Somehow got through the airport bureaucracy with my e-ticket and was soon on the plane to Chengdu. Here, I was met in the airport and handed almost Y5000 to some bloke. This was the point where I could have been sold a pig in a poke; I had no comeback if I had been ripped off. I had been given return tickets and a piece of paper which had a "Tour Group" on it. Mine was the only name in this tour group. It looked dodgy, a tour group of only one person, but there was an official looking stamp. Then, I cleared customs and got another flight to Lhasa. Against all odds I had made it, but what had I forgotten to do? I'll tell you later.

I got the public bus from the airport to the centre of Lhasa. Exiting the bus station, I got a whistle from a bicycle rickshaw who took me to the Chinese compound where I had booked a hostel and was staying. I should have got the Y10 taxi; I ended up paying Y40, haggled to the point of being ripped off by the Tibetan driver, who I was made to feel sorry for after he had struggled all the way across the city, over the bridge, to an island. My guest house was in a recently developed part of the city that was Chinese compound style housing. These are walled estates, with houses not unlike the terrace houses back home. There are amenities in the compound and a guard on a gate to stop any of the undesirables i.e. Tibetans, entering. These compounds are mainly occupied by the immigrant Han Chinese. The Han, account for over 90% of Chinas 1,350,000,000 people. There has been a government policy over the last fifty years and more, to encourage the population to stop moving towards the overcrowded cities in the East and start to migrate to the less populated and less developed provinces in the West. Tibet was "liberated" by China in 1951, since which time, the Han Chinese have been moving there. The Chinese compounds are slowly covering more and more of Lhasa and Tibet, and along with the new factories, the new roads and all other things Chinese, are slowly taking the place over. To be honest, it actually looks nice and ordered, but that's what it's supposed to be and not very Tibetan at all.

The hostel was run by a Chinese family that did not speak English. I'd found the place on hostelworld.com, a site that had never let me down, but although the family were welcoming, the place was not what I was looking for. Too far from the city centre, too Chinese. It was a homestay type of hostel, even as far as an evening family meal being offered to all the guests, catering for Chinese visitors to Lhasa. The whole of the compound was constructed in what looked like breezeblock. The houses were reasonably large, so much so that this one could be converted into a hostel. There was a courtyard garden as you entered from the street door. With some care and paint and accessories it would look pretty rather than just functional. I had already decided that I needed to take a look around Lhasa, with the intention of finding somewhere else to move on to. It was dark when I got the taxi into the city with another tourist from the hostel. She was Chinese, but spoke a little English and wanted to get herself on a trip to Everest Base Camp. We headed to the main street, Beijing Lu with its courtyard hotels and hostels. There are lots of information boards in the other "real" hostels in the City and it became obvious that I'd booked into the wrong place. Anyway, this gave me the knowledge to suss out a trip to Namtso Sky Lake.

I was up in the morning, walking into the city through a mixture of new build and derelict dirty streets. There was an area that was making prayer wheels and other metal objects. This was in a jumble of workshops, men beating metal into cylinders by the side of the street and others polishing up the gleaming gilt leaf. I took a few stares; this was obviously not a place where tourists usually walked. I got back onto Beijing Lu, found the Potola Palace and got my new camera out, but at the first attempt, only managed to take a video of my feet, that I couldn't delete. I am useless with any sort of technology, it conspires against me. I counted four or five hotels that contained large courtyards with restaurants, hotel accommodation, hostel rooms, tourist agency and bar all working together as one. This is where the western tourists were staying and there was note upon note asking for people to join together for excursions in jeeps to Everest or Kathmandu. This was obviously where I should have been. The tour agency in the Kirin Hotel had about the best deal to Namtso Sky Lake. Then it was just a case of having a look around Lhasa.

Essentially, the city revolves around two main sites, the Potola Palace, sitting like a white and red crown on a hill top, and the Jokhang, in the middle of the old city. It's a bit difficult to explain the difference between the 2, but Potola was the seat of government and the Dali Lama lived here. The Jokhang is a temple, and the spiritual heart of the Tibetan people. The Tibetan quarter, or what remains of it, with its stone block housing surrounds the Jokhang. The area around the Potola has been redeveloped, Chinese style. The pilgrims take in both sites, prostrating themselves in front of both buildings and walking, chanting, clockwise around the buildings and the maze of streets that lie in between them. This is also where you see bejeweled yak skulls for sale, yak butter (yum, yum -not) yak wool coats, yak kebabs, in fact, a hell of a lot of yak things. There are also mountains of Tibetan relics spilling out from stalls, prayer flags everywhere, incense burning. Wherever you look, people are chanting, preying, and prostrating themselves.

There is a specific way that the pilgrims prey and move around the temples on a "kora". This is a ritual act where they walk 2 steps forward, they touch their head, then their face, move to a preying action and finally bend down to prostrate themselves. Many hold wooden blocks in their hands, or have mittens. They have rubbed the large stone cobbles to the point that they shine, smoothly. After a few seconds, they will get up, take two steps forward and repeat again. Many Tibetans still wear their traditional costumes. Women with braided hair. White scarves adorn those who come to prey. Some women wear a type of apron; some that prey have a cord around their thighs. For the men, there is also a bit of a John Wayne influence in the dress sense, with some of the wealthier Tibetans now wearing the full ensemble of boots, cowboy hat and even shades. The other must have fashion accessory for the women at least is a face mask. Some say for modesty, some say to protect from the sun, others from the dust, but everyone has one. Outside the Jokhang, I sat in amongst the praying pilgrims. A mind blowing experience that made you almost believe that you could actually transcend to heaven. There were pilgrims sitting around chatting, the incense burning and the constant low hum of the chanting. I took some photos. My camera was taking all photographs in triplicate; I didn't know how to change the setting. That evening, back at the hostel I sat with the owner who helped me for over two hours to upload two, only two photos from my camera on to MySpace.

On day three I got an early morning taxi into Lhasa and began the jeep tour to Namtso Lake with 6 others. Two of them were a Dutch father and son. We followed the new railway line on the new road for 4 hour. Only one year earlier, this was a full day trip over rough terrain. We passed a pair of pilgrims on the road. Where they had come from or how long they had been travelling was anybody guess, but as we sped by them, we could see them take the steps forward, then prey, prostrating themselves on the road, before standing up again. Some pilgrims will take a year to travel from their homes to Lhasa. None of this made any sense to me in a modern world. What sort of religion would demand this loyalty and suffering? Surely, the Tibetans were leaving these backward practices behind in the past. We continued up into the mountains and from the sunshine through a cloud of snow. As we reached 5,200 meters, I started feeling the cold and began to rummage in my back pack. I had the horrible realisation that I'd left my jacket on the washing line at the Shekou apartment. Shit. How I kicked myself for getting pissed. How stupid was I? Who else would go to the Himalayas without a coat? Anyway, it was too late to do anything about it now. We reached the lake, which lived up to the billing of being one of the most wonderful natural sites I've ever seen. The blue of the sky perfectly matched by the lake and the mountains covered in coloured prayer flags, amazing, it almost made me forget how cold I was.

The camp was set up as groups of cabins, facing the lake. Each group of cabins was run by a family, taking in groups of tourists. Of the forty or so cabins, less than a quarter were occupied. We arrived as the weather clouded over and sleeted again, but within half an hour, it had cleared. I decided to take a look at the lake. There were ponies and yaks, all part of the tourist business, to transport the unfit or for photography. Their owners were even trying to extort money if you took a photograph anywhere near one of the animals. As the sky cleared, you could see why here is called Namtso sky lake. The blue colour and the white of the snow covered peaks on the distant shore looked like a perfect reflection of the sky and clouds. Here I was, on the top of the world and above us, just a thin coating of sky before the heaven beyond.

I next walked up to the cliff face, covered in prayer flags. Everywhere in Tibet, you see prayer flags. They are squares of cloth, in different colours, each with a printed picture or text. They are together on long pieces of string and hung from any landmark. The bridges across the river in Lhasa were covered in them. Wherever there was a sacred site, be it a cliff carving, a cave or a natural outcrop, there would be prayer flags. This cliff was most impressively covered. The top of the hill was maybe 300m higher than us, but there was a section of the cliff, that stood apart from the rest of the cliff, on a sort of giant mound, it may have been a "stack", formed when the lake was higher, or it may have been split from the main body of the cliff by the wind and ice. Here, the prayer flags in their thousands were trimmed from the summit of the hill, across the gap to the crest of the mound and down the other side to the shingle beach where we stood. An avalanche of fluttering colour. A mountainside dressed as if it was a king.

I headed back to the cabins and the weather worsened again. I ate in our dining cabin as the local hosts walked in and out, never closing the door. They would walk in, bringing in a blast of freezing mountain sleet, look at us, then walk out the other door, never thinking once about closing either one of them. Surely, they must have had more people than us complaining, but they didn't seem to understand. I thought about having a game of pool, on the outdoor pool table, but after the snow, it was obviously never going to be a good game. An hour later and the bad weather had passed again and I set off on a walk, this time in the opposite direction, around the headland and discovered a part of the lake that was still completely frozen. Ice and snow was churned up, meters high in front of me at the point where the frozen lake met the snowbound shore. There was nobody else around.

However, I was starting to feel the effect of the altitude sickness and things got progressively worse. My head was starting to feel like it was about to explode. Pressure and dizziness, shortness of breath with every step I took. I got to my cabin and gave up for the rest of the day. I just got into bed, fully clothed, just like I had drunk a dozen pints of real ale and ready to pass out. The following morning, the altitude sickness had got to a point where I couldn't move, apart from getting to the door of the cabin to throw up. Luckily, we were back in the Jeep by 11am and going back down the mountains to Lhasa.

I booked into Kirin hostel on arrival and by midafternoon I was back to normal. The next day I was ready to take on the Potola Palace. I set off early, around 08:00 with intention to book my transport to the airport and do a spot of shopping. I put my cash-card in the hole in the wall ATM machine, and had it declined. Often, in Lhasa, the banks remove cash from cash point during the night to discourage theft. "Maybe there is no money in that cash point," I thought, so found another. Around the corner at the next ATM it was the same story, no cash and a message on the screen asking me to contact my bank. I bank with the Halifax Building Society, Wood Green Branch, London. Panic set in. I tried to email the Halifax, but you can't contact them by email. I texted Lindsay, back in my flat, to see if there had been any letters arrive at home. At 4am in the morning in the UK, there was a fat chance of a sensible response. Amazingly, she responded but she couldn't shed any light on the matter. I phoned the Halifax. I had to do this on my China mobile because the UK one is banned in Tibet and I could not make an international phone call, another unbelievable stroke of bad luck. First I got an automated quote of my bank balance, well at least I had funds, I just couldn't get to them. The next call allowed me to re-register my card over the phone by using the keypad. This took about 10 minutes going through every option. Then I was told, automatically that I would not be able to complete my registration as it was out of office hours! I finally got through to someone. "This is an emergency", I said "I'm in Tibet and my card has been cancelled". The nice Scottish man on the other end of the phone started to talk about fraud in South East Asia and ask a series of questions. "Look" I said "can't you just re-activate the card, I've given you all my information and I'm running out of phone credit". "Ok," says he, "but it will take a few days to go through". I think I swore. The nice man put on his helpful voice. "If you really need cash immediately, I suggest you....." The phone went dead. My credit had run out.

With less than 20 quid to my name I still decided to visit the Potola Palace to take a look at what the Chinese will let us see. It is now a historical monument and that's the way they want it to remain. The first buildings here were from the 7th Century and inside the palace complex you can still see the extended cave on display where King Songstan Gampo reigned from and was married to his Chinese and Nepali wives. Much of the present palace was built by the "Great" fifth Dali Lama around 1645 and extends 400m East to West and 350m North to South. The area in front of the Potola Palace has been cleared and there is now a four lane highway and a very Chinese square on the other side. There is no statue of Mao, but one would not be out of place here along with the high flagpole and fluttering red banner of the Peoples Republic. In front of the walls of the palace, the Tibetan pilgrims were prostrating themselves. Such a juxtaposition, modern freeway and ancient, sack-cloth clad farmers. The Palace itself is one of those iconic places. It could only have been built by a near god, on an immense outcrop of rock, a palace on the roof of the world. It surveys all of Lhasa below it from its multi-layered, red and white buildings. It was built as a city within a city and you first enter a courtyard of white stone houses, originally a village inhabited by the servants of the temple monks. Up to 2000 people lived here at one time. There is a climb up to the

Palace wall proper, past more white stone houses with black painted window-sills, the coloured awnings flapping beneath the tiled eves of the buildings. A beautiful step back in time and a panoramic view of the city below. From here the Dali Lama could survey his kingdom. The section of the palace that we were allowed to visit was a mixture of narrow corridors opening up into rooms filled with statues and treasures. It was like an eccentric English Lord or millionaire had lived here, mixing the artifacts from all over Asia, piling them high in every room. The carpeted corridors and painted walls were thick with the richness of antique opulence. I saw the resting places of the Dali Lamas, each in a room with a gigantic gold stupa as a mausoleum and surrounded by statues of praying Buddha's and monks. There were books and scrolls lining bookcases, wall after wall. There were silk scarves hanging from the Buddha statues and wall hangings just about everywhere else. To call this place a treasure trove would not do it justice.

I headed back into the Old Quarter, taking a look at the shops selling bejeweled yak skulls and souvenirs. I'm not sure what type of person would buy a bejeweled yak skull, or where you would put one on your living room wall, they are far too big for the mantelpiece in my house. I bumped into the Dutch father and son from Namtso Lake. They wanted to go for a coffee, I don't really like coffee, but I followed and had the most random of convergences when I then met another Leader from my training group in Beijing. Beata was one of the women who were Tibet experts. I didn't know her so well, but she seemed as pleased as I was that we'd met someone that we knew and we arranged to have dinner with her group. This was another fascinating experience, now having my own personal source of everything Tibetan at my finger-tips for the price of a couple of beers. Beata was Hungarian and had studied Tibetan at University then had continued her studies in northern India. She was at Dharamsala with the Dali Lama and was in the second group of people let into Tibet when the country re-admitted foreigners in 1992. She talked about the changes since that time. She had taken the Tibetan people to heart, telling stories of her first encounters in Lhasa, whilst government informers looked on. Her knowledge of Tibetan Buddhism and culture was phenomenal. She also liked a beer, so we ended up in a Nangma. This is a Tibetan song and dance theatre and although the place we discovered was evidently run by and for the Chinese visitors, it gave me a good impression of what an evening of entertainment, Tibetan style consists of. There were a number of performances, singing, instrument playing and dancing and it was the dancing that we were also encouraged to join in with as well. I knew that I would have to come back to Tibet, there was so much that I hadn't done, so much that I didn't know.

15. Hello from the roof of the world, 08/05/07 (Lhasa)

(A) Hello from the Roof of the World

Hello from Namtso
Hello from the roof of the world
Where you find a rainbow
At the end of the road
Clothing a mountain
With all our prayers
So close to heaven
It makes you think you can reach there

Pictures by the lake
Out of some Other Earth storybook
A slight headache
But I have to walk and look
A little dizziness
I touch the edge of the ice-field
Again I'm breathless
A frozen expanse, truly a sight to behold

I shout out hello, hello
Breaking your spell for a moment
But as it started to snow

I'm at the mercy of the elements
All those trappings
That make you feel safe
Turn to nothing
As Winter reclaims this place

As night falls
The mountains hem in this world
In white and purples
Fingering the sky's black fold
That the stars fill
And the moon so bright casts a shadow
Time stands still
I'm on the roof of the world and shout out hello

B) How far To Heaven? 07/05/07 09/05/07 (Lhasa)

I saw two pilgrims on the road
I didn't know where they had come from
Lead face down, then one step forward
Moving slowly to heaven

Clockwise with the 'chou-for'
The baritone hum of the cyclic chanting
White scarves to the temple door
A gatehouse to heaven where the devoted are waiting

The prayer wheel spins in the Jokhang
Hands raised, a kiss, a bow, to knees
The devoted servant, flat, head below hand
Rubbing the stone smooth with prayer, not pleas

How far is heaven from here?
The pilgrims say they're getting near
You feel it in the atmosphere
How far is heaven from here?

If you stand still long enough
Stare into the gatehouse and listen
Moving, praying, every breath
You're almost taken with them

(C) Potola Park 7/05/07 Lhasa

Walking the tree lined boulevard
To Potola Square Park
Where the lake reflects the Palace
And the sun goes behind a mountain to rest
The sky begins to change colour
As the sun sets over the Potola
Another moment for me to capture
That can't be imitated on camera

(D) 7 Days in Tibet

The whistle of a rickshaw puller
Stalls selling yak butter
Poles wrapped in coloured prayers
Bejeweled yak skulls

Smoke that is Lingering
From burned prayers as offerings

Peeking through the courtyard door
Watching the women wash their hair
The most beautiful faces behind the masks

Security guards keeping an eye out
And the dirt from the street from the guesthouse

The large prayer wheel take a turn
Two pretty Chinese girls sit with a monk to learn
And there are photo opportunities for the other Chinese
With the digital cameras, dressed in T shirt and jeans

Women with yak hair around their waist
Hair in many coloured braids

A group of men sit on the ground chatting
Nothing to do now their pilgrimage is done
Rolled up mats and tied up blankets
in the hot sun

I compare this to day four of a rock festival
After all that booze and pills
It might get you as dirty
But could only mimic the spiritual

Early morning on the bus, immaculate women
School kids in track-suits, baseball caps and backpacks
Waving hello, they have school waiting
And the morning parade, rank and file presentation.

The following morning I got the bus to the airport. The security
was just as stringent getting out of Tibet as it was going in.
As I queued, there was a problem with one of the travellers
in front of me. A woman in her fifties was arguing with the
official. She had bought some alcohol miniatures; all were still
in the packaging of a selection box, unopened and technically
below the allowance of the total amount of liquid that you
can take on a flight, but the official wasn't having it. He was
telling her that the six bottles breached the regulations. She
was getting irate and wasn't going to leave them behind, so,
as we fidgeted, with somebody reminding the pair that we had
a flight to catch, she opened the first miniature, and downed
it. Then she did the same for the second, then the third, until
all six were drunk, and so, soon, was she. I made it back
to Shenzhen and had enough cash for the bus to Shekou.
Once there I was back in funds, so it was time to celebrate
again. Janie was still at the apartment and Philip was there
for the night. Off to the Irish bar and another crazy rock 'n'
roll night.

I was stupidly hung over and slow the following morning. It took me ages to get out of the apartment and off to the boat for my next trip. On my way through customs, I was still the worse for wear. I always think I'm going to be stopped because in China they test you by heat sensitive camera for avian flu. The symptoms are a higher than normal body temperature and sweating. Now, I can't remember a time when I haven't crossed the border, still beetroot red from the previous night's drinking, carrying a ruck-sac and a day pack and sweating in the 35 degree heat. Anyway. This time they stopped me, and I was running late. This wasn't going to be good. Luckily it wasn't me that they were concerned about, it was my luggage and they wanted to inspect my daypack. Inside I had a load of booklets that I was supposed to take to the West Hotel. These in turn would be distributed by the tour leaders to their passengers at our first group meetings. They contained info about the trip, travel tips, city maps and information. The customs officials seemed concerned. It turns out that the map of China on the front of the booklet wasn't quite right. How my Travel Company haven't got in trouble for this before I don't know, but Taiwan (a province of China according to Chinese government policy) was a different colour from most of mainland China. I was now being held at customs for the distributing illegal reading material. I missed the boat. Fortunately, they understood that I was only taking them to a hotel for a friend, "it was all a big mistake, no I wasn't working in China illegally, sorry, sorry. Can I go now?" The pamphlets are now probably at the bottom of the South China Sea.

So, my new passengers were not so impressed with me on arrival. The two Canadian women were the first to complain that there was no information prepared for them and nobody to meet them when they arrived. There isn't supposed to be, but they had expected more. There was a mother and twenty something year old daughter, Abigail. There were older Australian couples, Martin and Maureen, Robert and Rachel. The four singles were Dave, a 47yr old Aussie, a single bloke, who seemed to know English woman; Joan as if they were travelling together. There was more to develop there. We also had Barbara in her 50's and Andrea who at 22 had just finished University. I tried to salvage the negativity over dinner, but got a complaint from Martin, who had been eating at the local noodle shops over the last two days and thought that the meal on Knutsford Terrace was a bit expensive. Well, I was hardly going to take them to Chunking Mansions or some 'roach infested noodle bar on their first night was I? That would definitely have set the wrong impression. You just can't please all the people all of the time. I had an interesting enough bunch.

The following day we had to take taxi's to the train station, then a KCR train to the border, then cross, get money exchanged and enter the train station in Shenzhen for our overnight train to Guilin. This was the first time that I'd done the trip in this direction and I had recurring nightmares of the problems we always had with the trains. So, I gave them a long explanation as to what to expect, including the sleeping arrangements. Trains in China are either "hard" or "soft" sleeper. This has nothing to do with the comfort of the beds; however, my introduction to the Chinese railway went a little like this. I said, "We are sleeping "hard sleeper" class that is six to a cabin, rather than four to a cabin. Your tickets will read: number 1, top middle and bottom, number two, top middle and bottom and you are in the first compartment. In the next compartment, note, there is no number here, only your beds are numbered, there will be 3, top middle and bottom and four, top, middle and bottom. Is that clear? The response was "the beds are hard in this hotel, aren't they... why don't we get soft sleeper?" Try as I might, they were not listening. The Canadians wanted to know why we didn't fly. When we got to the train station in good time, they complained about us having to wait for too long. As I said to them, taxis, trains and border crossings can take a lot longer and we wouldn't want to miss the train, would we?

I quickly gelled with Robert, who was originally from Manchester and would have easily spent most of the trip just chatting with him. But that's not what it's all about. On the first night on the train the group bonded very quickly over a few beers. I was beginning to get a good feeling about this trip. They all wanted to do things in Yangshuo and I texted Rosemary with all the details and we organised a packed itinerary. On arrival in Yangshuo I went out to see Snow, and Monkey Jane. It's amazing to have people you consider friends in such a short space of time. Monkey Jane is so called because she does monkey things that Chinese girls don't do. She runs a bar and plays 'beer pong'. This is a game where you set up 6 pints of lager in a triangle on your side of the ping pong table and your opponent does the same at his end. Now, you bounce a ping pong ball into your opponents' pint and he has to drink it. It is not surprising that in a "winner stays on" situation, after a few games you are completely smashed. I found out that there were quite a few other leaders in town including Eugenie, Tang, Sheila, Janie and Esmeray, who had just done "hot cupping" at Dr. Lillyi's and was covered in round bruises across her back. She comically said that she had been raped by an octopus. So, once again I did the bike ride to Moon Hill with a hangover.

The Aussie couples wanted to ride tandem bicycles. Martin's enthusiasm for everything wasn't reciprocated by his wife and she was uncertain about riding a bike. Joan had a sore foot and would only ride pillion on a motorcycle. I had quite a demanding group, but I did what I could, and being the novice that I was, I still thought that this was usual. This is where I had my first real test (and it feels like a test) from Martin, the self-styled "scientist" of the group with more than a passing resemblance to the original Doctor Who. Martin seemed to be taking enough notes to write a novel. He asked about every river we crossed and what sort of fish lived in it, all the plant life we passed and what crops were grown and a myriad of other things. I wonder if he will ever find out that it was the "mei you mingzi" or "no-name" fish that lived in the river and "mei you mingzi" "no-name" tree that was growing at the side of the road. Luckily, George Chan was our local guide in Yangshuo and he could answer a lot of Martin's questions, but his constant analysing was getting to the others in the group. We could not eat at the old ladies house in the village this time. The village committee had thought they could be on to a good thing if they could charge for the tourists to enter the village. The upshot of this was that I did not have a budget to pay for the entrance fee and so were no longer going and the old lady was the one who was losing out. The pursuit of money was changing the lives of the villagers. They saw people getting wealthy in Yangshuo and wanted a part of it. We ate at another small house in another village. George showed us around, pointed out that the tiles could be re used and were hundreds of years old, whereas the mud bricks were maybe only a decade or so. Many houses were now replacing them with baked brick. George pointed at the windows that were half bricked up, as their purpose was to only let in some light and air and keep out the robbers. You would not think that a place like this has robbers, but paranoia along with superstition about the spirits play a big part in people's lives. On the doors of all the houses were pictures of Guan Yu, the warrior from the Romance of the Three Kingdoms saga. He was a protection god and was there to ward off robbers and evil spirits. I told them that Guan Yu had been a real person, who had been elevated to "God" status as one of the last things that the last Emperor of China had done. I mused with the group that maybe, any mortal could be elevated to God status, even I could become the "God of the tour leaders." Some laughed, but weather it was with me, or at me, I was not so sure. Inside all the houses, there would also be posters of Chairman Mao. He, was also revered, almost like a God and was still relevant to the lives of many of the local people, particularly the older generation.

Martin was asking how the mud bricks were made. It turned out that he had decided to build his own house out of mud bricks a few years earlier, something his long suffering wife was still having to endure. He had tried to create an energy saving, ecofriendly and cheap build house. Unfortunately, he had not got the consistency quite right and the house had subsided and was slowly washing away, much to the anguish of his long suffering wife. As we rode back to Yangshuo, we passed an irrigation system. This, to all intents and purposes, is a weir, across the Dragon River, that channels water. At the end of the channel, is a manmade foss, where the water drops into a hole and rejoins the main river below. The ingenious thing, is that the locals have constructed what we know to be an Archimedes screw in the hole. This is paddle driven so as when the water descends back to the river it turns the paddles, which in turn drive the Archimedes screw that pumps the water up hill to an irrigation channel. Let me repeat this again. It pumps the water up hill, purely from the force of the water going back down to the river. Neither I nor anybody had seen anything quite like this before. I have only seen a secondary power source used as a pump in the West, either wind mills, or steam in the pre mechanised era. Here, the Chinese had constructed something quite outstanding. Water which pumps itself uphill. Martin was making sketches and looking baffled. George told me, that although this was a relatively new construction, it was a design that had been used for hundreds if not thousands of years. Back on the bicycles again and everything went straight back to normal, as the group took pictures of farm women carrying babies in baskets on poles. They looked cute, but it cost them 5 Yuan per picture. They were unhappy about this, but grudgingly paid up. Then there was the water buffalo, dressed for another picture, and another one ploughing a field that also had its owner asking for photo money. They were slow learners.

Back in Yangshuo, Martin started as he meant to go on, asking question after question. We were in the hotel waiting for the bus to arrive and I was watching a local man trying to chop a branch off an overhanging tree. Quite stupidly, he was actually sitting on the branch that he was chopping and there were electricity cables all around. Martin also saw this and asked me why the man was doing something which was evidently as stupid as it looked to both of us. Another question that I could not answer. He didn't stop there, as we left Yangshuo, he asked if there were two crops being planted in the same field, then asked why there were stones around some of the tree trunks.

Then the whole group of Aussies would comment upon how green the countryside was, comparing it with the brown earth of Australia, then ask me about rainfall statistics, how it was stored and piped to the villages, was there any hydroelectric power. It was constant.

I had thought that everything was going ok, but you can't gauge for the random disasters that happen. Joan's mum died. Not something that you can really deal with. She still wanted to continue with her round the world trip and Dave, who knew her, spent some time consoling her. In hindsight, this was one of my most difficult groups, but at the time I didn't know it. Abigail had spent most of her youth growing up as a privileged ex-pat in South East Asia and has gone on to boarding school, private school and a very good job in H.R. where she would find enjoyment in getting whatever she wanted and making other people's lives a misery. My first run in with her wasn't that bad, considering. All I had done is prep the group as we left the westernised Yangshuo for the boat with an overview of what to expect regarding service standards, food and facilities. Once on the Yangtze River Boat with our guide Gerry, we went for dinner. Firstly, meal times in China are specific. If it states that the evening meal is from six o'clock, to seven o'clock, then this is the only time you can eat and it means that you have to arrive at six o'clock. If you decide to come at six forty five, there will be no food left for your group. This is the same in hotels and for breakfast. If you decide to arrive five minutes before the breakfast room closes, you will find nothing but some cold rice or noodles. If there was anything resembling western food, it would have been eaten a couple of hours earlier by those in the know. The hot plates for the food on the buffets are rarely if ever replenished, as everybody else arrived at the start time, eats in twenty minutes and then goes. This leaves the few confused and disappointed westerners, wandering around asking questions of the staff who think that you are stupid for arriving late. The unfathomable looking at the inedible. I had already briefed my group about the meal situation and that dinner on the boat is not the most pleasant of experiences and a bit of a shock after the niceties of H.K. and Yangshuo. It is a group meal, as it is in most places in China, and there is no such thing as individual portions or catering for individual tastes. If you ask for something different, you get a very puzzled look, as the food was ok for the last 100,000 customers, so why would it not be ok for you? However, when I explained this, Abigail raised her voice. "Well we have a Chinese speaker; he can order the food that we want". She asked for a portion of chicken noodle soup with some specifics, not too spicy, not oily. Gerry tried his best, but for her, the food was just as awful and oily as it usually was and contained bones. Abigail left in a huff, followed by her mother and I was left having to cover the cost of her meal.

I met with Amy again on the Yangtze because she was getting the same boat back as us after dropping off her last group in Yichang. It meant that I had an extra friend amongst the difficult group and some back up knowledge when I got the difficult questions or impossible demands. We disembark on the upstream trip at Fengdu before getting a private bus to Chengdu. Amy had asked if she could take our bus with us, it would be much cheaper and quicker for her. I suggested that if she would take the group around Fengdu ghost City, earning herself some commission, she could come with us. I also asked her to give us a short tour of Chongqing when we got there, as I didn't know the city and it would help me out. On the way to Chongqing, the questions started, about the church that we passed, about what the people did or worked as in the towns that we went through. Many people here were re-located as part of the dam project and there was some work in the towns, but the majority of the men would have to travel to where the project was still taking place, building new towns, roads, industries and would only come home at weekends or even monthly intervals. Over two million people had been re-located with the building of the Dam. People had been compensated and new houses built for them, but there were many stories of the people not getting enough money or being re-housed in inappropriate places. The new cities, designed just like our own British 1960's misadventures, were all concrete and curves and grand designs. I looked at the identikit white tiles on the houses and remembered the only place where I had seen them before. Blackburn shopping centre, built in the 1970's had exactly the same white tiles covering the buildings. I had to laugh at myself. In the cities, the long sweeps of four story houses had the ground floor converted into shop fronts, selling the same cheap products. There were a lot of idle young men. We travelled for mile after mile in traffic. On parts of the road that were still not improved, we had to wait twenty minutes before we could attempt to squeeze past the lorries, all loaded up with everything from rocks to motorcycles. We got to one long stationary queue, where Amy told us that it was the queue for the ferry. It must have been two miles long and the industrial output of central China was there for all to see. It was immense.

We had a quick check in at Chongqing before Amy walked us into the city. At the centre of the city is a monument to the liberation of the city by the Red Army at the end of the Second World War. Amy told us that this was the tallest structure in the city as she was growing up and at twenty something meters was now dwarfed by the surrounding buildings. She told me that when the city became a province ten years earlier and the first building that had been taller than the monument had been constructed; they had all been given the day off school for the unveiling. This building too had been dwarfed by at least a dozen other office blocks and as you looked around, the cranes and concrete half built apartments were scaling the heights. It was a fantastic example of new China, on the move, up and up, literally. The group had looked in the lonely planet and wanted to go to a pizza place. As much as I like the book as a tool, it is infuriating when passengers start quoting it at you as if it was gods own bible. Amy didn't know where this pizza place was, but could point them in the right direction. They were quite surprised that she hadn't heard of the pizza place they wanted, in a city of 32 million people.

I met up with the group and took them to meet Amy again in the Pirate nightclub, complete with staff dressed in pirate uniforms. "Shibber me timbers", there were no customers though and the music just as appalling as in every other night club in China. The passengers didn't understand that they were supposed to buy bottles of beer in sixes or whisky by the bottle for sharing. Strange drinking culture these Chinese have, but I like it. My group quickly moved on when they couldn't get a vodka and orange, I'm not sure what they expected, but it wasn't what they were getting. I spent the rest of the evening with Amy, playing the dice game and some other drinking games. The dice game was taught to me by Pierre. Each person has a shaker with five dice. You shake your dice and take a look without the other players seeing. Then you bet. The idea is that you assess how many sixes or fives or whatever there will be between the whole group of players. The next player has to go higher, then the next, higher still until one will call their bluff. Then all players reveal their dice and we count up the number of whatever was called. If the last call is correct they win, if the one who calls bluff is correct, they win, the forfeit is usually a shot of whisky, or as Amy and I were playing, a shot of beer. Another popular game is rock, paper, scissors and there are other games around counting and holding up either zero, five or ten fingers. You say a number and show hands at the same time, if you guess the sum of both players' correctly, you win. I was enjoying my night out away from my group with Amy's company. At one point, she asked me if I thought she was cute. Yes, of course she was, but I was trying not to think about that. She had a boyfriend and I had a new friend in China and I was very happy with the way things were working out.

The next morning we were off to Chengdu again. On the train journey, we found a girl that spoke some English and wanted to ask questions. After the "where are you from?" question, we were stuck trying to explain that we were all from different places, not a family, or friends and had booked the trip, on line. That got nowhere, the concept of a tour group, booking on line and not knowing each other before was too strange for the Chinese who travel as an extended family or work department. As I am English, she asked me if it was true, that when an Englishman would meet her (a lady) in a street, he would take off his hat, bow and say "how do you do?" Then she said "I have heard that Australian man can drink three bottles of beer in the same day". Well, yes, we agreed, they could, and sometimes more. More astounding cultural differences to ponder upon. On arrival in Chengdu we were met at the train station by a guide from Sam's agency called Kevin. He had a great spiel, cracking jokes on the bus to the hotel. He gave me a hand checking in as the staff didn't speak a word of English and couldn't understand my Chinese, although I knew I was saying the correct words. Then he immediately whisked us of to Holly's Hostel for lunch. All a bit quick, as we hadn't even had time to unpack and it looked like he was more interested in getting his cut and getting us out of the way as soon as possible. Then, before I knew it he was gone. I had to call him to get him back, there were no arrangements for dinner and I was in a part of town that I didn't know. He agreed to meet us later and confirmed our tour to the pandas for the following day. I took the group for a walk into town and showed them the sights. Andrea was the only one of the group who really wanted to be on the trip. She had been taught Mandarin and Chinese history at school and wanted the real experience. When we got to Tian Fu square, she was overjoyed at seeing the statue of Mao, whereas most of the others either didn't know who he was or just thought him some ruthless dictator, along the lines of all the propaganda that they had been given in the cold war. Some of the others in the group had been brought up on a cold war mentality and all its propaganda. The idea that somebody wanted to see Mao, did not sit well with them, in fact, the whole visit to China did not sit well with them. They had already commented that "it was not Communist, really, just look at them, they're happy and they're definitely not poor". They had marveled at the modernity of the cities and it didn't quite fit what they expected to see. The shops full of goods, the expensive cars on the road just didn't say "Communism" to them. But what was Communism? I tried to start a discussion, but just got knee jerk answers and platitudes from the uninformed. Unfortunately, at their age, there was no reasoning with them, they'd lived through the Cold War and couldn't see that they'd been given a large dose of propaganda to wash it all down. They even started to tell me that they were "disappointed with China" because nothing was "old". They wanted to see crumbling alleyways full of hidden temples lit only by lanterns. They wanted women in "Qipao style" dresses and parasols, being carried in sedan chairs over the muddy streets. They asked about foot-binding and wanted to see porters with long pig tails. If any of this had really existed outside a Hollywood film, it was a century too late for that. Andrea at least knew something of the country and I started to warm towards her, she was the only one asking sensible or informed questions.

At the pandas, there was a split in the group, with some of them very upset about the facilities and the treatment of the animals. The information given explained that they were solitary creatures, roaming over large areas. Here, they were in penned enclosures and many were in groups of two or three. The baby pandas, the highlight for most tourists were a group of six, all out on show for feeding time, with the keepers putting them in artificial trees, or encouraging them to follow and play for food. More of a circus act than a wildlife sanctuary. We also watched the video, very informative again about the pandas life and breading habits where we saw a female giving birth in a concrete cage and very distressed, that it almost crushed her offspring and a keeper had to step in to save the baby. True, there were successful births shown, but so much of it was all about how cute the pandas are and what a good job was being done to save them and breed them. As Andrea, Martin and Maureen got angry and upset about the hypocrisy of the organisation, Abigail paid Y1000 to have a photograph taken holding a baby one and another Y600 next to an adult one. There were rumblings of disquiet about the spoilt, arrogant girl and things did not improve.

I had left the group to their own devises whilst I completed my chores and met up with Chicory. When they went for a meal later on, there was another incident. Some of the group had wandered into a restaurant and were trying to order food. There was no information in English and it was difficult, but with smiles, gestures, pointing they were getting somewhere. That is until Abigail got involved. She began harassing the waitresses who were not actively serving her and started having a go at them for not understanding what she wanted. This hit a climax after a few minutes where she shouted at them "you are all fucking peasants". They understood that well enough. I only found out about this a few days later, unfortunately, too late to do anything about it. I should have thrown her off the trip for that.

A few of us had a couple of beers at Jin Li Street. I was spending most of my time with Dave and Andrea as the others who were not inclined to try anything different would just go to bed. I went to the bar that I had been in twice before and settled down as the Chinese tourists from out of town surreptitiously tried taking our photographs. Then I managed to do something worthy of a photograph. I leaned back on my bar stool and the back snapped and I was immediately pitched onto the floor in the middle of the shopping street. Great fun for the locals and for my group alike. The concerned waitress placated my complaints about the flimsy stool with a plate of French fries, so we all went home happy.

Then we went to Emei Shan. On the way there, I warned the group that it could be cold at the top of the mountain. I told them 5 degrees and Barbara replied "that's cold". I thought they'd got the message. We crossed the river at Le Shan and everybody thought that it must be the Yangtze. It isn't, it is just a small tributary, but the Australians don't have rivers of this size, so unless I could prove to them otherwise, they had decided which river it must be. The big Buddha at Emei Shan had queues that stretched for nearly two hours. The group complained one after another how long they had to wait, why had we gone there? why were there so many people in China? And why was there no restaurants for them to eat in? I was glad to get out of there. At Baoguo Monastery, Patrick was there to meet us again. I was trying to give the group an orientation and Patrick was to organise dinner, but when we got to Teddy bear Cafe, they spotted the western menu and that was it. Pizza and beer were ordered. I have said before that the Chinese versions of western food are not as you would expect. Whatever the picture you have in your head about what you have ordered, forget it. At Teddy bear Cafe, they do an English breakfast. It consists of bacon, sausage, eggs, tomato, mushrooms. That picture in your head probably looks good, but when it arrives, it is all finely chopped together and in a pile on the plate, served with chopsticks. So I got more complaints.

I had talked to Patrick quite a lot over the last two visits; he was quite an interesting character. He had learned English from a man who he still referred to as his teacher. This man had himself learned English before the Second World War and had sided with the Kuomintang forces. The Kuomintang had based themselves in Chongqing and also in Emei Shan for a period of time and even used one of the rooms we were now staying in as Chang Kai Sheks office. When the other Kuomintang had fled the country, he had literally "missed the boat" and been put under house arrest until after Mao's death. Finally, in the late 1970's he was allowed to teach again and Patrick had come to him. His teacher had told him that learning English was the future, as foreigners would one day be allowed back into China and would want somebody who would be able to help us. It was also how he could understand our foreign ways and learn from us. Patrick had taken his teachers' ideals to heart, including the Buddhism that he practiced and his dislike for the Communist government and its policies. This was exemplified in that Patrick had two children. On my previous visits, Patrick had said that the local people had thought him crazy to have a second child. He told me his story. His first child was a girl and they wanted a boy. When his wife became pregnant again, he hid her in one of the local villages. When the police came around to ask him where his wife was, he told them that she had run away to Shanghai with somebody else, or that she had run away to work the streets there and that he was glad to get rid of her. When the delivery date grew close, they went to Chongqing, in the next province, a city where doctors did not ask so many questions as long as Patrick was willing to pay them. His son was born.

The police were soon on to him. They arrested him and questioned him whilst in hospital. If he had a second child without permission he would be heavily fined, or imprisoned. They had the confession in front of him. If he signed it, he would admit guilt and immediately start paying his fine which would amount to around three years of his wages. He told them, that he could not read the warrant. The police said "You work with the foreigners, how can you not read?" Patrick replied "I can only read English" and the police released him. This was not the end of the matter and the authorities were pursuing him for payment. In most cases, the parents will pay, but not all. A child who is not registered cannot go to school, have medical care, cannot reside anywhere legally, and cannot legally get a job. An unregistered person is a non-person, with no rights and destined to a life on the margins of society. Patrick's plan was to get the fine down to something manageable before his son had to go to school. He had already got the fine to almost half of the original sum over the last three years and said that he could squeeze it down a little further before his son reached school age.

George was our guide again. As ever I had to jolly him along in his welcome speech and description of our trip up Emei Mountain. He got all the information in, including the temperature and our time at the top of the mountain, but later the following day, the Australians were standing in their shorts and "thongs", freezing. They were upset and blamed me by not saying exactly how cold it would be. I said that I had told them, a couple backed me up, but some still argued the point until one said that I had not taken into account the "wind chill factor". What am I?

A metrologist? These were grown adults. Meanwhile, Martin and Maureen had been having a disagreement. Martin had been sitting at the front of the bus on every journey, taking notes. The traffic in China is unpredictable, triple overtaking is common and Maureen had been exclaiming and covering her eyes on the last two bus rides, but this was just too much for her. Emei Shans winding mountain pass had busses swerving from head on collisions with only inches to spare. She said that she was having nightmares about it and finally left Martin and his notebook to take a seat at the back of the bus. When we started the hike, we had more issues. Joan was also having difficulties walking. She said that she had hurt her foot whilst travelling a month or so earlier and it just hadn't righted itself. The long walk up the 1200 steps took us around 45 minutes, with me having to talk her through it all of the way. The good food at Bettys and a few drinks with Andrea and Dave, ended the night well until the monastery manager, Mr. Li, rang them to say that he was closing the doors. Not bad, that on my third visit, I was on good enough terms that the monastery was ringing Betty to let her know how long I could still stay out drinking.

On the way back down from Emei Shan, there were some monkeys. We had run through the precautions about the monkeys before our walk, and all had food and water hidden from view. Rachel had even asked if George had been trying to scare us with tales of monkeys attacking as we hardly saw any on the way up the mountain. Most of the group were taking pictures, then Joan said that her film had ran out and proceeded to stop put her bag on the floor and open up her camera. The inquisitive monkeys decided that this was food. Anything like opening packages or unattended bags looks like an opportunity for food. We started to get surrounded, Joan was oblivious that she was the cause of all their interest. George had to double back, swinging his monkey stick, to the annoyance of the monkey friendly group who just didn't understand that we were about to be under attack. We ushered Joan on and through the monkey area with them hot on our trail and menacing. I was at the back. I had to take a swing, and then swing again, but they could see that I was an amateur and only the presence of the monkey police saved me from a bite or a scratch. At the monkey police area, Joan got her camera out again. For some reason, she gave it to one of the monkey police who opened the back and exposed the film. All the photos she had taken on the holiday were ruined. The monkey police man didn't know what he had done. He had never seen a camera like that before. Joan's trip had gone from bad to worse. There was nothing that I could do. We split the group into two, some doing the long walk and the older ones doing the short one. This is where I found out why Abigail and her mum were travelling together. I noticed a long scar along mum's chest. Abigail was acting as her mum's carer. It turns out that she'd recently had a triple heart by-pass and hadn't bothered to tell my managers or me about it. And I'd just scaled a mountain with this woman.

We have more time in Emei Shan on the northbound trip and there are a number of options for our final day. There is a "hot springs" which, is more of a resort with around fifty hot pools, some open air, some under cover, all with different mineral waters at different temperatures. Some of the group liked this, others, still had complaints about there being slippery surfaces and things to trip over. Others thought that the hot spring would be in some naturally forested lagoon. We never said anything of the sort, they are actually in a four star hotel, which I had thought would keep most people happy. There was also the chance to go with Patrick on a tour around the villages. They returned a couple of hours later, saying that it was the highlight of the trip so far. They had visited a Kung Fu school, calligraphy class, noodle factory, and the school where Patrick's daughter was, in class, practicing a play for "children's day". They had devised a song and dance routine, the Alphabet song from Sesame Street and Andrea had videoed it. It was a real life, trip experience. I only wish that I had gone instead of catching up with my paperwork.

Our bus driver back to Chengdu got our itinerary all wrong, dumping us at the train station with over two hours to spare. For once, I was glad of Martin's enthusiasm and desperate need to be at the forefront of something. He pointed to "Dicos" fast food; the rest of the group said yes and were happy munching on chicken burgers until the train came. Our next overnight train journey took us to Xi'an again. I walked the group around town and took them for dinner in the Muslim Quarter, which went as well as I could have ever expected with such a conservative group who just didn't want to try anything different. Their big complaint this time was that all the dishes were arriving at the same time and plates were being put on top of other plates. This is quite usual, but according to the group, it was bad and hurried service. Most went home after that, but I met up again with Andrea, Dave and the Canadians on the awful Bar Street before heading out of the South Gate. I had been told of something happening there and wanted to see for myself. When you near the South Gate, you can hear the noise. Only when you get close up can you see exactly what is happening. This is China at its best. Hundreds of people are dancing away to the rhythm of a drum and percussion section. This is all local people, just doing this as a way of relaxation, entertainment and exercise. They dance to some sort of random sequence, with leaders who hold sequined umbrellas, others holding handkerchiefs, doing some sort of strange conga-line. If you want, you are more than welcome to join in. It usually takes a few beers for any of us to do this, but for the Chinese, it is a sober, but fun filled activity. We have lost all this playfulness in the west. Our daily lives are so obsessed with doing the right thing, keeping up with the Joneses, not making a fool of yourself and being too dam wrapped up in ourselves and our ego's that we've forgotten how to have fun, unless it's got a drug catalyst. These people who have suffered all sort of hardships in China, just go out and dance. Just opposite the dancers, is a spontaneous choir. Anything up to 100 people, singing in unison. Usually one of the traditional "Long March" songs, rousing in its' collective rendition. Sang from memory, sang from the heart. Further along again are the kind of stalls that you find at a fair-ground, hoop the bottle of beer, throw darts at balloons. There will be street Karaoke, there will be another drum and percussion group working through a rhythm. This is a fantastic place and probably what sums up China to me more than anywhere else.

After that I continued with Andrea and Dave. We hit the jackpot and found the bar that played live rock music, called 'Music Man'. I like this city more and more every time I go there. Then, just to round off the night, I took Andrea to one of the nightclubs. These places are truly awful. The music is very loud and a mixture of local bands, Korean pop, some chart mixes turned into techno beat and even Bony M's Rasputin (that seems to be a favourite). The whole idea of these places is to get really pissed. It's not uncommon to see Chinese fall off their stools at the bar whilst playing dice. There is vomit all over the toilets. People try to dance with you. One man tried to hit on Andrea, saying she was beautiful. God loves a trier, but he didn't stand a cat in hells chance. Another portly bloke in shirt, tie and spectacles kept grabbing me to dance with him and his friends. He had even less chance. We managed a few dice games with the bar tenders though. They are usually as pissed as the customers. Then the girls started dancing on the bar podium. They are an incredible turn on. Andrea noticed me looking too. I said, honestly, that a lot of western blokes won't go back to western women once they've been with a Chinese. They're just so fit. Andrea said that she could probably dance just as well as the girls. I think there was something that I missed there.

The next morning, we went to the Terracotta Warriors with Jim again. He did his usual spiel about Xi'an and added in some more information. He started off by teaching us how to count, which also gave us information that different numbers had hidden meaning. The number four, pronounced "si" was similar to the word for "death" and so it was an unlucky number. Eight was a lucky number as it was in harmony, because it was four pairs and equally balanced. People want eights on their car number plates or on their telephone numbers and will pay a lot of money to get a telephone number with as many eights as possible. Then Jim taught us the four compass points and how they related to Beijing (Bei is "North" Jing is "Capital") Nanjing (The old Southern Capital). Dongjing (Dong meaning East) which is the Chinese name for Tokyo and Xi'an, which means Western Peace. Then about the four areas of Xi'an. To the North was a commercial area, where people would greet you by asking "so, how is your business going?" and such like. To the East was the educational area and people would greet you by asking how your child's studies were, or which university they were going to. In the South, was the cultural zone. But in the West, it was a poor area and people would ask if you had a job yet, or how your child was coping in prison.

The Terracotta Warriors was Joan's' thing. It was the highlight of the trip for her and we spent a lot longer there than usual, especially as it took her so long to get around with what we now knew was a broken foot. She had also been in a bit of a mood with Andrea, who had been sharing with her. She had actually commented on her late night out with me saying "does your mother know what you are up to?" it may have been in jest, but Andrea felt the heat. One thing that I like to point out at the Terracotta Warriors, in Pit 2, amongst the warriors on exhibit in glass cases, is the kneeling archer. Look at his back, there is a little bit of colour remaining. When the warriors were originally created, they were painted, but as soon as they are dug up and exposed to the air, the colours disappear. The Japanese and the Germans have both offered the Chinese government cutting edge technology that can preserve the colours of any new finds, but true to their ideals (or is it just a money thing) the Chinese have said "no" until they can develop the technology themselves. The Japanese want 20% of all the ticket sales to the Terracotta Warriors in exchange for their knowhow. Another intriguing exhibit here is the galvanized sword. It took us in the west until the 1950's to be able to chromium plate objects, but here we are, with a sword from around 220BC, with chromium plating. What is more amazing for me, is that you need electricity to be able to galvanize metal.

As usual we finished the trip in Beijing and an excursion to the Great Wall. It rained, which made me think of actually cancelling the hike. The Canadians had also only brought sandals to hike in and summer clothes though I'd warned everyone about the rigorous hike and changeable weather. Once again, they had wanted a comprehensive weather report, rather than listening and being prepared. Once up there, the mist and rain meant that you couldn't see more than a few meters in front of us. The wall was deserted. It looked like a scene from a Lord of the Rings film, following a path that lead to who knows where, broken pavements and the glimpse of a tower as the mist momentarily cleared. Andrea, being by far the youngest and fittest took the lead, then Martin, never one to be second at anything, ran on as well. Someone in the group looked at an abandoned Maureen again, long suffering on this trip and over the forty odd years of marriage. "I can't stop him" she says "I don't know how he keeps going; he is like this with everything, going and going and going and going..... He is like a machine". She was blissfully unaware of why we were doubling up with laughter at the thought of him going "at it". As the four hour hike through the rain ended the group were still actually laughing and joking and the sky cleared just long enough to see the outline of the next 7 towers unclicking themselves along the hill-tops. Spectacular. As we got off the wall they were whistling the theme from "the great escape", even one of the Canadians with a broken sandal was still enthusiastic. It was a memory that will stay with me a long time and a credit to those who had done the hike with me

I like the Youth Hostel in Beijing. It's sort of a home from home for me. Zhen the bar man knows me and always laughs about the condom snorting trick I showed him in training week. We've had a few very late nights/early mornings and even met the king of China once (his name is Guo Wang). Zhen, like most Chinese working in a western style bar, are doing it so than they can learn how to make cocktails and make a lot of tips. I'd tried to explain to him that this wasn't the way it worked in England, but the Chinese have adapted the humble pub experience. Now it is all about private tables, shared bottles of expensive whisky and cocktails and big tips, so Zhen was trying to work his way into one of the Chinese nightclubs. I assumed my usual position at the bar on my return to the Hostel and was joined by Dave and Andrea. This is how it was for the next couple of nights interspaced with trips to Hou Hai and being joined by other Tour Leaders Janie, Sheila, and Steven.

16. Return to the Broken Rainbow, 05/06/07 (Hostel, Beijing)

I return to the broken rainbow
My home from home, where I go
When I'm given that most valuable free time
When I unpack the world on my shoulders that is mine
Where I share with strangers, make new friends
Walk the streets of my new home-town again
Where my world is a little bit bigger than just me
At the broken rainbow's end is where I'll be

Too many late nights that I'm addicted to
And running around invincible like I was twenty two
Laughing in Tiananmen Square, I never would believe it
It took someone quite special and I'm glad we met
And had the time that could only be here and now
Because she will go on to achieve more than I will ever do
So I have no regrets and no urge to follow
As I write a song from this side of the broken rainbow

I'm sitting in the gutter, looking at the stars
Sharing beer with prostitutes at the street bar
The station clock chimes away another hour
Before the lights wink off, to save power
And nobody knows that I'm here for sure
In the twilight world amid beer and whores

Somehow I belong here, it's a place I know
My world at this side of the broken rainbow

17. The Ancient Observatory, 19/06/07 (Hostel, Beijing)

The ancient observatory
How I think how you used to be
A building filled with majesty
A statement there for all to see
With golden sphere to rival the sun
Measuring the sky into great partitions
One step higher than the lowly human
The centre of the universe on high solid stone

Now you are an island in the concrete
Surrounded by the six lane street
And a fly-over that has you at its feet
Encircled by high-rise, you admit defeat
And look out from your once proud turret and see
Across a vista of rushing city
Of concrete and glass and ultra-modernity
Thinking of how it used to be

Before the city wall was breached by roads
And the night sky was clear of smog
When you marked the passage of gods

18. The Great Wall, 19/06/07 (Hostel, Beijing)

Back upon the Great Wall
I walked across the castles in cloud
Living in a fairytale
Whistling the Great Escape as we walked out

Free from the dragons of the storm
Full of magical visions, we head home.

On one particular night it was just me and Andrea again and it was getting a little bit blurry after the ear licking incident (another one of my party tricks) then, for some reason that I still can't fathom out, I decided to follow her to Tian An Men Square. She said she wanted to see the flag raising at dawn. An excellent double entendre if ever there was one. We were both very pissed. There are a few good photos to prove it and I think that's the only reason why we didn't get arrested for laughing at the soldiers. At one point I was going to climb the national flag. At another I was going to have a piss in one of the litter bins. Both these acts would have put me in prison for a very long time. As we walked back into the hotel we bumped into Martin and Maureen. They just didn't quite understand that we'd been out all night and why we were laughing so much. Most of the next day was cancelled for me. I'm glad I paid the extra for the room.

Andrea left a day later, and Dave stayed on for the rest of the week, so I still had my drinking buddy's when Steven returned from the wall. We had another night out in Hou Hai where we sort of gate crashed his trips leaving party. It was also Eugenie's birthday, so we met up for Pizza and went out. As we both had synchronised time off at the end of the next trip in Hong Kong, we looked at booking a trip somewhere together. We decided on The Philippines because there were fewer visa restrictions for both of us and it was less than Y1000 for a return flight there. This became a bit of a farce. The first problem was paying for the trip. Although Eugenie had two bank accounts with money in them, her bank would not release the funds above a certain amount per month. I remember when I first got an ATM card in the 1980's and there was a limit of how much I could take out in a week. This was pretty fair, as I was un-waged and needed to live on a budget. Eugenie had to phone and argue with her bank in order to give her more than the monthly allowance and she discovered that although she had two cards, the amount that she could withdraw or spend was not double the amount if she only had one card. The farce did not end once this was resolved as it's not so easy for Chinese to leave China. She needed return flight tickets, hotel reservations, a copy of her bank account and a letter from her employer saying that she was returning to work and on what date. Eugenie hadn't got the letter from the employer, as the head office is officially in Australia, so on the first attempt, she was knocked back. We had to get the office manager in Beijing to sign. Eugenie had been trying to avoid this, as Cathy was prone to changing Eugenie's' work status to "Not Available" and with it dock her non leading allowance for the four days that we would be away. In the end, we went with Cathy's' signature and Eugenie furious that all these countries make it so hard for Chinese people visit, when China just allows all the foreigners in. She wouldn't believe me when I told her that it was as much China stopping its' citizens leaving and that it wasn't easy for foreigners to visit here either. She still seemed to think that there were a lot of us in China though, especially in Beijing and Shanghai, though for me, they must be extremely well hidden. It's all relative; she hadn't travelled to South East Asia or any of the other tourist destinations for westerners. Eugenie also helped me decide on some hair dye. This was harder than what meets the eye (literally) I'd been looking to do something with my hair for ages, as it had washed out to reveal red patches along with the brown and grey re-growth. It was a real mess, but there aren't many options in China and I certainly wasn't going to risk going into a hairdresser. I'd come away with much more than a hair job and my managers would sack me if they saw me leaving one of those places, no-matter what story I could come up with. So in the end I dyed my hair in the true spirit of Henry Ford. "You can have any colour you want as long as it's black"

Chapter 5

ROAM CHINA

*Our greatest glory is not in never falling,
but in rising every time we fall.*

Confucius; Chinese philosopher & reformer
(551 BC - 479 BC),

I had six days off in between trips, most of it spent between the office and my hotel room. I had met the usual incompetence from the office managers, so was trying to update my knowledge of everything Chinese the hard way. Leaders came and went and I met Mill, who spent time drawing out a map of Shanghai for me. "On my first visit, I did my own orientation walk before the passengers got up, just so I would know where to take them" she said. She had taken Chinese lessons "because, when you have a passenger needing to go to hospital, you just have to sort it out." She was recognized as being one of our outstanding leaders. She also suffered from a lot of prejudice, as, being a black American; the tourists to China were just not expecting her as their tour guide. I had also found myself wandering the streets in the cities that we had visited across China. Whenever I was without a group to attend to, often late at night, I could have got myself into all sorts of trouble, but luckily, there is not so much trouble in China. Everyone is frightened about being robbed, so much so that the windows on the twentieth floor of the apartment blocks have bars on them. It would take one hell of a cat burglar, more a Marvel Comics Supervillian, to rob any of these places. I had learned as much as I could of the language, whilst trying to learn as much about China, whilst dealing with the group for up to 18 hours a day. Often, I would have a book out on the train, or be plugged into my language lesson, when the question would come. "Where do we go tomorrow?" Or, "what was that village called?" Or "are we on time?" I was now reading through the information held in the office, printing off sheets that I thought were interesting or relevant and filling my forty page display file to the maximum. I signed up for language classes at "Frontiers" where I had private tuition for a couple of hours a day and I watched a lot of T.V.

This was mostly CCTV9, the only channel available in English. I would watch "Da Shan", a Canadian, who had a morning slot with "Learning Chinese". I watched the "Travelogue" girl, off with her backpack to minority hill tribe villages. There was always a welcome with singing and dancing, to the point that it looked very staged. Then we would see other Chinese tourists, travelling in Range Rovers, wearing all the latest designer hiking gear, hats, walking poles and all, just to have a stroll in the countryside. The news was always interesting for all the wrong reasons. Premiers Hu Jin Tao or Wen Jia Bao were off globetrotting, signing agreements with African nations or hosting foreign leaders. There were success story after success story concerning the modernization of China. Wherever there had been a problem, there was work towards a solution. Then there was "Dialogue" and this is where I started to understand more and more of what China was all about. Yang Rui was an expert interviewer with a broad knowledge. He would have panels to discuss the topics of the day, he would have searching questions for his guests and he put it all in a Chinese context. The West was jealous of the growth of China and was attempting to rein this in through policies on the environment, trading standards etc. that were not even being applied in Western countries. This was the history of Chinas' dealing with the West; always the foreign forces were trying to humble the Chinese. There was a scandal about paint contamination on toys made for export to the U.S.A. The argument was that the Chinese factory was complying with the U.S. paymaster's requirements. Then there was the interview with the U.S. Ambassador. Yang Rui was quizzing the Ambassador about the U.S. foreign policy with relation to China. He got him to re-affirm the commitment to the "One China" policy, which on the surface is about Chinese unity, Hong Kong and the two economic and political systems working side by side. When you dig a bit deeper it is about the status of Taiwan as one of the provinces of China and not an independent nation. The Ambassador agreed to this and said that there was no intention of aiding Taiwan militarily, or instigating regime change if they wanted to become independent from China (referred to as "the mainland"). The Ambassador said that the U.S. was not that sort of country and had no history of arming insurrection movements. Then Yang mentioned a number of Middle Eastern countries and the Ambassador was spitting feathers.

The rest of Chinese T.V. is very bad. There are a number of "historical dramas", based around the Ming or Qing courts, full of intrigue, love affairs, battles and murder. More up to date is the many series concerning the war with the Japanese, the Kuomintang and the liberation of China by the heroic Communist Party. All T.V. shows have subtitles. I'd been asked previously by someone why this was the case and when I had posed the question to a Chinese friend, the only answer that I had got from my Chinese respondent was "why do you not have subtitles?" On some things, they are a way ahead of us in the West. On a lighter side, there are the game shows, filled with cartoon pop-ups on the screen and stupid noises and there is the entertainment shows like the Chinese versions of "Idol". There is a complete culture of pop music in China that the West has no idea about, not that you would want to be subject to boy band after boy band. The faces of the boy band members are on the cans of Pepsi or Wahaha water, or at K.F.C. or their Chinese version, Dicos. Then there are even performance shows with the military, dressed in uniform performing with the ever fluttering Red Flag behind them. There are no Western films, no Western programmes, no foreign news. It was hardly a surprise that the Chinese people that I had come into with had such an obscure view of who we were. It was also becoming obvious that China was almost like a parallel universe to the West. Their versions of history, why things were the way they were had a completely different prospective from the things I had learned growing up. The main things that underpinned this was the idea that China was rightfully at the centre of the world. It was "The Middle Kingdom" or "Zhong Guo". For five thousand years it had been the most powerful country in the region, if not the world. Then, in the eighteenth century, the Europeans had come. At first, they were dismissed as barbarians. There was the story that until a chamber orchestra was shipped over to play for one of the Emperors; they thought that the West had nothing of value. History then tells us that the Europeans, worked together to bring China to its knees. Whilst the British and French were at war across the rest of the globe, they decided that China was a big enough prize to form a truce over. We slowly encroached on Chinese territory through trade deals and treaties that the Chinese signed at the threat of "gunboat diplomacy". Near neighbours, Japan were also getting in on the act, as they became closer to the Western powers. The Chinese were slow to realize what was going on as the Qing Dynasty court was corrupt and power obsessed. This finally fell in 1911 with the rise of the Nationalist Government under Dr. Sun Yat Sen, but much of the country remained loyal to the Dynasty system and was ruled by warlords. Japan began its expansionist policy, taking over the North East and installing the last emperor of the Qing Dynasty in power. This humiliation of China saw a rise in the power of the Communist Party. As the Second World War became an extension of the Japanese occupation, the Communists and the Nationalists in China fought each other as well as the Japanese. It was the Communists who became the people's choice as the Nationalists ended up siding with the Japanese invaders, against the Communists. As the Second World War ended everywhere else, it rumbled on until 1949 in China, when Chairman Mao finally defeated the Nationalists and announced the formation of the People's Republic of China on 1st October that year. The Nationalists, defeated, fled to Taiwan. Ever since that time, the Chinese government had laid claim to Taiwan as one of its 34 provinces, whilst the Taiwan government still lays claim to be the legitimate government for the whole of China. This is a point that most westerners do not understand. Both parties still claim to be the rightful government of China to this day. When the Nationalists left, they looted the Forbidden City and took the countries entire gold reserves. The Communists inherited a country, at the end of a fifteen year war, with the cities destroyed, with the crops failing and with no funds. They made the decision to close the door on the West, as, historically, every time China had dealt with the West; it had come out as a loser. Since then, there began a programme of agrarian reform, then industrialization, and finally modernization that has brought China to the cusp of being the greatest nation in the world, once again.

And so on to my next trip. I was really looking forward to this one. Sixteen passengers, all but two of them under 25. I was going to have a ball. Or at least I thought I was. There were a few people who had quite evidently booked the wrong trip. The first was the Irish girl, Colleen. I was heading down to Chong Wen Men Hotel to put up my introductory trip message about the first group meeting and all the other local info' when I got a phone call. It was the Chong Wen Men reception and there was the Irish girl there who was mightily pissed off because she had the wrong trip joining information. She had first gone to the Hostel, who had got in touch with the Travel Company's' Beijing Office and Cathy, the manager, who had then sent her off to Chong Wen Men. A bit of a mix up, especially as Cathy had not been any help at all and Colleen had been ripped off on a five minute taxi ride that she could have walked. If only someone had been around to help her. I had hoped that a 29 year old Irish girl, travelling on her own would be "good craic" as they say, but she was flustered about turning up in a foreign country with no one to help her and was obviously out of her depth doing any sort of independent travel. She told me that she worked as a teacher, "with the sisters". I'd got my stereotyping very wrong. She then asked me about the bike ride on day 14 of the trip and the hike between the Long Ji Rice terrace villages on day 18. She didn't want to do either and wanted to know what other options could I give her. She had been told, when she booked with STA that I (the leader) would sort everything out for her once she was on the trip. I think STA were more interested in making a sale than giving out the correct information. If someone does not want to do the included activity, there is no alternative and no compensation. If she does not want to hike between the two villages, she would have to find her own way from one to the other by bus. I suppose I could get the guide to write down some information and point her in the right direction, but that would be all. Just one look at this overweight, flustered girl and I knew she would not be capable of negotiating public busses in rural China.

The rest of the group arrived the next day. I'd put my notice up and had suggested that the early arrivals could have lunch with me. This was a shot in the foot, as all it did was get people asking me questions about things that I wanted to explain more thoroughly in the group meeting. They had too many assumptions about what the trip was all about and all wanted to do different things and I had to pour cold water on it all as I kept saying that we had to stick to the itinerary. I never made that mistake of meeting any of the group before the actual group meeting again. That night we had the usual group meeting and I got the usual response of "you've only been working for how long? Do you speak Chinese?" and "what will the weather be like in Hong Kong?". The ones that I had met in the afternoon didn't help as they had already decided what they wanted to do, as they had decided that they were now experts and were telling the new arrivals all about what to do in China. Then they started talking about malaria and how likely they were to get it. I'd not heard of any malaria cases so far in China. It seems as though when you go to the doctor in the U.K. he looks at a computer program on a screen and the areas with malaria turn red. Evidently, China is one of these areas, so he prescribes malaria tablets. I told them that as far as I knew, there was no malaria. "But..." they kept saying. Well, I wasn't taking malaria pills and neither was anyone I knew. I later looked this up and China is pretty malarial free with no account of a tourist getting it in the previous four years. My group were a bit of a mixed bag. A British Indian girl who had just spent a month teaching English in the north of the country. Another Irish girl, who seemed more out of her depth than the first one. A Swedish couple, who seemed more independent than the others, an English boy and girl who were friends at University, travelling together, but not "together". But the outstanding pair were the father and daughter John and Janet, travelling together. In my trip notes, there had been a medical warning. The daughter had cystic fibrosis

With my company's travel and tours; there is quite a lot of information in the brochure concerning the style of trip. It talks about the physical and culture shock rating. There is a day by day guide as to what the group will be doing and what optional activities you could do. You would hope that anybody spending over $1000 on "the trip of a lifetime" would do a bit of reading up on where they were going and what they had actually paid for. I don't expect the group to know everything, that's part of the adventure and of course, the literature states that things can and will change in a developing country such as China. Nevertheless, for both me and the group, it was a strange start to the trip. A basic trip has no included activities, so that means no guided tour of the Forbidden City. In fact, the group has two days in Beijing to occupy themselves. We, as tour leaders are around to help out, however, it was a bit of a shock to most in the group when I had to explain that the Optional Activity List, which was quite extensive, was just a suggestion of the things that they themselves could do whilst on the trip. It was not a list of the things that were included as group activities. Many of them seemed to be offended that I was not going to organise their next two days and guide them around, to each and every different places, all free of charge.

I'd taken a couple of the early arrivals to lunch and did the whole group dinner thing on the first night. This was a bit of a surprise to most of the group, as they hadn't expected to share plates and didn't know what any of the food was. There were the questions of "is it safe to eat?" as if I'd take them to a place on the first day in an attempt to poison them (though, in hindsight...). They asked; all concerned, about the safety of the food that we would be eating. Up until this point they must have been thinking that it was burgers and pizzas all the way. They were concerned about the water. "What about salads?" they said, and I replied "what salads?" and then the ice cubes, to which I also replied "what ice cubes?" John had brought his own knife and fork and told me that he was a vegetarian as his daughter looked on, puzzled. As we talked about the next two days in Beijing, I said that I could get a guide for the Forbidden City, at a cost of 200 Yuan, or less than fifteen pounds between whoever wanted to go, which deterred all of them from signing up. Then I left them to it. I offered dinner on the second evening, but it was only John, Janet and the Irish girl Colleen who came along. I assumed that the others were being truly adventurous and sorting themselves out. I think they found K.F.C. and didn't venture beyond the road at the front of the hotel.

We arranged for a 7am departure to the Great Wall. Most of the group was late and two of the girls arrived at around 7:15, only to tell me that they had to go to the shop first to get water. We left during rush hour and our three hour journey to the Wall took four hours that day. I reminded the group about punctuality; it seems that this was a new word for many of them. I told them that if they were late for a public bus or a train, then the rest of us would have to go without them. The girls were chatting away so much that I may as well have been talking to them in Mandarin. It was on the trip to the Great Wall, that I first realised how little John and Janet knew about the trip that he had booked. The bus dropped us off at Gu Bei Kou, a very rural part of the Wall and we met our local guide for the trek, Hai Long. He was in his forties, dressed in combat gear and spoke only a little English. We needed someone to guide us through this part of the Wall as much of it was across open fields and countryside and not on the crumbling Wall at all. As with all the Great Wall sites, we had quite a climb up to the actual structure. John took me to one side as the three of us and the Irish girls were bringing up the rear. "You know of my daughters' medical condition. What emergency measures are in place if something goes wrong out here? Is there an air ambulance?" My honest reply was that there were no emergency measures. There was an air ambulance in Beijing, but it was not on standby for us. If anything happened, he was to contact his insurance company and they would have to do the rest. He could not believe what I was saying. He thought that because he had booked a trip, then our company would be dealing with whatever problem arose. True, we had people in the office that could help out, but it was news to him that we didn't have a hotline to the Beijing emergency services. The pair of them and one of the Irish girls Colleen was struggling particularly badly. She was cursing the weather and saying that she had not been told that this was going to be a 10km hike in 30 degree heat. She had the same notes as everybody else and I had talked about our trip to the Wall, but was still telling me that STA hadn't mentioned anything about these included activities, or all the optional activities that she had wanted to do over the last two days in Beijing, but no one was around to take her to the places that she wanted to visit and she certainly hadn't expected to pay for them. It was later, in her feedback that she stated that she felt "like a fucking ATM".

After half an hour, we finally got onto the Wall. Janet was out of breath and crying. She could not go on any further. She was mostly frustrated that she could not do the hike like all the others. Colleen was also ready to call it a day. So the two of them and John went back to the bus. The other Irish girl now started panicking. She did not like heights. If you have ever seen pictures of the Great Wall, you should have an idea what to expect and the trip notes are quite clear that we hike along the top of a wall, but this was obviously lost on her. It was her one chance to return to the bus, but she decided she would give it a go. Half an hour later, faced with a scramble where the Wall spanned a gorge, it was too late to change her mind and I had my second girl in tears on the same day. Who were these people? What were they thinking when they booked the trip? It took hours to negotiate some of the steeper sections, holding hands, saying "I can't make it". Then, slowly maneuvering the girl along the defile. Hai Long had not seen this before. He couldn't understand it. At one point, we came across some farmers who had set up a check-point and asked us for money to pass. This was just a scam, as they knew a group of foreigners passed this way, around the same time on the same days every week. I refused to pay and ended up ringing the office, getting Suzy Li to chat to them. It was Suzy's first week as the new Senior Leader and she was getting a lot of work, as she actually answered peoples' questions and helped out the leaders. It was a nice change having someone in the office who was trying to support us. The only other help I had been given in the office over my first months was from Li, or the leaders who were always passing through in a hurry.

We stayed at a hostel on the Great Wall at Simatai that night. Some of the group actually thought that we were camping on the wall, but that is neither allowed, nor advised. It is, after all, a wall. Simatai has a couple of restaurants and the hostel had a bar that looked over the reservoir. It was quite pretty as the sun set behind the wall, above us on the hill. I looked around the village that evening, where the villagers had erected a homemade film screen across the road by tying a bed sheet to lamp posts. On it, a war film was showing, probably glorifying the Chinese victory over the Japanese as usual. Once again the social aspect of the Chinese was confusing my tourists, who assumed that it must be some special occasion. You never have far to go to join in with something, have a good time, be entertained, and meet people in China.

We had a night back in Beijing, where most of the group had booked to see one of the shows, but we were so late returning that many went without having dinner. I ate with John and Janet. Apart from bringing his own knife and fork on the trip, the only preparation he had done before coming to China was to watch a documentary and visit the local Cantonese takeaway in Tooting, South London where they were from. I got a little bit more of their story. Jane's' condition was degenerative and the doctors had said that if she wanted to travel, she should do it sooner, rather than later. She had said that she wanted to see a number of things. Ayers Rock, the Great Barrier Reef, the beaches of Thailand, as well as The Great Wall and Terracotta Warriors, both, by chance it seems, were in China. So they went down to STA and they sold them this trip along with a couple of others down through South East Asia. This was their first time travelling. They hadn't got a clue and my heart went out to them. When the group was talking about their lives, going to university, travelling the world and getting good jobs, it became obvious that Janet's' life would be so different. She did some work with kids, wasn't going to university and didn't say too much about the future. When I asked John about himself, he said that he had given up work 18 years earlier to care for his daughter. He had nothing in common with his co-travellers.

We went on to Xi'an. We stayed in a hotel to the South of the City Wall, I did the usual orientation walk and then they all wanted feeding. I took them to a local snack café, where I knew they did wontons, and as they wanted to just order small snacks, I thought it would be ideal. However, they wanted something more western, of which there were a random couple of dishes which were bad interpretations of the real thing and with them all trying to order individually, it just became a confusing mess for the waitress. Some left for the place advertising pizza. As with all basic trips, the Terracotta Warriors is not included. The company that I work for gives the group the "option" of getting out to the museum site by public transport. Once I had written this up on the trip message, along with drawing maps, bus numbers and info of the other sites to see in Xi'an this had them all thinking that I was abandoning them or not doing my duty. They all started checking their notes to see if I was lying to them and checking if I was ripping them off. There was another option of hiring a bus from the local operator and taking a guide. They decided that they would take the hire bus option, but not the tour guide; it worked out at less than three pounds per person. As they looked at me, I agreed that I would take them to the Terracotta Warriors, at my own expense, when there were so many other things that I wanted to do in Xi'an. We had the afternoon in Xi'an, showing them around the city, the Muslim Quarter where we ate dinner at my now regular Number 57 Restaurant (I can remember the number, not the un-pronounceable name) as I could pre-order the food there. After this, I lost some of the group in the street bazaar, asking what all the Middle Eastern style foods were, but I got most of them to see the local singing and dancing outside the wall. We even managed a few beers on Bar Street, but none of them wanted a late night.

I arranged for the bus to meet us in the morning, keeping it through to the afternoon in order to visit the Big Goose Pagoda on the way back from The Warriors. Once again, we left almost an hour late, waiting for the same girls. We went to the site and apart from the notable exceptions; the group were bored of the Terracotta Warriors within two hours. It was still two hours of my free time when I could have been doing other things, but that had gone un-noticed. So we continued on to the Big Goose Pagoda. Once there, the Swedish couple said that they had already seen it the day before and would get a taxi back to the hotel. A couple of the girls were also not interested and the last thing anybody heard them say is that they might share the taxi back with the Swedes. The Big Goose Pagoda was built in 652 during the Tang Dynasty and was rebuilt in 704 during the reign of Chinas only Empress, Wu Zetian. One of the seven storied pagoda's many functions was to hold sutras, or books and figurines of the Buddha that were brought to China from India by the Buddhist translator and traveller Xuanzang, more commonly known as Tripitaka. If this rings a bell, then you must remember the T.V. programme "Monkey Magic", a 1970's offering from Japan. I had started to talk about this T.V. programme with monkeys on flying clouds, a pig and a fish God, all protecting a monk who was played by a woman. It was all too farfetched for them. A pity, because the actual story that "Monkey" was based upon was "A Journey to the West". This is an ancient classic, full of stories about the quest to bring back the Buddhist scriptures from India and the trials undergone by the travelling companions en route. The Temple complex housing the Pagoda had ornate courtyards and prayer halls. The main one had the most wonderful walls, carved with the ancient scenes from the story of the Journey. Surrounding the complex were acres of parks and gardens and every evening, the largest musical fountain in Asia would come alive. This was a big draw to the Chinese, but my lot were no more enthusiastic than I was about seeing it.

One hour later and it is departure time and we are all back on the bus apart from the Swedes and the two girls. "Has anybody seen them?" I asked. "No" came the reply. So we went back to the hotel. This was always going to happen with 14 darlings who would chat chat away. Well, half an hour after our return to the hotel, I was met at the front door by 2 distraught girls, one in tears, getting out of a taxi, because the bus had left them. It's funny how 14 other people managed to get the departure time right isn't it.

Then there was Shanghai. The worst experience of my working time as a tour leader so far. I'd never been there before, so I'd asked everyone I knew about the place. Mill had drawn me a map, others had come up with suggestions. Andrea, who had travelled on independently after our last trip had emailed to say it was a great place and had been to the Propaganda Museum and Sun Yat Sen's house. I had my trip notes, so what could go wrong? As we left the train station for the taxi rank, I said (paraphrasing the trip notes); "This is where we meet up in 3 days' time when we come back to the train station in taxis. Please remember it!" I pointed at the large blue sign for Shanghai Railway Station. I got five taxis with surprising ease and 15 minutes later we were all at a Hotel that beforehand had only been a handwritten address in Chinese on five "post-it" notes. I was very pleased with my ingenuity. I should have quit whilst I was ahead.

We were located a twenty minute walk away from the centre of Shanghai, we were on the other side of Suzhou Creek, near Zhapu Road. Instead of going out first and getting my bearings, I decided to immediately do an orientation walk and ventured off out with the 16 trailing up to 100m behind me across the river, through the building sites and onto The Bund, Shanghai's famous riverside walk. We all looked across the Huangpu River to the Pu Dong Area, Shanghai's new glistening heart. Full of new skyscrapers and the giant spheres and buildings shaped like globes that formed the World Trade Centre and the Oriental Pearl Tower. I told the group that only fifteen years ago, none of this existed and it was just a poor shantytown on the wrong side of the river. I told them that in the late 1990's half the world's cranes were in Shanghai. John wondered why they had all gone. "Was it because of all the building?" he asked me. It took me a little time to clearly understand his train of thought. He thought I was talking about the birds called Crain's. Half an hour later I realised I'd not taken the right turning. The information I had been given was to look for the Peace Hotel and take that street. This would be Nanjing Road, Shanghai's major artery and shopping street. Unfortunately for me, the Peace Hotel was being re-furbished and was covered in sheeting. I never saw it. It's difficult trying to double back with such a long line of people. Some were getting hungry and dropped out after spying a KFC. A good decision on their part as it was another 20 minutes before I got us to the Nanjing Hotel. Once at Nanjing Hotel, the darlings then asked, where they were going to eat and what were we doing next. I calmed my reply down, pointed at the 20 or so places to eat in downtown Shanghai, then said "you have free time....." I said that I would grab something to eat in Yoshinoya, the fast food restaurant and take people on to the Shanghai Museum once I'd eaten. Most were not interested in more walking, so I said I would organise dinner for the following day. I needed a break.

In the next twenty four hours, I got to know the city by getting hopelessly lost following the travel company's' booklet map. It turns out the map provided, was not a map at all, just some sort of evil puzzle. Four or five people had drawn different sections of Shanghai and they had somehow been cut and paste together in such a way that if you thought you could follow a road from starting point to destination, you would somehow find yourself in another part of town. It was a cross between a maze and time travel. Roads that were actually half a Kilometer apart appear next to each other on this map. It was a hapless task, and I had it. Shanghai is all about buildings. The Bund that we had walked along is famed for its European Colonial style and the solid blocks of grey stone built buildings, many resembling old banking houses that you would find in London or the other British cities. Around the Ren Min "Peoples"

Park were the gothic art deco tower of the Park Hotel and the, "flying saucer" topped Radisson Hotel, both pre Second World War iconic buildings. Then, around the park were the newly built History and Planning Museums. Connecting the park and the Bund is Nanjing Lu. This is the main shopping street in Shanghai and all the western shopping outlets are there. There are also all the Chinese brands, many of which have more than a passing resembling to their western counterparts. A shop selling sportswear had a "swoosh" very similar to the Nike insignia. Another looked at first like a misspelled Adidas. There are also hawkers trying to sell just about everything. The latest fad, whether it be the trainers with wheels, or the plastic jelly like "creatures" that you can splat against a hard surface, only to see them take shape again. There was the remote controlled flying thing, anything and everything imaginable was on sale. There were the people selling the two magnets, which made the annoying vibrating sound when you let them come into sharp contact with each other, they are possibly one of the most pointless souvenirs that I have ever encountered. Most of these trinkets I had seen in most places where there were tourists in China. There were the more aggressive sellers too; carrying cards with pictures of handbags, watches, trainers and hassling you to go to their shop. There were people trying to get you to go to their art show, saying they were students and it was the last day of their exhibition. Others saying that they knew a good place to have tea, or a tea ceremony. There were also girls, who would come up to you and ask if you wanted a massage. I was getting used to being phoned in the hotel rooms and asked if I wanted "an mo" and I had walked past numerous neon lit hairdressers and massage places on my late night explorations, but this was the only place where I had actually been approached on the street for sex and it was the main shopping street in China.

Around the hotel, there were a lot of "foot massage" places with scantily dressed girls hanging around. This wasn't new to me, there were many places that we had passed through that had hairdressers and massage places with their pink neon lights that doubled up as brothels, but around Zhapu Lu, it was on a different scale. On my first night, away from the group, I walked the streets, as I would in any new city, and was surprised at the number of places with girls idly playing cards in soon to be demolished shop fronts. These places were pretty basic, cheap knocking shops. I ran into John, who told me that he had gone into one of the bars, for a beer. He had been ushered upstairs, to where there were women just wearing towels. He had not been expecting this at all. The next day, as promised, I went to Nanjing Lu, booked dinner and was pre ordering the food when a couple of the group arrived. It was nice of them to search me out, as the others had decided that they wanted to go to the pizza place. It was one of the girls birthday the following day and they wanted a celebration of sorts and not Chinese food. I left the bewildered waiter, who thought that I had just scammed him. Very embarrassing and it could have been even more so if nobody had come to tell me of the change of plans.

My first visit to Shanghai had not been a good one. Getting back to the train station to leave Shanghai was even worse. As we waited in the hotel lobby for the Taxis, Irish girl Colleen actually said "I bet you're glad to be leaving Shanghai". "Don't speak too soon" said I. How I mark those words. We split into into five taxis, each of the passengers holding their train tickets, we sped off..... In the wrong direction. I soon lost sight of the other four taxis and started shoving my train ticket in front of the drivers' nose. "Chur Zhan", I said, he agreed, but carried on going as we passed signs for the airport. I tried again, "chur zhan" and he just kept on going. I was starting to come up with all sort of scenarios for how the other passengers in the other taxis were coping. How would they get on the train to Guilin? I decided to ring the Local Operator. "You are going to Shanghai South Station", I never even knew the place existed. I then had visions of my passengers, also realising that they weren't going to where they thought they should be, arguing with the driver and then, after deciding that they were being abducted, throttling him and taking over the wheel. Needless to say, when they all turned up, bemused, angry, at Shanghai South, they were about to throttle me instead. No amount of explaining was going to get me out of this one, I even showed them my trip notes with the reference to meeting back at the station that we had arrived at.

It was a twenty four hour train ride to Yangshuo. I couldn't get there early enough. I knew the group would appreciate the western food, the bars, the idyllic scenery and I knew I could get a birthday cake there too. I drew out the map of Yangshuo for them, took them around all the major points, bank, internet, market, riverside, best places for food and drink. I took them for an introduction to local massage, acupuncture, hot cupping or any variety of Chinese medicine at Dr. Lillyi. I took them to see Henry for Kung Fu or Tai Chi, if they wanted, to book later. There are so many other things on offer in Yangshuo and the group seemed a lot happier about being there and at least I could regain a little bit of respect. Some wanted to go on the River Cruise, this is just a couple of hours on a bamboo raft and very un-cruise like if you were expecting a real boat, but it gets you into the heart of the countryside, where the picture on the 20 Yuan note was taken. Others wanted to see the "Light Show", which is a cultural song and dance on a magnificent scale on the Li River. Then, there was Cormorant Fishing. This is a strange local occupation where a fisherman has a bird, called a cormorant, trained to fish for him. Fisherman and birds go out in the evening, in their small bamboo boats on the river, dressed in traditional reed jackets and conical hats. The birds will sit on a pole across the boatman's shoulders; they are actually tied to it on a long thread. The Cormorant is then encouraged to dive for fish. The ingenious part of this, apart from the training, is that the bird has a cord tied around its neck and therefore cannot eat the fish. Ingenious, but also not in the spirit of responsible travel as far as I could see. A generation ago, this was the way that people fished and probably still do in other parts of rural China, but in Yangshuo, it is a spectacle for the tourists and I started to tell the group as much, most of it falling on deaf ears.

As for the evening meal and birthday, I managed to pull this one off and organised a table on the rooftop bar for the sunset a Monkey Jane's. I had asked the group to pre order their food, so as to speed things up and most of them had filled out their requirements on my list that I gave to Jane an hour before we went to dinner. I was glad that I was getting things right again. However, things never go quite according to plan. I saw the "baked potato" arrive, cut like a series of fat chips with a dollop of tuna and mayonnaise on top. This was obviously not what the girls expected, so I went back down to the kitchen with it as the remainder in the group completed their food orders. Nobody had ever shown the chef how to stick a potato in a microwave oven for ten minutes, then to cut it, crisscross style and put the filling inside. Most of the cooks in China have never actually been served in a western restaurant, let alone worked in one and although Jane used to do a lot of the cooking, she now employed others to do this and they just didn't have the know-how. I returned to the group table. Many had seen "Beer Fish" on the menu and as it was a local dish, had all ordered it. That meant four beer fish. After two weeks in the country, they had still not got it that food was for sharing. The four beer fish arrived over an hour later and could have fed half of the group. What's more, the fish came complete with tails, heads and bones, so largely went uneaten. At least the birthday cake was a success and so were Monkey Jane's Mojitos.

There were other leaders in town again and we were all comparing notes on our groups. The Roam China trip has a reputation for having difficult customers as it attracts "gap year" students on a round the world trip. Many have been sold it as a filler from S.T.A. They offer flight deals on round the world tickets and they manage to get the travellers to go to Beijing and out of Hong Kong before visiting Thailand for its beaches and full moon parties then on to Australia. There were stories of disappointed groups, not having any idea of what China was like before they arrived. I was told of entire groups who would not eat the food. Leaders, who had catered for "vegetarians" for over two weeks, would find their passengers leaving McDonalds with a burger, only then letting on that that they didn't trust the meat in China. There were other groups where they would only eat rice with soya sauce, for days on end. Others brought their own food with them and would still be opening cans of baked beans two weeks into the trip. Then there was the whole "optional activities" thing, with the group not understanding that they had free time to explore around by themselves. The expectation level on this basic trip was often much higher than on the "original" ones, where the groups actually wanted to be more adventurous and go off by themselves. This was all ringing true about my trip; I felt that I was not alone. I raised the subject of the Aussies not liking the large bottles of beer, jokingly saying that they were obviously not the men that they thought they were, as it was only a pint and teenage girls in the U.K. can be found knocking back pints the length and breadth of the country. So an Aussie, piped up. "By the time you get to the bottom of the bottle, the beer is warm, that's ok for you, but we want cold beer". Same old Aussie ignorance again. "Drink faster" said I.

It was around this time that everybody started asking me why I wasn't planning to set up my own business. For most Chinese, the idea that you can set up your own business is a status symbol. This is more apparent in Yangshuo where so many, once poor farmers have become rich, almost overnight. It is part of the Chinese dream. They have a saying, that being happy is being able to "Sleep until noon. Spend your day counting the money your business has earned until your hands get tired. Then go out and celebrate every night with family and friends". The Chinese people I knew were constantly suggesting that I open a bar, or guest house or a tour agency. For many of the Chinese leaders, it is what they aspired to. A few years working for this international travel company would get them the money, the know-how and the contacts to set up by themselves. The local guides were one step behind on this, knocking on the door of my managers to become leaders, whilst at the same time trying to start up a business themselves. In Yangshuo there were a lot of foreigners involved in business. A foreigner can't actually own a business in China, a Chinese will always have to be the majority shareholder and that is a risk very few people would take unless they could trust the person or people who they are in business with completely. When it comes to the crunch, Westerners have no rights in China and your business partner could just sell up and run off with your investment. I'm not one for being a businessman anyway. I've worked and ran small businesses on the behalf of the Universities I worked for and I knew how hard it is. If you are committed to making a profit, you will spend every hour available at work, trying to make a go of it and this changes you. In a bar, or guest house, you will be the first up, last to bed and inevitable consuming an unhealthy amount of alcohol in the process. You see your friends as potential customers and the people who work for you as potential thieves. This is not the life I want to live.

In China, and I saw this in Yangshuo, there is a bit of a mafia going on. People pay back handers for leases on land and permissions. There are some strong arm tactics going on as well. The people at the top of the pile in Yangshuo were uneducated peasants only 10 years before and in so many ways they were still those peasants. They believed that they were doing well and would flaunt their wealth and power. They were all trying to outdo one another and all suspicious of everyone else. Rumors were everywhere. Monkey Jane had an uncle who was the head of the police. Which smoothed things over for her, but the back biting about her success in the village was constant. Everybody was trying to set up a business, but most had no business sense at all. Richer people from outside, firstly Guilin, then other cities were trying to establish businesses in Yangshuo and they all looked like identical candidates for failure. Not being able to present a restaurant correctly, or decide where they would pitch themselves in the market or even be able to advertise themselves were simple failings. So many businesses would just open their doors and think that the public would come and buy. These were also the sort of people who were suggesting that I could set up a business. The drive, to one day be a rich business owner was overwhelming, even against such odds. These poor people, all wrapped up in the governments "feel good" expanding economy were ready to pitch their lot in on the chance of making it. I looked at all the places I visited, I could see that there were gaps in the market, especially if you could do something slightly different or of a better standard, but nothing would tempt me to get on the band wagon. Or should I call it "gravy train".

We did a bike ride in over 30 degree heat. I knew that Chinese summers were hot from my last visit in July 2002 where the big temperature gauge on the side of the Train station had always been at 38 degrees. I'd found out subsequently, that this was the official temperature, as above 38 degrees, the workers were allowed to stop work, so the official temperature never got any higher. George was our guide again and I had got him to take his motorbike and Colleen rode on the back, as she could not ride a bike. She spent a lot of time squeezing up to George. He was quite nervous, thinking she might want to take him home; it had the rest of us all laughing. That night we stayed in a farm house "The Outside Inn" away from the main town of Yangshuo, in Chao Long Village next to the cooking school. It is in one of the most idyllic settings in between the karsts and overlooking the rice paddies. The Dutch owner has done a fantastic job in restoring the old farm houses and installing modern conveniences, but it is still rather rustic. Being in rural China you would not expect anything different and it is all part of the experience. Then one of the girls saw a spider. Then another girl saw a spider, screams went out and girls went running around between the old farm buildings. There is only so much you can do when confronted with the inevitable. I may not sound too sympathetic, but you are going to get spiders and so many other things around old farm buildings. I didn't want to let the rest of it get to their imagination. I went on spider clearing duty.

At around 11pm, I got a knock on my bedroom door. One of the girls had been vomiting and had diarrhea. This is pretty usual, so it's just about re-hydration and reassurance. But this had gone on a stage further. She was now hallucinating. Her friend was rightly concerned, as was I. Rural China is not the best place to start hallucinating. The language barrier is bad enough, without having somebody speaking in tongues at her diagnosis. How would the local doctor understand what was mad and what was not? As I checked on her, the obvious diagnosis was sunstroke. I got as much water as I could and tried to contact the local operators. Nobody apart from the assistant manager at the cooking school was answering their phone. At least she could organise transport and the hospital if it came to that. As I checked on the patient, she had gained lucidity and we stayed with her for long enough for me to think she was ok to be left where she was. The following morning, she was in no fit state to leave and travel to the rice terraces and undertake 2 days of hiking, so I left her in the care of her friend, with instructions to re-join the group a couple of days later. There is not a great deal else I could do.

By this time, we were on day fifteen and almost at the end of the trip. We'd hiked the Great Wall and visited 3 major cities. I clearly remember John, sitting in the farmhouse courtyard, along with the others in the group, asking "So what is a Basic trip?" He had never read the notes. Back in England, he had just gone into STA and let them do it all for him. He had sadly been under the miss-apprehension that he had booked some sort of all inclusive tour through China, for 700 pounds! Always remember, if it looks too good to be true, then it is too good to be true. He thought he had gotten the deal of the century. I know our travel deals are cheap, but that would be ridiculous. Since then everything had shattered his expectations. I had really felt for him has he struggled with every activity. He couldn't eat the food and was not really a vegetarian, but had thought it best to pretend to be one in order to avoid getting sick from the meat. Now we were in Yangshuo, he was tucking into a meat feast pizza. It came to light, that he had even considered just getting a flight straight to Hong Kong from Guilin. He had asked Rosemary, the local operator about the possibility when they met for one of the activities. His philosophy on this was that I would look after his daughter for the last week of the trip. He hadn't actually told me about this plan, well, it wasn't as if I was his favourite person after I'd put him through the seven hells what is adventure travel in the last two weeks. He had told Rosemary that he just couldn't carry on any more. Apart from the food and cultural difficulties he'd faced, he was an easy target for the tourist touts. He must have increased the income of every beggar and hoodwink-merchant fivefold as the money came out of his pocket after the least bit of persistence or slightest sob story. We found out that on the Great Wall he had paid around ten pounds for a book, which was in Chinese. At the Forbidden City, he has been asked to visit an art gallery with pieces made by students and he had come away with a couple of expensive, overpriced paintings that were impossible to carry whilst back-packing for a couple of months. In Shanghai, after I had left him at the museum, he had gone on to a "tea ceremony" parting with a lot of money and came away with the sort of stuff that you would be embarrassed to find in a very bad Christmas cracker. At Moon hill, he had the rest of the group laughing as he parted with money to all the ladies who were following him up the steps. Colleen even said "you must have put all of her kids through college". To top it all off, even in West Street in Yangshuo, he had got talking to a woman who had asked him if he wanted to find a girl, for sex. He had seen enough. He admitted, he was soft hearted and found it difficult to say "no". He said that he was looking forward leaving all this behind and going to Thailand. Once again, I was astounded by his naivety. The tourist hassles in Thailand make China look like a walk in the park. He just said that he wanted to get to the beach. I asked him what he had booked. He replied "A place not too far from Bangkok, I don't want to stay there, I've heard bad things about Bangkok. Instead, we're going to a beach resort to get away from it all." And the name of this beach resort.... "Pattaya". He was taking his daughter to the sleazy sex capital of the world.

The highlight of this trip for me was going to the Long Ji rice terraces. I'd never been there before and was in the capable hands of Farmer Tang. He had been recommended as the best local guide and was a diminutive forty year old who had been guiding for about ten years after teaching himself English, quite some feat for a Yangshuo Farmer. He picked us up at the Outside Inn and we bussed it via Guilin to Long Ji and the village of Da Zai. The bus up to the last village was full, we had to stand and Farmer Tang had to convince the driver to take us all. The bus can only, legally, take so many people, so it had to leave the bus station, with only some of the group already on the bus. This had those on the bus panicking again whilst the rest of us waited around the corner for the bus driver to stop and let us squeeze on. I thought at the time that it was not good practice for us; tourists taking up all the room on the local public bus. We flouted even the Chinese health and Safety regulations, something that I thought almost impossible. The road up to the rice terraces twists and turns. Not unlike the road up to Emei Shan, there are sheer cliffs, hairpin bends and triple overtaking from the crazy drivers. I was taking it all in along with the fantastic scenery, until, one of the girls pointed at the Irish girl who was afraid of heights. She was quaking in her seat, at the point of tears again. I've no idea what they expected me to do. I can't make the rice terraces flat; they wouldn't be terraces any more. We stopped for a few minutes to cool the breaks, where water was hosed onto the steaming pads, something that I still don't understand and neither did anyone else. Then we were off again, climbing and curving as far as the steep hills would let us. We arrived at the car park, at the valley bottom of Da Zai village, where we had a forty minute hike up to the guest house. The Irish girl was once again asking if there would be any places where she might fall off a rice terrace, or have to cross any bridges. Once again, I was astounded that she had booked a trip, not knowing anything of what she was doing. A rice terrace, by its very nature, is a steep hillside made into steps where you can farm on the flat portion of the step. Farmer Tang took the lead, offering us a lunch stop at the first village. All that was on offer was noodle soups and basic fried vegetable and meat dishes, so that didn't start with a good impression. After Yangshuo, I think they were all hoping for more western cafes, they had been spoiled and were back to real China with a bump.

At forty years old and only 5 foot tall I've never seen anyone trek through mountains with such ease as Farmer Tang. The villages here are all of wooden houses, quite large, usually 3 floors, built on the sides of the hills. Stone paved pathways twist between the houses, ascending and descending through the village and up through the rice terraces. It is one of those iconic scenes of China. Water buffalo plough the fields; farmers are knee deep in the paddy. Then terrace upon terrace, like a layered cake. We walk through all this, immersed in this picture of China. Much of the way of life here has not changed in hundreds of years and it is a region that is home to some of Chinas Ethnic Minorities. These are people who are not the Han Chinese, that make up over 90% of Chinas population, but the other ethnic groups that include Mongolians, Tibetans and 54 other ethnic groupings. Most of these Ethnic Minorities live in rural China and observe a culturally different way of life, steeped in thousands of years of history. Many of the ethnic minorities have their own language. A good number have written script, though for many peoples it is based on the Chinese Characters that have been used throughout the region for over two thousand years. Many have retained "animist" religious beliefs and like the Han Chinese, practice ancestor worship. The Taoism and Buddhism that has swept over China in the following millennium has intertwined with the local cultures and the traditional stories. Up until relatively recently, the ethnic minority people have been marginalised from the majority of the Chinese way of life. They occupy the worst land in remote places. The Chinese, over the centuries have either tried to force them out of China, or to destroy them. Now they are subject to the countries boundless economic growth and way of life that reaches right into the communities. There is a sort of "Han-isation" going on and this is most known about in the West when we read about Tibet, but it is happening with all the minority people across

China. We stayed with the local ethnic minority group, the Yao, halfway up the terraces, in Da Zai village at a place called Jing Tan. Farmer Tang took the more enthusiastic and energetic of us for a walk around the terrace scenery points. This took us almost to the top of the rice terrace hills and looked over the sweeping valleys. Farmer Tang explained that Long Ji translated as "The Dragons Backbone" where the larger steps of terraces were known as "dragons" and the shorter ones as "tigers". Different formations of the terraces had their own names, such as "seven stars looking at the moon" and "nine dragons, five tigers". Along the way up to the scenery point, we met the women who would try to get us to pay money to have us take pictures of their long hair, or buy their hand made clothes and jewelry. This ethnic minority is famed for never cutting their hair and I, of course tried to get them to take pictures of my long hair. They were not very impressed at all.

It was here that the issue of the trek was raised again. I had already left two people back in Yangshuo and had clearly stated that this was an option for those who did not, or could not, do the walk. They all made it up to the guest house, a forty minute hike climbing up and along the terraces, but now, they wanted to know how they were going to get from here to the next village. The next village of Ping An was a ten kilometer hike over the Long Ji, or Dragons Backbone, by stone pathway. Farmer Tang, borrowed a piece of paper, painstakingly, marked out a route, mapping the Da Zai bus stop, the 50 minute drive to He Ping bus stop and then the hour drive to their destination, Ping An bus stop. After this would be the twenty minute hike up from there to the Li Qing Guest house where we would spend the following night. Farmer Tang was painfully precise and would draw out a story, with dates and times and names, just to get a seemingly quick point across. What I found out was; after being a guide for 12 years, he had been asked many questions by tourists. Most of these were the stupid questions that I often got. How high is that mountain? How long will it take to walk up it? Will I get tired? How much water should I take? Farmer Tang had taken it upon himself to know all the answers to these ridiculous questions. It would take 34 or 38 minutes to walk to scenery point one. The highest point was 1882m above sea level.

Farmer Tang told us that the rice terraces had begun to be built at the end of the Yuan dynasty, around 700 years ago. At that time, the Yao and the Zhuang ethnic minorities both lived on the fertile lowlands. However, the Han Chinese were expanding over these areas and with weaponry and improved agricultural skills, they came to dominate. The ethnic minorities were pushed up into the hills and began to terrace these hills in order to plant rice and other crops. This continued throughout the Ming and Qing dynasties, with the Han Chinese growing ever more powerful in the fertile lowlands and the minorities being marginalised. The outcome has been some of the most spectacular scenery. I had heard from other leaders that passengers often asked the question "Why don't they just farm the flat land, when it must be so much easier than building the terraces?" well; there was the answer and full of historical significance.

It was in this guest houses that I found, what is to date, my favourite menu. It sort of read like this:

MENU

CHICKEN DISH

Chicken with rice
Chicken with noodle
Chicken with vegetable

RICE DISH

Rice
Rice with Chicken
Rice with pork

Rice with vegetable
Rice with egg

VEGETABLE DISH

Vegetable with rice
Vegetable with Chicken
vegetable with pork

PORK DISH

Pork with Rice

STUFFED

Eggplant with pork
Eggplant with chicken
Eggplant with vegetable

I think you get the picture, I asked for Chicken with egg fried rice. They didn't have it - it wasn't on the menu. "Stuffed".

The beverages section was even better. One of the lads wanted a beer. Beer was priced very reasonably at 7 Yuan, around $1 or 50p. However, they didn't stock that beer, so he got given a different one. For this he was charged Y10. The argument that followed was resolved by Farmer Tang explaining that the beer he wanted was no-longer available and hadn't been for 2 years, just after the menu (yes, it was the only one, laminated for posterity) has been drawn up. The people that owned the guesthouse could not read the menu, as it was in English and would never damage it by writing on it and changing the prices, because it was the only one. We live and learn. Farmer Tangs guiding was excellent. He explained about the rice cultivation, local people and their customs. He told us how the village used to work as a sort of commune, where traditionally, the whole village would get together to build houses for the elder sons and newlyweds. The village chiefs would also allocate land to each family to farm. This is where tradition and the Communist system had seamlessly merged. As with most areas of China, the average amount of land farmed by a family would be three "Mu", where a Mu is 666 square meters. With all the terraces being different widths and shapes, the only way to do this fairly was to divide the hill from top to bottom, giving each family a roughly equal share and roughly similar large and small terraces. The water supply, irrigating all the fields from top to bottom was the responsibility of all the people in the village to maintain. On the terrace there would mainly be rice, but some other crops and animals, usually chickens and a pig. The undercroft of the three story houses were also used to pen animals. The family used the second story as a living room and the upper floor as bedrooms for the extended family. They were quite large houses, especially as you consider they are constructed on steep hillsides and without real foundations. Instead of digging down, there would be stones gathered and piled up to form a platform, or in some cases, a large block of a corner stone upon which the load bearing walls of the house would be raised. With tourism, these traditional houses had been easily converted into guest houses. Another knock on effect of the tourism was that the local people, especially the women with the long hair, were now hassling the tourists for money. Times were changing. The village was filling up with guest houses and we could hear the distant explosions of the new road being blasted through the hillside. We all managed the walk from Da Zai to Ping An, although it took longer than the four hours that it takes the usual groups. Here, we stayed at another breathtaking guesthouse, Li Qing, run by Yi Ben and his family, a Zhang minority people in this village. We were perched on the side of the mountain and overlooking the village, the rice terraces and the valley below. Once again, Farmer Tang, tirelessly, offered to take us on another hike to one of the scenery points, there were few takers. We had one of the best group meals at Li Qing Guest house and a celebratory couple of beers. Farmer Tang had to take me to the bus stop in the valley, as he had another group waiting for him and could not come back with us to Guilin, where we would be getting the train from the following afternoon. In the morning, I looked out and we were above the clouds. A moment I will never forget.

19. Nine Dragons and Five Tigers,
    25/06/07 (Long Ji/West Hotel H.K.)

I follow the ancient slate path
Up, up, through the ancient hillside
Crossing the streams gurgle and laugh
Women ask if you want a photograph
Of them unwrapping their long long hair
Or will you buy their basket of homespun wares
When all I want is a photo of the land
Where the clouds float beneath the hill where I stand

Where man moulds nature on an immense scale
Layered caked sculpted out of the hill
Two dragons fighting, watch the water they spill
Silver belts coiled to make snails and trails
And the village squeezed in the crease of the hill
Walking the crooked path between the wooden buildings
The donkey, loaded, two baskets to fill
The playful dogs, the leap-frog of the chickens

We climbed the mountain to view point one
To see the rising of the sun
Nine dragons and five tigers
To overcome a challenge, each one of us
Like the people that sculpted this land over centuries
We are changing our lives, our worlds, our realities
Each one can count a battle and a small victory
Changing what we've done and changing who we be

And as I get lost in this rustic scene
The romance of village life in my daydream
I hear in the distance, a dragons roar
Dynamite, for the construction of the new road.

20. A Boy and a Girl 19/06/07 06/07/07
    (West Hotel, HK/Yangtze Boat)

Playing at being white ghosts
Invisible hide and seek in Tiananmen Square
With only strange glances to dodge
Invincible, with alcohol. Running without a care
In this world, or any other world
Just a boy and a girl
Caught up in the crazy world
Of being a boy and a girl

Then on the other side of China
Three weeks and a thousand miles later
We both had so much to tell each other
Strange how it was so natural to be together
Talking as we were walking
When the rain came, we were sheltering
Then drinks in the Eight Fine Irish Men
Pictures from our trips again
Remembering being in Tiananmen
Reliving that special time when
We were caught up in the crazy world
Just being a boy and a girl
Brought together again in a whirl
Two of us in such a big big world.

It was a little nerve racking taking the group on the journey
back to Guilin, partly because it was a journey that I had
never done before and included me changing busses. Farmer
Tang had assured me that the bus drivers would wait for the

"wai guo ren, foreigners" at the appointed place. I also had to cope with the Irish girl being terrified as we skirted the gaping chasms as we descended the rice terraces. It was about this time that I got one of the most typically stupid questions that I had ever been asked. I had been pointing out the local people from the bus, saying that this was market day, so they were all going to market. Then one of the girls asks me. "So what will they do tomorrow?" and she genuinely thought that I would respond. Back in Guilin, we had "free time" and once again, the unadventurous people were expecting me to provide a coffee bar and an internet café rather than heading off with me to explore the town. Guilin is one of the major tourist destinations in China and deservedly so with the city peppered with limestone karsts, often with little temples on top of them. The train station is relatively modern and built to cope with the millions of tourists. We had the usual long wait and had our bags with us on the long lines of seats. The Chinese were gathering and inquisitive as always. We were entertained by the big T.V. screens that showed adverts on a loop for skin whitening. All girls want white skin as it makes them look less like a farmer and more like someone with an office job. Some people went to the toilet, which in a big modern station should not have been such an experience, but we had forgotten, we were in China. The toilets were only dimly lit and a centimeter awash with water and dirt. No, problem, the squats, were raised. I noticed that a number of them did not have doors. Even of the ones that had doors, many men were just squatting there, on view, squatting, pushing, smoking, maybe on a mobile phone and shouting. I decided to take a cubical at the end of the bathroom, with a door, and close it. Here, I noticed that the design of the toilets meant that as I squatted, with feet either side of a channel, I could peer down between my knees and see everyone else's shit flowing down the channel, with each flush from further along the line. It was somewhat apt. Over this trip I had been putting up with all sorts and is where I had also been getting some other corkers. When the train would stop on the line, I would be asked "how long for?" The guards could not tell me an answer, nor would they budge from the original arrival time at our destination, though with a hundred or so kilometers to go, it is so obvious that we will arrive late. Disappointment with my lack of ability to see around corners, read the future, or mind meld with the engine driver or signal controller is a big failing for my groups who need to know everything, but can't do anything with the information anyway. Then, as we would arrive at the station, I would get the question "What is the weather like outside?" Back in Guilin, I had checked my emails and found that my next trip had not been booked. This was especially shit because I had 5 Americans on this trip and they are notorious for being demanding. Another problem is that My China Mobile phone does not work in Hong Kong (and you thought it was now part of China). Well, this meant that as the train was hurtling towards the border, I was frantically calling all the people on this side about my 7 passengers and arranging accommodation and transport for the following week before my phone went dead. I suppose it's all part of the job, but the yanks wouldn't see it like that.

We finished the trip in Hong Kong. Different people on different budgets, some wanting to eat locally, some wouldn't be seen anywhere near a food stall when there was decent western restaurants around. I actually split the group for the last night dinner with instructions and directions to get to a bar with happy hour drinks for our final goodbye. So, Hong Kong is supposed to be easy is it? As it is about the only place where the group orders their own food, I got some other ridiculous questions. Looking at a twenty page menu with over one hundred dishes, they would ask me "So what is the steak like?" Or "How big is the portion, will I need something else?" or even, "Will I like it?" Finally given the choices that they'd been after for the whole trip, they couldn't make a decision. They seemed to think that I should know every item on the menu, their likes and dislikes. Then, of course, the prices were the same as the prices back home in London and they balked at paying five times what they had been paying in China for a beer. I had to split the group into those who would pay more from those who would not. Half

I took to the Temple Street Market Hawkers bazaar, which is some of the most authentic local food in the middle of a street market. The others came with me to an Irish pub for bangers and mash. When it was all over I was somewhat relieved. Andrea was also back in Hong Kong after her three weeks of solo travel and we hooked up. We all had a few drinks in the Eight Fine Irish Men bar and swapped stories and photos. She had made it to Tibet (through my contact, Sam, in Chengdu) and had pictures including those of monks having discussions on philosophy and completing each point with a slap to the earth. Now, Andrea and I are pretty close, but when, in her Bogan Australian accent she suggested "would you like to see pictures of me monks debating" I really didn't know what to expect!

Chapter 6.

THE BLIND LEADING THE BLIND

"The point of the journey is not to arrive"

Rush (Rock band, in the song "Prime Mover" 1987) quoting Mao Tse Tung

I left Andrea in Hong Kong and met up with Eugenie. We had booked a trip to Manila in the Philippines. At only Y1100 for a return flight this was one hell of a bargain. Getting there was no problem and we only had one person trying to rip us off in a cab before getting to the hotel. The hotel had seen better days, obviously an old colonial haunt in a rambling building with courtyard and polished wood and stonework, now lit by 40 watt bulbs. We headed out to the Intramuros, the old Spanish part of the city that surrounds the old port and fort. A lot of this area was under renovation and had been given over as a museum with the history of the imprisonment of the Filipino Liberation Movement by the Spanish. After an hour or so we went back through the city, following the run down streets to a modern shopping centre arcade with lots of food outlets. I foolishly ate Kare-Kare, which turned out to be tripe in curry. A lot of Manila has the feel of a city on the edge. Buildings in a bad state of repair. People living on top of each other down alleyways with no daylight. At least these people were housed. This was better than the large amount of people on the streets, trying to make a living, whole families sleeping rough. Manilas' reputation is just what the guide books and T.V. reports suggest. Unfortunately, I think it took Eugenie a couple of days for her to see what the place was all about. Coming from middle class Beijing, you don't really see this type of place, even on the tours around China; it's a different sort of poverty. Considering that we didn't really have a clue about where to go and what to do, things were working out ok and we started to plan a few activities. I'd noticed that we could have a day trip to a volcano. Before we had booked the trip, Eugenie had asked whether I preferred a beach holiday, or shopping. I'd said "neither" and so far it was going to plan. We decided to head off into town in the morning to compare tour prices.

As we exited the shopping mall, a bloke came up to us, asking if we wanted to change money. My gut feeling was to move on, though Eugenie had said that the rate that he was offering was a good deal and said we would see him later. I re-booked my next tour with the five Americans, via email, just as 2 of them would have been landing at H.K. Airport. This was going to be one hell of a nightmare to walk in to. Then we found the man I'd nicknamed "Scarface" again, just waiting for us outside the internet café and smiling the smile of a long lost brother. He really wanted to change our money. He said that we had promised to see him. Now, you know how it is, when you are hanging around with someone a bit younger, who gives the impression that you are a bit boring because you just don't "do things" and always take the responsible approach. Well I was sort of getting that vibe off Eugenie. She might not have meant it, but that's what I was getting, the feeling that she was thinking I was being boring and far too cautious. Not an "adventure traveller" at all and too much like her pathetic groups. So, we followed "Scarface" to his money changer shop. It was so dam obvious what was going on, but Eugenie thought she could get the better of the con artist, so after counting, re-counting, arguing about fakes and re-counting again, she put the rolled up bundle of notes, tightly in her fist and into my money belt. Right, maybe we had got away with it. Back at the hotel I realised that we were $40 down. Eugenie was furious. I tried to explain that this was what was always going to happen and that we couldn't out-con the conmen. They made a living out of it. Eugenie wanted to go to the police. In Manila, I'm sure everyone has heard of the corruption of the police. We didn't stand a chance of getting any money back and could spend hours in a police station filling out forms. Worse than that, we could be led right back to the lion's den. I had visions of "Scarface" following us back to the hotel and taking the rest of our money, just for being cheeky and downright stupid enough to think we could nail him. Anyway, I still agreed to go along to the police with Eugenie. Coming from Beijing, she had no concept of what I thought we were walking into, but she was upset and I decided I'd go along with it.

Eugenie is an amazing girl. I have never met anyone quite like her. True, she is uncompromising, organised to the point of being anal and a control freak, but she can make things turn her way. I don't know how she did it, but before too long we were in a police car that didn't look too dissimilar to a beat up version of the Starsky and Hutch jalopy, with a bloke in a Bob Marley T shirt and his side-kick. We began a slow cruise of the area. Nothing much looked like it was going to happen, the police were not interested and Eugenie said they were complaining about the job not being worth it. I recognised a street sign and explained a little more clearly where we'd been ripped off. Within 10 seconds we had parked right outside the money changer and were following the police up to the counter, they knew the place. This could be the stitch up (stitch up being what could be happening to my face in a few moments). One of the girls from behind the counter was easily recognisable. Within a couple of minutes one of the policemen came back with the woman who had actually done the switch. What happened next was much more what I'd expected from Starsky and Hutch with a Manilan "Huggy Bear". Instead of arresting the woman, there was a negotiation as to how much she'd ripped us off and how much we were going to get back. The woman was actually allowed to leave and come back with $30. Well, I thought, it's something, let's go. Not Eugenie she argued with the woman and told the police that we should have all the money back. Sure enough, she returned with more cash. That was going to be our lot. We were driven back to the police station, said our thanks to the police chief who told us that we would not get the full amount because the rate was too high, then left. We hugged each other for dear life when we got down the street, neither of us believing what had actually happened. The police had taken their cut, the conmen were free to con another day, and we'd got our money back. Unbelievable.

Our stay in the Philippines was only 4 days, but apart from being robbed, we also managed a trip to a volcano via a Jeepney factory. These are extended Jeeps that act as local busses, decorated with gaudy signs and fluorescent colours. We also visited a Catholic church with a bamboo organ, all of which took a bit of explaining to Eugenie. Obviously, she had never seen anything quite like this before, including the unhappy man hanging from the church ceiling. On our last night, we had a meal in a traditional restaurant, complete with a trio of singers/ performers who took it upon themselves to serenade us. This was awkward, as I had to say to Eugenie that they were serenading "us" like we were a couple. That didn't go down well and with her fuming at the situation, I tried to tell the musicians that we weren't "together", for which I got puzzled looks, before I just paid them to leave. With Eugenie, nothing is ever simple. Earlier that day, when I had relented to her desires to go shopping, I had been standing in some clothing store as she tried items on in the changing room. When I told a cute shop assistant that Eugenie and I were "only just friends, not even really close friends", she popped her head out of the changing room and gave me an earful again. "What do you mean we are only just friends...?" Only just friends had not translated to her.

I will give one more Eugenieism. When we returned to HK and picked up our work stuff from the hotel, I found her going through my money and straightening it. (Why? I don't know). Unfortunately, she didn't realise that some of it was the wrong way around and not all in one bundle because some of it was my money and some belonged to the company. Since then I wasn't able to figure out what cash was mine, whether I've made a mess of my accounts, or whether I owe the company any money.

21. Untitled, 29/06/07, 06/07/07 (Yangtze Boat)

Only momentary solitude, still planning my ways and means
Whirled like a typhoon across the South China Sea
Waiting for a reply, a confirmation from my destination
Reflecting upon everything that's come and gone and may be

My tired face, flecked with the sun
And too many late nights starting to catch up
The grey coming through at my temples
And my eyebrows that need trimming and touching up

I don't know what to do with my hair
It's neither one thing or another
I can't really look like I want to
And there's no one to impress if I could do
And nowhere to go, with no body
So, I'll just carry on being this version of me

A couple of beers in H.K. or Yangshuo
Meeting up with some people I'm getting to know
It's about as good as it's going to get
And I'm certainly not ready to trade it in yet

These streets are becoming familiar
I'm comfortable, in another bar
Becoming recognised and regular
In half a dozen places across China.

Back in Hong Kong and the trip with the 5 Americans that I had only just confirmed as booked. I was expecting Hell. It turned out that 6 out of 7 of the passengers were teachers. Could it get any worse? I would be getting question after question and not a chance of getting full marks in my feedback. The trip started on 1st July. I had one way of turning this one round. Where oh where could I find an endless supply of Budweiser for American Independence Day? Yes, I had the answer, Snows Bar, '98' in Yangshuo. Things actually went much better than expected. I'd been through all the places en-route 5 or 6 times before, and after the questions set by Martin "the scientist" and others in the past, I was starting to sound more like a native. This is a dam steep learning curve, but it was beginning to pay off.

The first couple of days went well, the group asked questions, but not of the ridiculous variety. They seemed interested in where we were going and all aspects of China that I could relate to them. On 4th July, we had the bike ride in Yangshuo; once again the heat was up towards 40 degrees. Even though I had told them about the dangers and my heat stroke victim in my last group, they were ill prepared. A couple of them were really suffering on the ride, but it wasn't until the next day that we realised that Sonny from Carolina got sunstroke after the bike ride. It didn't help that in his dehydrated state, he went out celebrating Independence Day. We had also gone on to "Cooking School" afterwards and done the guided trip with our chef of the day "Leo" through Yangshuo market. This is interesting for us Westerners, a covered market selling everything edible. There were markets similar to this, in the North of England, only thirty years ago, but only a few people in my groups are old enough to remember them. There was bench after bench of vegetables, many the sorts of things that you don't see at home. Choko, bitter melon, winter melon. There are tables full of tofu. On the floor and in plastic tubs there are fish, Cray fish, shell fish and all varieties of seafood, all about to become food. A woman was buying a fish from an aerated bowl, serviced by a plastic pipe blowing in oxygen. The fishmonger, picked the selected fish out of the bowl, smacked the fish on the back of the head with the back of her clever, then chopped the fish head off and gutted it. The fish head was still "gasping". So were the group who witnessed this. All around there was water being tipped out of the bowls, fish trying to jump free and splashing around on the wet floor. There were frogs in net bags, five or six frogs in each bag and the bags were jumping as the frogs slid over one another and tried to make a leap to freedom. All this I had seen before, but on this visit, as we entered the meat section, we could hear the dogs barking. We stopped to look at the pig faces, then the cages of rabbit, the cages of chickens, then the cages of rabbits and chickens together. There were four ducks, in plastic bags with a hole for the heads to pop out. Moving on to the next benches, everywhere you looked, there were the dismembered legs and innards of cows and pigs, hung up. Then Leo said, "Would you like to see the dogs?"

People still eat dogs in China. It is not a common thing, but in certain areas, such as this part of the South and especially at particular times of the year, dogs are the dish of the day. Group after group has asked me at the first night meeting "will we eat dog, will they give it to us and we won't know?" as if there is a Chinese conspiracy to get Westerners eating dog, probably with an eye on increasing the export market; those canny Chinese businessmen, eh? To which I always answer, "No, dog is a delicacy, it costs far more than most other dishes, so you won't be served it". That is usually the end of the shaggy dog story, but today, we were early enough to the market to see the dogs. Hung up, in a corner of the market were the dismembered dogs. The hair had been burned off them, but it was obvious that it could be no other animal. Behind the meat hooks, were the cages of the live dogs. They could have been family pets; they looked no different, just like the meat looked no different than, say, lamb. People get very emotional about eating dogs and I have had my times as a vegetarian, so on principal, I don't think we should eat meat. I'm just not very good at being a vegetarian, especially in China, where it is all but impossible. Nevertheless, aside from this, the thing about eating dog is the way it is killed. The dogs are beaten to death as it is supposed to make the meat taste better. That is what we had heard when we had arrived in this section of the market. The dog was now laying there, bloodied face, in front of the caged dogs that were looking on, awaiting to take their turn and meet the same fate.

That night I went to Bar 98 again, but it was quiet. I was chatting mainly to Snow, Ton Ton and the other bar girls. Around midnight, there were not so many customers and Snow asked me if I wanted to join them in the night market for food. I was hoping that more time with one of the bar girls would lead to something, after all, I'd be spending a lot of time coming through Yangshuo and it was a good place to be on my time off. Yangshuo night market was close to the day market and the bus station, on what was used as a car park during the day. Stalls set up, mainly selling food and it was all local Yangshuo people eating there. We sat down and the local delicacy of beer fish was ordered along with some snacks. I wasn't up for a big meal, so I asked one of the cute bar girls what the snack was. She looked at me rather strangely, and then Snow, laughing, did a translation. "She is eating ox penis" laughing some more. There is something about even a cute girl, chewing on an ox cock that puts a dampener on any amorous thoughts.

We had a long journey to Yichang with an ill Sonny and by the time we were on the boat he was feeling particularly unwell and we hardly saw him for the three days. On this journey, we had Emily from Yichang as the boat guide. She always takes us to the Dam and is full of information about the project and the city of Yichang. There was nothing that she could do for Sonny; the only course of action was rest and a lot of fluids. There had been heavy rains, typical of the "Monsoon season" which part of China suffers from. There was a flood which moved 2.2 million people from the Yangtze valleys and I was calling Amy to see if she was ok. She was completing a trip in the opposite direction, and then getting the speedboat back to Chongqing, so I wouldn't see her on this trip. The bus journey from Feng Du, along the Yangtze valley was quite hair-raising. I've never seen so many boulders just laying in the middle of a road. A hell of a lot of China has been rapidly constructed and in my opinion is un-structurally sound so don't be surprised if there is a major landslide in the near future.

Chicory came to Sonny's aid in Chengdu. We all went to the hospital, where he had blood tests and a few hours later was given a prescription. The hospital system was remarkably modern, clean and efficient. The doctor spoke English although Chicory was on hand to help. The only thing that was out of the ordinary was the medicine itself. If you want medicine in China, it will undoubtedly be Chinese medicine, not the sort of pharmaceutical products that you are used to back in the West. It was a Chinese traditional remedy, coming in five small glass voiles with straws to drink from. It was here were I found that Western medicine is still not widespread, people prefer the traditional. This includes looking for pain killers such as packets of Panadol, or aspirin in the chemist shops, they simply don't have them. Something else that everyone seems to take for granted in the West just isn't necessary or available in China.

For any of the girls travelling, there are no tampons either. This is partly to do with China being a patriarchal society that doesn't want girls inserting things in their vaginas. Nevertheless, two days later and the Chinese medicine had done the job.

The group I had was my best group so far. They were genuinely interested in China and in what I had to say and participated fully in the whole trip. In Emei Shan, Sonny was feeling better and we all did the hike to the Monasteries. On the way there I was pointing out the bad "Chinglish" signs and also the ones a concerned with how to conduct yourself on the mountain. There were "Cherish the monkeys at the point of entertainment that are good friends of mankind." Then the sign proclaiming the "Socialist Viewpoints about Honor and Disgrace," a "do's and Don'ts" of rules and regulations. There were eight of these, which started with "Take loving your homeland as an honor, regard endangering our homeland as a disgrace." It included "Take being honest and promise-keeping as an honor, regard benefitting ourselves without returning as a disgrace" and ended with "Take hard work and struggle as an honor, regard extravagant and dissipated as a disgrace." There was a phone number for feedback at the bottom of the sign that I was sorely tempted to ring. Other signs included "Do not chase or beat animals." "Avoid superstition." "Do not wear clothes exposing the neck and the shoulder." I asked Sonny if he had ever seen anything like it and to my surprise, he said that in the "Bible Belt States" there were signs that were very similar. Some signs that we had definitely not seen before were the ones in the toilets, I even encouraged the women to take a peek into the gents to see them. Above the urinals, was the pronouncements "It is civilized to get close to urinate", which was ok in the context, then "You can enjoy the fresh air after finishing a civilized urinating", which again, I could go for, but "Thinking of making things easy for others before urinating" just had me, err, pissing myself laughing. Then the girls came back from their toilets, to tell me that they had exactly the same signs in their squats. Now that just didn't make sense. As we all laughed about the signs, our tour guide, George came over and asked what we were doing. Then he told us that most of the translations for the signs were his. How embarrassing.

Once again Patrick surpassed himself. We took his "cultural tour" and visited a school, then a Kung Fu school where we had a demonstration by the trainees. Then by rickshaw cycles we moved on to a noodle factory, then a calligraphy artist who translated our names and gave us individual good luck messages. We saw an artist glass blower who could make the twelve Chinese Zodiac animals and just about anything else. We had a local meal, with dishes that I had never heard of or seen before and all delicious. What was the highlight for us though was meeting Patrick's teacher. He was now an old man in his nineties and we were told the story of how as a young man he had joined up during the Second World War and fought with the Kuomintang. He had trained as a pilot and flown both Migs and a Douglas. One of my group; Len had been in the U.S. military and commented that this man was possibly the only man alive who could claim that. We were told that Patrick's teacher had tried to flee the Communists and get to Shanghai at the end of the war, but he had literally, "missed the boat" to Taiwan. The rest of the Kuomintang had left, taking the government, the intellectuals and the entire countries gold reserves to Taiwan where they set up a government in exile. This is a government that over the next fifty years still claimed to be the legitimate government of China. Patrick's teacher, along with thousands of other unfortunate Kuomintang soldiers was arrested and tried. Unlike many others, he was not sentenced to death, but was placed under house arrest in Emei Town, Sichuan province. Here he stayed for almost thirty years. We were told how as he became desperate, he gave up hope and was going to kill himself when in the mid 1970's he had heard of power struggles in the Communist Party, of Mao's failing health and the chance of reform. He outlived Mao, and gained his freedom from House arrest the following year. In the 1980's he was allowed to teach and took students, one of whom was Patrick. I did have one other highlight on my trip to Emei Shan. I also had my birthday on this trip, which had us all eating birthday cake on a street market cafe in Emei town. Patrick had organised this and turned up, balancing a birthday cake on the handlebars of his motorbike as he rode. His wife and children came along too and we stayed out later than the 9pm monastery curfew.

In Xi'an we had another couple of really good nights out. One of the group; Sue, was a music teacher and thought the singing and dancing outside the wall was one of the most amazing things she had ever seen. I like Xi'an. It has a vibe in the evening that is just one step better than the other places I visit. Outside the wall there is spontaneous dancing, street karaoke, drummers and a choir that sings along to traditional opera pieces, mainly songs about "The Long March" and Chairman Mao's struggles against the Japanese and the Nationalists. All this is made up of local people, who, just go out every night and just join in. For us to do the same it would take about 8 pints, and for me, it usually does. Others in the group joined in the dancing. They were really loving the trip, so much better than my last group. Most of the group liked a drink and we stayed out at Music Man one night, with one of the couples enjoying themselves so much, that they got up to dance, much to the amusement of the locals in the bar. On another night, we stayed out late, eating and drinking at the street stalls, the authentic local experience. When I got to Beijing, the hectic pace was taking its toll and getting through the Forbidden City was a struggle for one of the couples and she threw a strop. This was the only real down side of the whole trip. I was also informed by Sonny that Mao's Mausoleum looks just like the Carolina Coliseum. This, evidently, is a football stadium. I'm still waiting for the pictures.

A change in the schedule had left me with a change of trips and no days off in between them. In the Beijing Hostel there was the usual coming and going of the leaders. One of the leaders Jane, who I had not seen since just after the training was telling me of her trials over the last couple of months. She complained about the bitches that had been on her trips, unable to handle travel, food, heat, lack of toilets, whatever, and that there had been nothing like a decent male in any of her 5 trips. Well, I thought, I'm not doing too badly then. She told me that the nearest she'd got was sharing a bed with a 40 something gay bloke, things were bad. The beer continued and we were joined by Lyn. Pierre came and went with his new group of ten girls (lucky bastard) and the beer continued some more as we exchanged more gossip and stories. It was then that Jane cracked. It turns out that the gay bloke wasn't the nearest she'd come to a shag. In fact on one of her trips, there had been a lesbian, and after 3 weeks of a shit trip and everything else that goes with it, she decided, "what the hell" and gone for it. If things ever get that bad for me, I know it's time to leave the job

So, my managers in their wisdom thought it was time for me to have a "blind trip". This was a visit to The Grasslands. This is a fantastic opportunity to travel there and was one of the places I really wanted to go to. It was a chance to see the wilds of the nomadic high planes in an area very remote from civilisation and tourism. The Grasslands were a place of Tibetan villages, ancient monasteries, remote and what I had dreamed about when I had first decided that I want to be a tour leader. However, the reality was that it would be me who was leading the trip and I hadn't got a clue what I was leading the 8 unsuspecting tourists who had parted with some well-earned money for the trip of a life time.

I hadn't had time to read any of the trip notes as I hadn't actually finished my last trip when I was starting this one. So, when it came to the First Group Meeting, I went through the usual spiel, telling them the itinerary over the next few days and that we would be off to walk the Great Wall of China the following morning. It was only at around midnight, when I finally got around to printing off a copy of the notes that I found that we didn't have to walk the Wall. In the morning, I sort of played the whole thing down, saying how hard and how hot it was and that walking the Wall was only an option and that they would have to pay the entrance fee themselves. Unfortunately,

5 out of 8 thought that this was a fantastic idea. So, for the second time in 4 days, with only 3 hours sleep and a body that stank like a brewery from the night before, in 40 degree heat. I walked the Wall. The things I have to do to please some people, I just hope they appreciate it.

The late booking of the trip had thrown up another problem. I didn't have enough tickets to get all of us from Beijing to Xi'an. My train ticket only went as far as Jai....... it's a place I'd never heard of, let alone had any want to visit. My passengers were somewhat concerned about my imminent early departure from their trip. I doubt if this is what they really expected when they parted with their well-earned holiday money. Adventure travel? They were certainly getting it now. Luckily, Esmeray was taking the same train, and she said she'd look after them. Between us we'd hatched a plan to keep everything ticking over until I made it to Xi'an. All I needed to do was get there. The prospect of spending the night/early morning in a part of rural China, un-trodden by white man, with more money on me than the average Chinese will see in a lifetime was quite daunting. The passengers offered to look after the trip money for me (how nice).

I had a piece of paper. Written on it in Chinese was something akin to a humiliating plea and beg to stay on the train until a bed could be found for me to continue the journey through to Xi'an. So, with paper in one hand, mobile phone in the other with my Beijing agent, Xiao Feng also begging on my behalf, I began a 3 hour lesson on how to feel like a stupid foreigner. Even though this wasn't my fault. In the end, bribery also played a part and at around 1am I was shown to a bed, much to the relief of me and my passengers.

In Xian, we did the usual trips around the Terracotta Warriors, wall, Muslim Quarter and got the group out for a couple of drinks. I was glad that this time around I had the perfect partner to have fun with in the shape of Esmeray and on the second night I think we stayed up until 5am, after a visit to Music

Man and a night club, drinking at the street stalls. Esmeray, originally from Turkey had been working as a local guide in her home country before getting a job with our travel company in the Middle East. Morocco, Egypt and the surrounding countries kept her busy for a couple of years, and then she got the offer of China. She would sooner have gone to South America, as it was "the" new destination for our company's' leaders, but hey, why not China. She had flown into the country the week before the other new arrivals, not knowing a thing about the place. She had lived an extra-ordinary life. From Turkey and a privileged upbringing, she had gone to Germany, squatted, moved to Barcelona and lived in a squat there for a couple of years before finally returning to Turkey. We both liked punk music and had both lived the lifestyle, I sort of had found my bosom buddy in China. And she was certainly not bad looking either. Esmeray was also going to do the Grasslands trip in 1 months' time, so I said I'd write down as many notes as I could for her. As we talked, there was a thunderstorm and the rain was not looking like it would stop, so that night, Esmeray took the spare bed in my room.

Our next train ride took us out west towards Gansu Province. We got off the train in Lan Zhou, a town once with the dubious claim to being the most polluted city on earth. The Chinese are rolling out industry to the provinces. The work it brings and the income to the population is greatly received, but the price is bigger than many understand. Whilst in the train station and trying to find our bus, we were subject to a scam with somebody dropping a roll of bank notes in front of us. The idea is that we pick them up and either we get arrested and have to pay someone off, or we give someone some of our own money in order to keep the bank notes, which invariably turn out to be fake. This is one of the very few times that I have seen anything like a scam in China. It was odd in a way that it was in such a remote place, but I suppose the remoteness made it every bit "Wild West". The centre of the town was all new construction, a large paved town square, high rise offices surrounding the square and train station and a hotel where we went for the buffet breakfast. But as far as civilisation went, that was about it and although our travel company run a trip through here every week, we were treated more like strangers than we would be even in the most predictable "Western" saloon. We had a private bus and we moved on to Labrang, also known as Xia He, with the worst ever toilet visit en route. I have to mention it, as it was also in the trip reports that I had been reading and I was writing out notes for Esmeray to follow on her Grasslands trip the following months. This toilet was a foul pit, you could see the maggots crawling over the shit and sanitary towels and what's more, it cost us Y3 for the privilege of using it.

From Lanzhou to Xia He, we passed rolling green hillsides with towns full of people dressed in traditional Muslim costume. Not the full shebang head to toe burka that you get in England, but definitely Muslim with head scarves and flowing long clothes. There were Mosques with silver topped minarets that shone in the sun from the clear sky. I saw street markets and a general vibe that was definitely not what I would generally associate with being Chinese. I was surprised that it was so obviously a Muslim area. It could have been a different country. Then, in Xia He / Labrang, the scenery changed again, with the Muslims making way for the Tibetans. A real mixture of Chinese and these other 2 distinct cultures. It was quite an eye opener. Over the next week I came to realise that these Tibetan Grasslands, although not in the Chinese Tibet Province proper, were more Tibetan than the areas that were tightly controlled and influenced by the Chinese government to the South and West. Historically, these people were nomads, and many still were, but the Chinese government was also trying to control these people by constructing villages and facilities for the nomads to move in to. You might think that providing a house, school and employment are all good things, but here it is changing a traditional, self-sufficient way of life. The facilities are a way of controlling and educating the Tibetans into the Chinese way of life. Our Guide, Drujia, was excellent and had no qualms in spelling it all out for us. It was the sort of stuff

I thrive on. I learned more on this trip and got more involved than I had at any other point since starting work in China.

Labrang was a small town built around a monastery that was founded in 1709. If it wasn't for the monastery, it would have looked a very bleak place indeed. Set into the barren hillsides of the grasslands, not too unlike the moors of Northern England, with just the one road leading through town. There was a line of shops, of the two story concrete variety that you get everywhere with open front that were selling a few soft drinks, provisions, pilgrimage goods such as incense and pictures of the old Dali Lamas, but there wasn't much else. Our guest house was a converted courtyard house and very atmospheric. All wooden panels and beams. Opposite was a restaurant, run by a Nepali man, who had family in Tibet as a result of the constant emigration of refugees to Nepal fleeing Chinese persecution in Tibet. This town was a very strange juxtaposition of life in Chinese Tibet, or is that Tibetan China? We visited the monastery in Labrang which is a smaller and possibly more rustically beautiful version of the Potala Palace in Lhasa. Drujia took us on a "kora", or walk around the outside of the temple, spinning the prayer wheels and explaining the background to Tibetan Buddhism. The monastery is one of the largest and most important in Tibet and although the main hall burned down in 1985, it was replaced by a new building. The monastery has a mixture of Tibetan and Han Chinese styles and contains 18 halls, six institutes of learning, a golden stupa, a debate area, and houses nearly 60,000 sutras. There once were more than 2,000 monks in residence, but now there are only 500. Labrang was the home town of the Dali Lama and this part of Ando Tibet was very much in the forefront of the pro Dali Lama and Free Tibet movements. I was told that the locals did not like the Chinese. The leader one week in front of me was Suzy Li, a fantastic Chinese girl, but Drujia had said that the local guide would not take her or the group out to the countryside to see how the locals lived or practiced Buddhism. Neither would the guide give any information that was anti-Chinese, so all the background information to Tibet would not be talked about. We went out into the hills and saw Tibetan families staying in tents, cooking on open fires. These "ovens" were just cut into pits in the earth, highly ingenious and very effective. We saw the yak herds and visited the outlying monasteries including the ones destroyed during the Cultural Revolution. We also saw the new villages where the Tibetans were being moved to. Guide Drujia said that there was nothing wrong with their old villages (though they lacked running water and the most basic amenities) and they preferred the semi nomadic life. However, the Chinese authorities were building houses with water and electricity for the Tibetans to move in. There were also schools, clinics and factories. The Chinese I talked to saw this as improving the lot of the Tibetans. Many Tibetans were living a better, healthier more comfortable life and had an income and an education and many were happy with this. Drujia enlightened us. Once you moved to the house, you became registered there. You could not become a nomad again. At some point you would have to start paying for the house. Yes there was work, but not enough and the Chinese were the bosses. The school educated the children in Chinese propaganda, not Tibetan culture and it was also another way of registering the population. The one child policy was only now starting to make an impact here, whereas for the previous twenty years, in this and other rural parts of China, the policy was unmanageable. Now, each child and family was registered and the government knew who was breaking the law.

As we travelled, Drujia also introduced us to elements of the pre Buddhist Bon religion. A monastery was newly built as there was a resurgence in that faith, though it had been marginalised by the Buddhists Chinese and the Communists. We saw an ancient village, laid out in the shape of a Kalachakra or "Wheel of Time". Drujia said that the Chinese, who had tried to destroy it in the Cultural Revolution, now wanted to turn it into a tourist attraction, setting up souvenir stalls and charging money for people to visit. He wasn't sure which action was worse and the Chinese had re-named the village "Ba Jiao City" or "Eight Angle City" completely obliterating its former identity and religious significance. High on the hills surrounding the village and the temples, there were ceremonial spears planted, which we climbed up to see. Drujia said they were placed there to commemorate the Tibetans giving up arms and fighting against each other. Back in town there was another tour group, led by Sharon, an English girl who I had never met before, but had the reputation of being one of our outstanding leaders. She introduced herself and later that night I was directed by Drujia to the only bar in town. This was a small place but had entertainment that was Tibetan songs and dances. I particularly liked the fake plastic hands, used as a "clapper" that we were given for us to give applause. Sharon and her group were all getting very involved, it was a pity that mine didn't fancy the outing and as such, I decided that it would be better if I did not stay too long. The other highlight, so to speak of the bar was the toilet. Out here they are communal. Just one long pit extending along a wall. The idea is that the men go to the left and the women to the right and you all do your business together, squatting down. One of the women in Sharon's group had braved the toilet and came back particularly astonished. She said that never in her life would she have thought that she would share an open toilet with a Tibetan monk.

We left Labrang and our next stop along the highway that crossed the grasslands was Langmusi, a smaller village full of character with its water wheels over the diverted stream. Once again it was surrounded by hills and high pasture. There were the usual small market town shops and the encroachment of tourism meant that there were a couple of eateries too. I was surprised to find one with a menu in English that purported to sell "The best Yak burgers in the world," possibly the only yak burgers in the world, I thought. The town also had two monasteries and once again, Drujia came into his own. He pointed out the "Tankor" paintings, a "Wheel of Time" that represented the world we live in and also the cycle of birth, death and reincarnation. At the centre of the "Wheel" were pictures of cockerel, pig and snake that represented the pride, laziness and jealousy that were in all people. Encircling this were depictions of people in different states of awareness, steadily becoming more enlightened. The outer circles depicted Demi Gods and Gods, both of which could not reach enlightenment as they were too obsessed with fighting each other, or too powerful to consider the Buddhist teachings. These beings inevitably would be reincarnated as lower life forms and not gain enlightenment. On other walls were Buddhist prayers in Tibetan script. These were a sort of cross word that could be read in vertical, horizontal or diagonal and the squares were coloured to from a picture. Then, we had the chance to walk inside the prayer hall. From the daylight, into the half-light and there was an overpowering smell of old incense sticks, treated wood and Yak butter candles. This was a heady mixture and we were suddenly in a Buddhist half world with the low murmur of the monks praying filling the hall in a thick murmur. The wall hangings and drapery added to sensation that you were somewhere else entirely, not on earth anymore and very conscious that you might be intruding on something very holy. I am not religious, but these guys have that affect. There was a sand Mandala. This is a Kalachakra or "Wheel of Time" made out of different coloured sand and laying on a flat surface. It was very beautiful and mesmerizing. I stared at the compartments, rooms depicting scenes and people going about their daily life. I stared to the point of tunnel vision and felt that could have fallen into the Mandala itself and stood in one of its many rooms.

That night, Drujia took us to a more local restaurant where we ate a stomach and blood sausage by candlelight because the electricity in the town failed. The stomach was an inflated ball, filled with heated stones and (yes, you've guessed it) yak meat. One stab with the fork, the stomach deflates and the meal, more theatre than taste, was, literally, a letdown. Drujia decided to take us up beyond the monasteries the following day to see a "Sky Burial" site. This is part of the old Bon Religion that has continued its practice into Buddhism. When a person dies, their body is taken to an altar, on a high place and left for the birds to eat and carry off. Drujia had taken part in these ceremonies and said that we had to be respectful of the rites and didn't get too close to it for fear of upsetting the locals. That night, back in Langmusi we met Bella, who I had met in training in Beijing and was one of the Tibet experts working for us. She was with her group and everyone went to the local bar-come community hall and got involved in the Tibetan dancing "Nang Ma". This is a group dance, with everyone forming a circle, or circles if there is enough of you and doing a sequence of movements. I remember doing "The Slosh" at Butlins holiday camps as a child in the 1970's, for those of you a little younger, think "The Locomotion", or even "The Hokey Kokey". I got up, then everybody got up and along with all the beer, we were having a pretty good time.

I had spent a lot of time talking to Drujia. He had told me his life story of leaving Langmusi as a young man, walking to Lhasa, then on to Nepal, crossing the border and being hunted by the Chinese army. If he was found fleeing China, of which Tibet is a province, he would have been shot. He told me many Tibetans become refugees, fleeing their homeland. Many then cross the border again, into India. This is all a humongous undertaking, travelling over a thousand miles on foot and crossing the Himalayas. Once in India, they head to Dar a Salam, the court, or government, in exile for the Tibetan people and home of the Dali Lama. More importantly for some, it is where the Red Cross will provide free education and a home and food for all Tibetan refugees. Drujia had walked from Langmusi to Dar a Salam as a teenager and spent a few years there. Here, he met many friends, learned English and had a good education, but like so many Tibetans, he longed to return home and in his twenties, undertook the whole return journey back to his family again. His story was not uncommon. We stopped off on the road and went to a Tibetan "fair" where we met his friend Kalsang. He was another guide for our company and owned the guest house where we had been staying in Langmusi. He had also journeyed to Dar a Salam and that is where the two of them had first met. As we chatted, they talked about the Chinese leaders that were now leading trips to Tibet. "We don't want them" they said. "We cannot teach the tourists anything with them around" they continued, saying that we were changing hotels because the Chinese didn't want us staying with Tibetans. Other people at the fair were asking us if we liked the Chinese, we knew that the correct answer was to say "no", I tried to be diplomatic, but I could see that there had been no diplomacy where the Chinese had been involved as far as these Tibetans were concerned. On a lighter note, we did manage to play basketball with the local children who were blissfully unaware of the politics being talked by their elders.

We had a fantastic homestay visit for a night in a very small village. We stayed in a courtyard style house, some livestock shared the courtyard, and the toilet was a pit out in the field. We helped the mother and daughter peel potatoes in front of the big stove for our dinner. We took a look around the village and before too long we helped the locals (all women doing the work) move logs for housing up the village "street" which was nothing more than a steep muddy pathway. It's here, amidst all the wandering livestock that I also coined the phrases "Mind the Yak" and "Stand clear of the closing boars". It was definitely the most rural and authentic homestay that I have ever been to. After dinner we helped the daughter with her English lesson, trying Tibetan phrases until we were told that she was speaking a local dialect that would not be understood beyond the few villages in a few miles radius. That night, we were given mats and blankets and all had to sleep in one room. I took the initiative. It was warm enough for me to sleep out on the balcony under the stars, another timeless memory for me.

22. In Amdo Tibet, 26/07/07 (Amdo Tibet)

(A) Grasslands

It's good roads all the way
From polluted Lanzhou to blissful Xia He
With one stop for noodles and mutton
And the toilet from hell all for fifteen Yuan

Fields of rape, barley and wheat
The glint of the silver minaret
The towns on the frontier
This isn't really China here

Away across the grasslands
The herds of sheep on the roadway, crossing

White tents around a dug out oven pit
My land and my people my home
Living history, living land
Living spirit, monks and shaman

Wheels spinning prayers out across the grasslands
Every spirit receives a blessing

The wall of the mountains, strong and unyielding
And the clouds acting as a ceiling
The pass through the chasm below
And the village in its shadow
Looking like the album sleeve of a prog rock band
Or a fantasy novel in an enchanted land

The village planned like the wheel of time stretches below
And the hills summit crowned with the prayer arrows
Then you hear about the tourist atrocity
That the government has planned for the ancient walled city

(B). Enchantment 28 July 07

Peeping into the chanting hall and holding my breath
Uneasy about entering this twilight enchantment
The butter candles, each a small life, travelling on a path
All senses on an overload with nervous excitement

Being drawn into the sand universe of the mandala
Falling into the picture
The rooms in the different houses that spin
Into the magical musical box, I fall in
Falling to the rhythm of the chanting
As the wheel of time starts slowly spinning
And then I'm in another world again
Full of the colours of a Gods palace in heaven

Casting the spell of incantation they're weaving
With each warp and weft of prayer they are creating
A blanket to smother us, to bundle us up all prepared for
carrying
Off to some heaven, off we are flying
Out of the temple, the spirits still clinging
My head still stuffed full of chanting and teaching
Bewitched by the spell, the world becomes nothing
But then I'm out in the sunlight, like the Samsara fish,
jumping

And the click of a camera from some other place
Brings me back, through time and space

(C) Untitled 29th July Langmusi

The jumble of roof-tops in the valley
Houses poured into the crack that the stream has made
Surrounded by the land that protects and provides
Like a green wave crashing over the mountain side
The rugged stone circle of the rocky crowns
Breaking through the thinly stretched grassland
That is like a net trying to hold them down
As the rock breaks through, pushing up, beyond

Challenging the air, bathing in the sun
Clouds take shade in the lea of rock face.

We had one last stopover with Drujia in the village of Tangor. This Tibetan town had been "developed" or rather, hastily constructed in concrete by the government. It stood high on the grasslands, remote, isolated and looked in every way like a frontier town. The Tibetans rode into town on horses, dressed in cowboy leathers and yak skins. They eyed the girls in the group, meaningfully. High desert dust and sand blew along the streets in the cold wind. You could imagine there being a fight at any minute. The government "improvements" had meant the construction of a concrete parade of shops, mostly now Chinese owned, selling Chinese goods. There was only the one hotel in town and the lack of soft furnishings, a common theme throughout China, only made the place seem colder and less inviting. The windows in the rooms didn't close properly, the heating was feeble. Once in our rooms we discovered that one of the toilets didn't flush, another one was blocked. The first was remedied by simply turning the water on, but this took everyone on reception and the manger to get the handyman out to deal with it. The blocked toilet was more of a problem. It was obviously blocked and when the lad in the group flushed it, the stinking brown water in the bowl rose steadily to the top of the pot. However, rather than tackling the problem at the drain end, these Tibetans were more used to the "squats and long drop" toilets rather than anything with plumbing. So they just stood around and flushed it again until the water spilled over the top of the pot and onto the floor as we all were pointing and screaming at the hapless hotel staff. Drujia had us eat in the hotel dining room, there was not so much choice in town and we also had some entertainment in the form of a local Tibetan teacher who played us some Tibetan folk songs on his guitar. Then, it was goodbye to Drujia and we were off the following morning to Songpan and the Traffic Hotel.

In the trip reports I had read, I had been warned about this place and Suzy Li had left a note suggesting that we should change hotels, but I had not followed it up. The complaints from Kalsang were ringing in my ears. "The Chinese want to change the trip to take money away from us," was what I was thinking, but as it worked out, Suzy Li had everyone's best interest at heart. All seemed good at first as we were met by the local hotelier and also the local cafe owner, both who spoke English. We had a stroll around town, another very pretty place, with an enclosing wall and ancient street. You could see that there was an established tourist trade here with the souvenir shops and tour excursions. We booked to go horse riding the following day. I had one slight concern. This was for my passenger, Steve, as at around 6 feet 5 inches, he was a similar height, and probably a larger weight than tour leader "Big" Nigel. I had been reading Nigel's trip report and amongst all the information and sprinkling of jokes was a paragraph about him being called "too fat" for the horse. The Tibetan horses are more like ponies and although they are hardy creatures, surviving on the Himalayan grasslands, they are not the largest of animals. We would find out how they would faire the following day. We ate Tibetan style again for the last time. We'd had enough of vomit tasting Yak Butter Tea and other delights by then. As we went to bed, I got a knock at the door. One room still didn't have hot water. I went to see what I could do. As I was explaining this to the floor attendant, I got called over by my passengers Steve and Amy. "There is a rat in our room", and there was.

I didn't actually see it, but there was enough evidence for them to want to move. The floor attendant was completely unhelpful, saying that there were no other rooms and seemed to think that a "rat" (though I only had the Chinese to call it a big mouse) was not a problem. The couple moved across the hall and doubled up with Stacey. I went back to my room and sat on my bed texting the other contact that Suzy Li had given me, saying that I was in the town staying at Traffic Hotel and that we may have to move hotels and asking if there was room. As I did this, a large rat ambled across the floor of my room and under my bed. I changed the text message to "definitely" have to move. Later that night I was awoken again as another rat scurried across the top sheet of the other bed in the room. In the morning I was up and out early, not just because of the rats, but because I was starting to feel a little unwell. I threw up and had the shits, but thought little of it and assumed that it would pass. I went over to see the other hotel and they said they would have rooms later in the day. Excellent, we could move. I went around knocking everybody up and told them the good news. The last person I visited was my passenger Paul because he was in a side corridor and had not been part of the fun and games the night before. He answered the door looking like death warmed up. Concerned, I asked him if he'd not slept well. "No", he said. There had been at least 2 rats in his room all night. He'd spotted one dropping from the ceiling and after that he'd kept a vigil with the light on until morning. Poor sod.

We moved over and the rest of the passengers went on a horse trek. I'd started to feel worse and actually took to my bed in the new guesthouse. This was the first time I'd been ill in about 5 years. I literally shitted vomited and sweated out whatever my ailment was over the next 24hrs. As for the horses, Steve said that he was definitely concerned for their welfare, as they were struggling to take his weight. Then it was back on the bus again and a ten hour drive to the more familiar territory of Chengdu. Chicory was our local guide again, what a relief to be back in her safe hands and everything went perfectly.

There were actually seven leaders in Yangshuo when we were there and it was also the birthday celebrations for Thai-chili. We all did the round of all the bars. I gave Esmeray the notes I'd written, we had a fantastic night out that ended up with lots of tequila and dancing on a stage in a Chinese nightclub until 4 in the morning. Somehow it took my passenger Stacey 3 motorbike taxis to get back to the hotel; we were only around the corner. After about 3 hours sleep I left Esmeray in my bed and went on the obligatory bike ride to Moon Hill again. Needless to say, I still hadn't climbed the thing and wouldn't do that day either. There was one thing that I did notice. Out of the usual on the bike ride was that one of the karsts was in the process of being demolished. This is spectacular scenery and it is supposed to be a national park, but some company was quarrying a karst and looked like it would completely obliterate the stump in a matter of months. Next to the remains of the karst, a new development of a hotel and resort was being built. I suppose the local government official would see this as progress and take a sizeable back hander as part of the bargain. The following night was just as crazy, I danced with Sheila as always and had some video footage of me recorded by Lyn when I was trying to show everybody the "Madness, One Step Beyond" dance. That was a real hit. Philip was providing some of the music with his mandolin in Bar 98 and it was Thai-chili's birthday celebration. Her birthday was going to be at some point in the next trip, so we decided it was close enough to celebrate. Pierre was also there with his group. It looked like they'd been partying their way through China. I bumped into Pierre's group the following morning and they still hadn't got on their bikes at 10am. I found out later that one vomited within 20 minutes of starting the bike ride and another had to give up after 40 minutes. Before I left, I ran into Steven, also from training. He had done a few Tiger Leaping Gorge trips, so I picked his brains about them. Andrea, from a couple of trips ago was coming back to China and we'd agreed to meet up and travel through Yunnan Province together.

The trip ended in Hong Kong as usual. Hannah, the big boss from Australia was in town and we were going to have interviews with her at some point during her stay in the city. Somehow, Esmeray had managed to wangle it that we were sharing a room. Nice one. Tang was also about and most of the other leaders would be passing through soon too. The other thing that was passing through H.K. was a typhoon. As we arrived it was Typhoon warning 4 (whatever that means). This soon increased. The group had found a fantastic place on the harbor front to have our final night dinner, called "Blues on the Bay". We watched the light show and then slowly, went to the harbor front restaurant and ate while we watched the storm come in. Within half an hour we couldn't see Hong Kong Island and then the rain came down. Somehow still managed to get the restaurant to serve us whist sitting outside in true British "whatever the weather" style. We finished the night off in the Irish Bar again along with Esmeray and Tang.

I had a big hangover the following day again and just had to go for a curry with Esmeray. As we walked back to the hotel we noticed that most of the businesses were closed. Then the rain hit again, hard. Things were blowing over in the wind such as shop sign-boards; this was a Typhoon warning 8. Somehow Esmeray managed to get to the airport before it was closed. Unfortunately I left my boat crossing to Shekou too late as I had my interview with Hannah. For some reason unbeknown to me still, she asked if I wanted to carry on working through the winter and of course, I said yes, so it looks like I passed the probation. If she ever read any of my emails, she might well have reconsidered. So, I actually spent that night in Chungking Mansions. I never would have believed that 5 years after leaving that shit hole, I'd be back there again. I joined Pierre's group for their final night get together along with Philip who was now in town. I left them before it got really out of hand. I think Pierre had been extremely popular with the girls on his trip and now they wanted a taste of Philip. I wasn't going to stand in their way but left them in the middle of a "dance off" but wasn't sure who the prize would be.

23. The Tail of the Typhoon, 12/08/07 (Yunnan)

The tail of a typhoon was blowing in
Across the harbor to smother the buildings
The authorities on air, announce the warning
"A level eight is coming"

Blown about by all my feelings and pains
Too many goodbyes and girls with no name
The power of it all, pumps through my veins
I am washed baptised again

As I sit in Chungking Mansions
With a curry from the Indians

Chatting with my new best friend
From Turkey, about living in Green Lanes
And Citizen Fish and Punk Bands
With a hangover too big to understand
I thought I was back in London Town
As outside, the rain came down

I'm standing in the Typhoon rain
I'm standing in a hurricane
And whirled back to London Town
Just for a second, as the rain came down.

Things went smoothly the following morning and I was in Shekou and typing up my trip report and accounts by 11:30. Andrea was also on her way in to China. We'd agreed to go to Yunnan province and hike Tiger Leaping Gorge together. Those of you who know anything about me must think that I've gone completely bonkers. Rather than spending a week slobbing about and drinking beer in the Irish bar in Shekou, complete with rock band, I'd decided to give myself the hassle and expense to travel halfway across China in order to do a 2 day hike up a 3000m high gorge. I remember my dads' old saying. "A man has two heads, but can only think with one at a time", guess which one I was thinking with. Anyway, she arrived around 5pm, just as I'd finished my paperwork and we went out to the Irish Bar, with Pierre in tow. Remembering what had happened the last time I did this, we didn't have a late night, so I was fully packed and prepared for our trip to Yunnan in the morning. I suppose this is where the Andrea Jennings curse started and not a single mode of transport arrived or departed without a hitch from then until I returned to Shekou without her. In 5 months of travelling with paying customers around this country, I've generally been on time, found hotels with a minimum of fuss and not taken anything from them or left anything behind in them. Enter Andrea and I may as well have been straight off a banana boat. I couldn't actually blame her for most of the things that went wrong; it's just that they did.

We left Pierre in the morning as he went walking off down the street with a cup of coffee in his hand, so French Canadian, so Pierre, I'd never met anyone quite like him. The authorities, whoever they are, in their wisdom had demolished the bus shelter that our airport bus was supposed to stop at. So it didn't and we had to wander off down the road in search of another one. Our plane was delayed 2 hours, meaning that when we finally did get into the Camilla Hotel in Kunming, we were a bit short of time and my travel company's' contact, Pauline, had knocked off work. We did the sensible thing and tried to plan our return trains to Guangzhou and Shenzhen for 7, and 5 days' time and also a bus to Qiaotou and Tiger Leaping Gorge for the following day. The only option on my train was hard seat (no beds) on a 30 hour journey. Andrea couldn't even buy a train ticket until the following morning when they were to go on sale. Most train tickets in China do not go on sale until 7 days before the departure date. This became a bit of a problem, because there were no direct busses to Qiaotou, so we would have to get one to Li Jiang, leaving around 9am. The woman in the hotel business centre said she would be in before 9 and try to buy the ticket for her. Meanwhile, the only real option for me was to fly. So, an internet visit later and I'd parted with over a week's wages, but gained an extra day in Yunnan. I also bumped into Sue, the music teacher from my excellent group of 2 trips ago and she gave us another run down of what to expect at TLG.

The woman in the office was true to her word and Andrea got her ticket and we got the bus. I received a text confirmation from my travel company's contact, the Sunshine Hotel in Li Jiang, so things looked like they were working out. Our first impressions of Yunnan were that it was a lush green province of rice paddies, which turned into rolling countryside before becoming hills. We passed traditional villages by the side of the new motorway that cut the ancient through with the modern. Old style farm houses had tiled roofs with mock fish carved on the eves. The fields were full of a curious style of haystack. There was a central pole, or in some places, a tree had been used and the hay was built in a tube all around the pole until it was topped off, conical hat style. I'd never seen this anywhere else in China. We arrived just before six o'clock, giving us over an hour of daylight to find the hotel. Andrea had the maps that I'd sent her from my travel company's library, maps being the important plural word here. The bus station had been moved and it took us a while to get our bearings. Half an hour later, we still had not found the entrance to the Old Town, but as I stood outside the Black and White hotel, saying that I was sure I'd read somewhere about a "Black and White" hotel, Andrea then said that it could be on the "other" map. Yes, the other map that showed quite clearly how to get into the Old Town, opposite the Black and White Hotel. Things didn't improve. The Old Town is a rabbit warren of winding streets that are impossible to negotiate. The address given in my travel company's trip notes for the hotel just didn't exist, so as the sun went down we headed for the Youth Hostel. An impossible twist and turn through the cobbled streets again. There were some wooden sign posts, saying "you are here" but even to the experienced map readers like myself, only a mad man would try to map Li Jiang. It was alleyway after twisting alleyway all set in between the small hills and there was no way to know which way you were ultimately heading. It was dark by the time we got to the Youth hostel which was full, so we ended up in a Chinese Hotel, because it was the nearest place that was open and things were beginning to look desperate.

I was really impressed with Li Jiang. All the things I'd been told about it were derogatory and likened it to a tourist Disneyland town. In some ways it might have been that, but the Old Town had character and masses of people. The area has a history of over 2200 years, from being a settlement of the Naxi people, who still made up a sizeable minority of the population. It was founded as a Southern Silk Road settlement in the late 13th Century and became famous as a trading station on the "Tea Horse Trail" from India, through Yunnan and into China. There was an earthquake in 1996 and a lot of rebuilding had gone on since then, but to the untrained eye, the Old Town of Li Jiang looked very well preserved. We were close to the town square. There were rivers that flowed through the town, contained between stone footpaths and crossed by numerous bridges. There was a wooden water wheel as the centre piece of the town and the narrow, wooden building lined streets would wind back on themselves until they opened into courtyards. It was all very pretty. Almost every building was a shop of some sort and the Naxi and Dongba ethnic minority traditional cultures were on sale in the form of artwork with poems in the ancient languages. Many people still wore traditional dress. As the night grew on we wandered by the river, all lit up with red lanterns, stopping at cafes and the numerous bars for a drink. At one point, people were placing lanterns in the stream to watch them float through the town, there was quite a crowd gathering and having fun and when we got to the bar area, we watched groups of Chinese chanting at each other, across the narrow river from the 2nd floor of the bars, like football supporters. This was a fun place and already I wanted to come back.

The following morning we decided to get bus tickets to Qiaotou, what should be a 1 1/2hr journey away. The local travel agents couldn't help us, so we walked to the bus station where we'd been dropped off the previous day. Here, we were told that this was the wrong bus station, the other one being quite a walk away, elsewhere in town. This ballsed up our plans, so we decided to go back to the hotel and taxi it to wherever the bus station was then, hopefully get on the next bus out of town. The next bus out of town was at 2:30, which was over 4 hours later. There was nothing for it than to enjoy the splendors of what Li Jiang had to offer in the shape of a decent English breakfast with a pot of proper tea from one of the Western-friendly tourist cafes. Then we went on a shopping expedition that saw me come away with a ridiculously multi-coloured hat, chosen by Andrea.

This latest cock up put the pressure on our hiking time. Instead of being a leisurely stroll over 2 days, it looked like I was going to have to keep up with a very fit 22 year old who was used to running up the side of mountains. I however, am much more built for comfort rather than speed and a lifestyle of twenty years of drinking and smoking was not the preparation recommended for doing TLG in record breaking time.

We arrived in Qiaotou around 4:30. The weather had held off so far. We met Margo, a very eccentric Australian who lives there and acts as a local guide and information guru. She was constantly checking the road for errant travelers who were going to wander up TLG by themselves, get lost and die through injury and exposure (was I really going to do this?). So we were fed and watered as we chatted with Margo about the hike, the people we knew at my travel company, such as Steven and Bruce who had both done many trips through the area so we passed as much news as possible in half an hour. Margo kept darting to and from the door of her "Gorged Tiger Cafe" which was no more than a wooden hut, yelling at the foreigner hikers passing bye to be careful. Then at the locals to keep their distance and stop ripping off the tourists. An illuminating and somewhat invaluable stop-over as Margo was one of the local guides used by the company that I work for. Next came the hike. Not too bad at first, but of course we had to get to the Naxi Guesthouse before nightfall. This just meant that we had to keep up quite a pace on the long slow incline up the side of the gorge for four hours without a break. As we gained height, the views of the gorge improved, even if the weather was not the best, the drifting clouds gave it some atmosphere and scale and also helped me cool down a little. This was tough going for me and I was glad whenever Andrea would slow to take in the view, or photograph the fields full of sunflowers or the golden chocolate of the swollen Yangtze River, far below us. The first bit on the first day actually went well. I renamed the place "Horse Shitting Gorge" because that was what there was a lot of. You couldn't get lost on the trail, just follow the line of turds. We made the guesthouse by 6.30pm ish and booked in for the night.

The really difficult bit was going to be starting off early enough the following day to complete the Gorge in time to get a bus on to Dali. The following morning we were ready for a 6am start, but it didn't get light until nearly 7, so we were already an hour behind schedule. We shot off over the mountain-side at a rare pace, until around half an hour into our trek, we heard a voice shouting from about half a kilometer behind us. We turned; it was the girl from the Guest house. "Youshe, youshe!" she cried. I thought for a minute, then looked at Andrea. "You have given the key back in, haven't you?" She furtively produced the room key from her bag and ran back to the girl over the mountainside. When she returned, I don't know if her red face was from the exercise or the embarrassment. However, I rubbed it in. "Youshe, that's Chinese for Key, don't 'forget' it".

She soon got her own back as we then had to do the 32 bends, which even by her standards was a hard climb. This put us even further behind schedule as I needed regular rest breaks. What did surprise me was that at a slow steady pace, I could catch my breath again after only a few seconds and with a few slugs of water I was back on the way up. The scenery is quite out of this world at the top. Then, we walked along a path built along the side of the gorge. A real sort of mountain path with steep drops to the river below. This only became a problem when a heard of goats happened to be walking in the opposite direction. I don't know too much about goats apart from the story of the "Three Billy-goats Gruff" in which a goat pushed a troll off a bridge and into a river where he drowned. I reckoned that a troll was probably bigger than me and so the goats would have to be passed with the upmost caution otherwise I was going to go the same way as the Troll. I am also afraid of heights, so walking along the outside of the path, exposed to the 1000m drop with the goats between me and safety had me shitting myself. Andrea knew nothing of this as she also confessed to not feeling at ease around the goats. I should get an EQUITY card for my acting skills as I even got a photo sitting down on the cliff road with my back to a group of them and the gaping chasm. Anyway, just about six hours after the start, two stops and a couple of stumbles later, we made it to Tina's Guesthouse. The end of the Gorge Trek, "to voyage where no unfit man had gone before". By a stroke of luck, we got picked up within minutes by the bus and were negotiating the landslides back to Qiaotou. We picked up our bags and said goodbye to Margo as a rainstorm hit. Then we were on a bus to Dali.

Dali is also set in amongst the hills of Yunnan, but on the gently sloping shore of the Er Hai Lake, the 9th largest lake in China. The area was traditionally settled by Bai and Yi peoples, another two of Chinas ethnic minorities over 4000 years ago. The city has a complex past, first coming to prominence during the Han dynasty when it was annexed by China, but it was also the capital of its own state between the 8th and 13th Centuries. It is a walled city, with much of the Ming construction still standing. The major sights are the three towering pagodas that dominate the city and are now lit up, nightly. We got lost again looking for the hotel in Dali and in the end had to phone to be picked up by the hotelier, Mr. River, so I can quite confidently say we had a good look around the town. I didn't think that Dali was as nice as Li Jiang. That goes against everything else we'd been told about the two places. The buildings are of a traditional style again, but more like those seen in other parts of southern China rather than Li Jiang. They are solid, built of grey stone and clean cut and square. They have balconies overlooking the wide, paved straight streets that are now pedestrianised. Not the winding cobbles of the other towns. There are streams along the side of the roads, but they too are straight and boxed in by the stone slabs of the pavement. The small rivulets in town run alongside the roads and pathways and there are bridges that form beautiful vantage points. It was actually so late when we finally checked in that all we could do was eat and then I prepared for my onward travel. Once again the Jennings curse had struck and busses were booked out leaving me with having to take an alternative route and an earlier bus. Well, only one last night, what else could possibly go wrong? We headed into town to find the Bamboo Bar and Steven's contact and friend there, George in amongst the two streets of western bars and cafes. Andrea stopped to get some money out.... and her card was rejected. Surely, this was about the last deal of misfortune.

We spent far too long trying other ATMs and thinking that I might have to give her money, which I could never guess on when I would get it back. Finally she managed to get cash out on another card, which solved any future problems about her travelling and getting money back to me. Then we found George. As Steven had promised, George was an excellent host, the beer was flowing and the conversation would have gone long into the night if it wasn't for me having an early start for my bus in the morning. Nevertheless, we had a very pleasant end of our trip together.

24. Yunnan, 12/08/07 (Yunnan)

Back to the mountains crowned by clouds
The flat valley patchwork of green rice
Slant roofed houses around walled courtyards
The electric line and the dirt road to where the distance
reaches the sky
And the clouds come halfway down the mountain
A sash befitting a beauty queen
The tail of a Typhoon, a smokey coiled Dragon
Wrapping the horizon and looking down on the scene

25. Remembering Something for Kate,
    16/08/07 (Apartment, Shenzhen)

Do you remember how it rained so much
But we had sunshine in the top of the mountains
Getting lost in the Old Town of Li Jiang
Listening to the opposing bar crowds chanting
Hiking the gorge at a misty sunrise
And having to run back to hand the room key in
Last minute bus rides through the villages of Yunnan
Last minute condoms and another farewell kissing

I remember how you asked me to show you the stars
In a north hemisphere sky you had never seen before
The sound at the top of the Empire State, listening to cars

Was the shoals of the Yangtze in its Tiger Leaping Roar
The chocolate river, flecked with silver wrapper
The weaving bus rides, praying we weren't late
The dancing heads in the sun-flower fields
I will always remember Something for Kate

26. More than Distance 25/08/07

It's all got to mean nothing
Because that's all it can ever be
When you're hoping that there will be another meeting
In some time we might have free
Should I try to try, or try to forgetting
That there's anything between you and me
There's more than just distance between us
Much more than either of us could ever be

A text message across the miles
Another valued friend
The picture on MySpace will always smile
And the memory that will never end
You and I, different forks, different roads
And we can't see what's beyond the next bend
There's more than just distance between us
Much more than either of us can email and send

There's a page on saying goodbye
In my phrasebook in mandarin
That starts 'I'm happy to have met you'
And ends with 'Dzai-jian'

There's a page on saying goodbye
In my phrasebook in Mandarin
And it makes me want to cry
When I get to 'Dzai-jain'.

There was not really any time to do any sightseeing in Dali. I
only saw a snapshot of the town whilst I was there. I was

getting ready to leave for Kunming and say goodbye to Andrea, possibly forever. I checked my phone messages. (I only turn my UK phone on every couple of days, half the time it doesn't work and it saves the battery for when it does). I had a message from Mike (aka Moo) my flat mate back home in London. It read "We've had a small fire in the flat, everyone's Ok. I'll email you the details later". My world just ground to a halt.

Chapter 7

KEEP THE HOME FIRES BURNING

Be not afraid of going slowly; be afraid only of standing still.

Chinese Proverb

I love Lindsay with all my heart. I could not ask for a better friend than Moo. However, they are both a little crazy. When my other friends learned that Moo and Lindsay were taking my flat on whilst I was in China, they all questioned if I'd finally lost my sanity as well. "They'll burn the place down....ha, ha, ha" I heard them laughing. "You'll come back and there will be nothing left of your house, ha, ha, ha," Only to be followed by "There will be mad parties every night of the week, they'll trash the place, ha, ha, ha," How we all laughed. But I wasn't laughing now.

What constitutes a "small fire?" Would they have necessarily contacted me if it was nothing to be bothered about? Has half the house gone up in smoke? The houses around mine? I started thinking, I've lost everything. 20 years of hard work gone up in flames. I'm going to have to go back to England and somehow find a job and somewhere to live and somehow start paying the thousands and thousands of pounds of damage off. It looked bleak. I tried to contact Moo and Lindsay, by text, phone, and email, (of course they wouldn't have email, their computers would be melted lumps of plastic now). I got no reply. "Everyone is Ok", who is everyone? There should only have been Moo and Lindsay in the house. I started thinking, what were they doing? I had visions of yet another wild party, with a house full of the people that some of us had nick-named "The Camden Circus" along with every gothic-punk oddball in London. Moo and Lindsay had been running around naked with burning torches made out of their own underwear. That was it. There was no other logical explanation as to how there had been a fire in my flat. I felt completely lost and powerless. I was waiting for a message from one of them, not knowing what my next move was going to be. Odds on, whatever happened, it looked like it was goodbye to China.

Andrea did what girls do best, and by God I needed it. Then, with my head full of oh so much going on, I left Andrea in Dali, probably for the last time, this time and carried on to Kunming, checking my phone every few minutes all the way there. I got a text from Lindsay, saying that things weren't too bad and that the Housing Association had been informed. In some ways, this didn't help because the Housing Association thought that I was the only person living in the house. They did not know about my friends and they would probably want to see me to at least sign off some paperwork to say that the place was ok for habitation. This is not the sort of news for a born worrier on the wrong side of the world.

When I got to Kunming, I had a nice surprise because Philip was there. I joined his group for dinner, which at least stopped my paranoia for the evening. It meant that I got a quick tour and a look at the eateries around the hotel. Philip told me a story of one of his group not recognising the mosquito net hung over his bed for what it was. He had thought that it was some sort of hammock to sleep in. When he had tried to get in it, he had brought the whole thing crashing down. Philip had spent most of the year since training, doing the Hanoi to Hong Kong trips, or Hanoi to Beijing, then the return journey, so it was the first real time to catch up and have a beer apart from the drunken nights in Yangshuo. The next day I flew back to Shenzhen and the apartment. When I arrived, Lyn was there, so there was nothing more for it then to head off to the Irish bar to watch "Mind the Gap" knock out some rock classics and get drunk. This we did for two days. The first night was particularly memorable for it taking us nearly an hour to walk the 500m back to the apartment as we were so drunk and Lyn kept having to sit down because the ground was moving too much for her. It was on this occasion that I found out that Lyn was also writing. Some poetry and a blog of each of her trips. A different style to mine, with pictures and stories, but we felt that we had a lot in common and became firmer friends.

I also got a phone call from the West Hotel in Hong Kong. They asked me about my passenger Mr. Wong, who had turned up for the trip, but wasn't on their list, so how was I to pay for his hotel accommodation. This became intriguing as I didn't have a Mr. Wong on my passenger list, so I fired emails to the head office in Australia, trying to get to the bottom of this. I phoned the West and took the decision that if he wasn't on my list, then he wasn't one of my passengers. No accommodation had been booked through China and we were supposed to be on a train in 2 days' time and there wouldn't be any tickets booked either. I braced myself to have one hell of a troubled time on arrival in H.K. When I got there, Mr. Wong had been dealt with. It turned out that he'd booked onto my trip, then cancelled and booked onto another starting in Beijing in 2 days' time. Unfortunately, he'd got it all mixed up and Mr. Wong had found himself in the wrong city, on the wrong day, trying to get on the wrong trip. He was definitely, Wong.

I got an email from Moo, and Lindsay. Let me see if I can get this right. The fire was started by a joss stick, which had burned and ignited a can of "cat flea" spray. Moo had got to the fire before it had got out of hand and saved my house. It had been one of those ludicrous events that should never have happened. (Ever remember the sequence in Police Academy when the nerd-rookie cop throws the apple over his shoulder and starts a riot?) Well to me it sounded like that. Moo coming back from work early and finding the blaze was another almost unbelievable stroke of luck. They said that only some papers and stuffed toys were burned because they were stored behind the wardrobe. I'm not going to think that my life's work of poetry (covering 25 years in over 400 pages) has gone up in smoke along with the teddy bear I've managed to keep since a baby. It's better not to ask any more questions than are strictly necessary. Lindsay said she would paint the room pink for me. Umm.

I had been really looking forward to this trip because I was supposed to have a trainee. This is pretty good considering I'd only been in the job 4 months. My trainee was to be a 22yr old Chinese girl called Ruby Liu. Did the management really know what they were doing? I was playing out the fantasy of seeing how I could train this innocent young girl. Oh, what demands could a Westerner put on an inexperienced Chinese. This was going to be fun and free Chinese lessons thrown in.

Unfortunately, it turns out that the girl never passed training in Beijing. Defeat snatched from the jaws of victory again. Ah, well.... My new lot of passengers seemed another reasonable bunch again. In Hong Kong we ate at Blues on the Bay and I found myself in Murphy's bar with Sarah, Lyn and their passengers. As I watched the televised Premiership football, the two American girls started to make comments that didn't make sense. They had been looking at the clock in the corner of the T.V. screen showing how many minutes had been played. Then they had looked again and the time was not what they had expected. At fifteen minutes into the game, they thought that the clock should have been ticking down to zero, as it does in all American sports and there was only fifteen minutes left to play. They had decided that they could endure that, for my sake and were waiting for the game to finish for us to continue our conversation. Utterly confounded, as the time on the clock increased and they started questioning how I, or anybody, knew how much of the game was remaining. The concept of a game of 90 minutes (ok, with extra time, but I didn't want to complicate the situation still further) was lost on the yanks. They weren't prepared to wait for over an hour, so they decided to leave.

Off into China the following day, still very concerned about the lack of info about my house fire. I got a call around 5pm whilst I was in Shenzhen train station buying some noodles for the journey. It was from Circle Anglia Housing Association, or some agent representing them. "A fire has been reported, and we have not been able to get in touch with you" (bloody China mobile doesn't work in H.K.). "Yes' I replied, a small fire.... nothing to worry about" I was hiding in the toilets in order to get away from the echoing Chinese announcements that would surely give the game away. "It was a kitchen fire?" they asked. "No", I said, "Bedroom", sounding as knowledgeable as you can about something you have no idea about, but knowing your life as you know it depends on a convincing lie. "It was put out by my flat mate and he called the fire brigade, no real damage". I could hardly hear what the girl on the other end was saying; something about an inspection and that they'd call me again later that day. I said that the Fire Brigade had said that there was no structural damage to the house and that there was nothing to worry about and that my phone was on all the time if they needed to call me. I prayed that would do the trick. I stayed awake until after midnight waiting for the "afternoon" call. It never came.

I'm glad that this was a trip I'd done so often before. I had enough stress thinking about the house. I had a group that ranged in ages from the young English, chemistry PhD student, to the English University professor from Manchester. So, 23 to 36. I had two couples on the trip, both Australians, both late twenties, but then I had Helen. There are certain types of passengers that just make life more difficult. Americans are usually the worse. Nothing is ever good enough for them and they demand things from the trip that are just impossible in China. English gap year students, or those just finished are just as bad, they also have a superiority complex and don't like the fact that some bloke from Blackburn is leading them around China. There's the intellectuals, who want to know all the answers to everything. Then there's the "independent women". This category is bad because they have the superiority complex of the gap year kids, but they've already travelled and just never think that I'm up to the job. They also compare everything with what they've seen/done before, never quite getting it that "this is China", a place unlike just about anywhere else in the world. Helen fitted firmly into this category. She also argued the toss about most things, having an opinion on everything, including things that she knew nothing about. I particularly liked the way she was interrupting a conversation about Chinese politics before saying "Who?" when someone raised the subject of Chairman Mao. This was all in the first twenty four hours, before we had even got to Yangshuo.

Yangshuo, being a bit of a party town, usually gets everybody to let their hair down. However, my group was unusually restrained. The Aussie couples were not up for drinking, which was a real surprise. Frank and Frances were off on a trip to Europe and Canada, with the intention of working there, so were on a budget. Helen was also on a sort of budget, but at the same time was telling us all how much she had got paid as a H.R. consultant in Sydney. My only previous run-ins with H.R. people had not been good. They have over inflated opinions of themselves and seem to take joy from other peoples misery. They are tough, to the point that they try to see weakness in everybody else. Helen was also out for herself, in every possible way. She was moving to London, where she thought it no problem to get back into H.R. and earn a mint. I reckon she was in for a big shock in moving to London, a city at the heart of the world, with whatever skills she may have gained in Sydney. She started to flirt with Frank, and then said that all Aussie men were wimps. You could tell that she just wanted him to try to prove her wrong by making a move on her in front of his girlfriend. She was a nasty piece of work

We did the bike ride in Yangshuo with George. Once again, an excellent day out. George told us the story of how Yangshuo and the karst scenery came into being. He said that there had been a man from the North of China who had come to Yangshuo, when it was all flat land and decide that it would be a good area to raise cattle. He returned the following year and brought with him some goats and a camel. However, in his greed, he forgot to give praise to Buddha for granting him this new land. He fell asleep and Buddha sent a strong wind over the land. When the man awoke, he could not see his animals, instead, the land was now covered in the karsts hills. He asked, "Where have all my animals gone?" and Buddha replied to him, "They are still here, but I have changed them into the mountains and the rope you used to tether them has become the Li River. He looked around and could see that the mountains were indeed in the shape of his animals, he could see a goat with his horns and a camel crossing the Li River.

On arrival back at the hotel, I was passing the envelope around for tips when Helen piped up. She announced to the group, that the group should not tip the guides. Then said with glee that on her last trip, she had got the group to agree with her and the guides had gone without tips. This had confounded her previous trip leader, as many of the local guides were so appalled by the lack of tips that they said they wouldn't work with the leader again. This was Helen having some sort of power play. I told her to refer to the trip notes where is distinctly says to bring money for tipping guides. I told her that this was what she signed up for when she booked the trip and that she should not try to influence the others in the group. I passed the envelope around and some money went in. Round one to me.

We had bad weather on the Yangtze River and our local guide, Emily, who had so often been my excellent guide at The Dam was unable to encourage the group to anything much on the trip. I'd contacted Amy, we arranged to meet up again and this time tried another of Chongqing's bars and got toffee swirls and snack food from the complex around the Trade Winds restaurant. This area is a favourite hangout for the Chongqing young and trendy. This turned into another late night full of dice games and joking around. We talked a lot about ourselves and the pressure she was under to get married, although her relationship with her boyfriend was not going anywhere. She was putting all the work into her job and wanted a better life, she was even planning on buying an apartment, this is an amazing step for an unmarried girl in China and with her mother being divorced, and there were no family handouts. Dad had left years earlier and was working somewhere in Tibet. Divorce, although not uncommon in China, is still not as readily acceptable as in the West, there is a stigma attached to it and the family for not staying together and the patriarchal society demands father figures and male roles in everything from work, to ancestor worship. The one child policy has had so many different impacts in Chinese society, the policy itself is only strictly applied to the cities, those in the countryside can have more children, if you are an ethnic minority, you can have more children. The status of women in China has improved, as, with only one child, the parents are as determined that their daughter will get a good education and a good job as any son. One thing that the Communist Government didn't recognise was that when a daughter gets married, she joins her husband's family, leaving her ancestors un-worshiped. In a country trying to battle with its superstitious past, the Communist party just didn't care about these things, unfortunately, for the population, ancestor worship and superstition play a big part in the culture. In the morning, I was in a bit of a state and forgot the room deposit. Then I nearly broke my leg as I fell off the train fully loaded with backpacks at Chengdu station. Nights out with Amy could lead to all sorts of trouble. The group were not impressed.

Nevertheless, things worked out ok for most of the trip. I even thought I'd won Helen around at one point. This is when she discovered "Chicken Wing". We were at Baoguo Monastery, where she found what appeared to be a dead kitten. She took it to a restaurant where we'd just eaten and got some food. The cat survived the night. A day later, Chicken Wing was well enough for his de-fleeing (no inflammable cans of spray here) and first bath. We took pictures and I blow dried him with my hairdryer (my 1 luxury item in my back-pack). We left the kitten in the safe hands of Patrick and I said I'd let the other tour group leaders know about the cat and adopt him when they came through.

I had found that my only drinking partner for most of the trip had been the 36 year old Chemistry lecturer. Most of the others were in bed early, but I did manage one good night out in Xi'an, where I kept most of the gang together until about 2am. This was the night that another one of my tour leader friends from training, Jane was in town. We went through the gossip and updates. It turns out that things had got a lot better with her sex life than when we'd last met in Beijing. I quickly found out that she'd been shagging one of the passengers who was in his 40's (she's 30). He had been on the trip with his mother in law. Strange but true and how she'd managed this one I don't know. He was also a millionaire owner of an Australian company and told her he'd fly her over there and leave his wife. Watch this space is all I can say. She also relayed another story which had been growing on the grape vine over the last few weeks. One leader had got drunk whilst leading a trip and came off a motorbike. He had then lost his job, but somehow begged to get it back by saying he would give up drink. What the curious part of the story is, that the manageress, Hannah, is then reputed to have sucked him off. I just had to find out more.

In Beijing once again and no-one was around for a drink for the first few days, so I got my report done in double quick time. I was supposed to have had a week or more off between trips. I'd had the specter of doing a couple of "blind trips" (luckily short ones, and I knew most of the places on route) back to back coming up. I'd decided that I'd have to brush up on my Chinese and booked lessons. One of the trips was going to be a "comfort trip", known for elderly, well off, demanding passengers and I knew that I would just not fit the bill of what they wanted in a leader. Anyway, with less than a week to go before my previous trip ended, the schedule changed. This happens quite a lot, but I've been lucky with most of mine and have been able to plan ahead a little. What head office had given me were two different "blind trips", back to back, covering a month, going from Beijing to Kunming and, yes, hiking Tiger Leaping gorge. Did the company actually realise that I was probably the most un-fit leader in their employ? Somehow, they had decided that because I'd done it before, I could do it again, this time leading a group of 11. I only had 1 day off in between my last trip and this royal double-header that I was about to endure. The Chinese lessons got squeezed into 4 days whilst I did my trip reports and had a quick look at where I was supposed to be taking the new group before we made it down to TLG. It looked as though we also had a 2 day trek to a desert thrown in, just to liven up the trip. Wonderful. More places that I didn't have a clue about and another series of question of "how hot/cold/difficult" etc. that I just couldn't answer

Luckily, Janie was doing the trip 1 week in front of me. I met her in the bar just as she was leaving. She'd had a week off to research it and had been in contact with our camel trek guide. She handed on what info she could and said she'd text with regular reports. It's times like this that you really value your work colleagues. Lyn was in town for a couple of days. She had a friend over from the U.S. visiting and I'd agreed to take them to the Great Wall as part of my trip as, quite strangely, Lyn had never been there. She had been given the tour leading job after training, then had been sent down to do Vietnam trips, just like Philip and Steven had, so had never actually been to the wall. On her next trip she would have to take passengers there, so I agreed to help out and told the group that her friend was another trainee. This time of the year was also Mid-Autumn Festival and we went to the Hou Hai Lake for a beer and watched the local people lighting lanterns and letting them fly off into the Beijing night.

27. Music Fills the Night-time, 02-03/08/07 (Xi'an Haida Hotel)

Music fills the night-time
Coming up from the apartment blocks below
Revelers, still full of music
Turn on their radio
Hot Summer nights, the best time
To hang out by the window
The feeling takes hold, the bottle I neck
Then back into the night I go

Conversations swirl with another tunes beat
As the radio waves catch hold
And cut music through the night air heat
Another story to be told
The city-serenade
To the background of the radio

And the traffic and the street pulse begin to fade
Til we're all just part of the world below the window

Here comes that song again, rising through the air
And a ghost walks through me and there's magic everywhere

How this year has gone so fast
And spun me like a prayer wheel across the world
Those songs, floods of memories from my past
A special moment, a special girl
All left behind, well, nothing is lost
And in its time, time for something new
So I walk the city as music fills the night-time
A creature of the night, with a whole night of nothing to do

28. Lanterns over Hou Hai 08/09/07 (Hostel, Beijing)

Will you watch the lanterns fly away
With me across Hou Hai lake
Before you go?
Each one a small burning soul, see it fly
Journeying on into the starry sky
Like the people I know
Here I am at this journeys end, watching those journey on
Those lights that bring a smile to my face are too soon gone

29. Lead On 18/09/07 (Bell Tower Hostel Bar, Xi'an)

The kick of a drum
A familiar guitar tune
To start another night-time
In another hostel bar room
Another group of expectations
That I can never exceed
Or provide the dream or solve the problem
All I do is lead

And I've got to do it my way
And be true to who I am
I'll show you some painful truths
And expose another sham

And if this isn't what you wanted
Well, it's as real as it's going to be
If you thought it was sugar coated
Well, it's much more bitter sweet

Another bottle of beer
Another time to contemplate
To re-group, to re-assess
Plan the time line to a future date
Whilst still trying to live every second
Cram it in, immerse myself
To become part of this land
To distill its chemicals

To re-interpret with reference points
To re-package in bite-sized chunks
Three thousand years, the third largest country
With all the contradictions of history
And religions with too many deities
The environment, traditions and nationalities
Trying to understand where it all comes from
What's happening, where it's going. Lead on...

So the sun goes down, but never on me
As long as there is electricity
And the drum beat kicks in again
New beers and new friends
Taken to another country in Xi'an
The dance begins and we all move on
Snatched away in the swirling anthem
And I'm left kicking to the beat of a drum

I was hovering around the hostel again a few days into my trip
when the leader who'd lost/regained/blow job'd his way into
history turned up. He related me the story, about getting drunk
in a village, crashing a bike into a rice paddy and his phone
no-longer working because it was all muddy. He'd got the call
from head office in Australia a week later (we thought he'd had

an interview in H.K.) where the manageress had "sacked him off", not "sucked him off". These Australian accents just don't translate too well. Now he is bothered about the story getting back to the office, because that will surely be the end of him.

This story was only out-done by another leader who had joined us. He'd been on a trip with a load of girls including a high powered U.S. female lawyer. At one point she'd mentioned to him that some of her female colleagues had been to S.E. Asia and tried "it" with a girl. He thought nothing more of it until the last night when the conversation came up again. As the story goes, he ended up taking her to a place he had heard of in Hong Kong where the two of them and a Filipino girl spent most of the night doing the things most only dreams about. China is a very surprising place.

I had a group of 7 for the first leg of the trip. A good mix. Only one older passenger, Jack, 51 from Yellowknife. "Where is that?" I hear you ask, well, it's in the Northwest Territories of Canada and 1000km from the nearest city. He'd brought his banjo with him and was travelling for a year. Over the next weeks he gave us an insight to life in Yellowknife and there is no way that you'd want to live there. There was a Kiwi couple, a little younger than me and technically "on honeymoon". The other four were younger singles. Two English lads, Pete and Pat, and two girls. One English called Natalie. One Irish called Sandra. Pat was so obviously gay when I first met him that I had to tell him that it was still technically illegal in China and that he had better take care of himself. Pete was a lad, in every sense of the word and had spent 15 months travelling Australia and around. There was the archetypal difficult English post gap year student, Natalie, who had to question my every move. I couldn't fathom out the last passenger yet, Irish girl Sandra, 28, decided to come to China and was going on to Nanjing with a group from her work to learn about acupuncture. She'd also booked on the Tiger Leaping Gorge trip, but didn't want to walk the gorge, interestingly. From the outset, Jack was happy to drink anywhere and was asking whether there was a possibility of having a jam session (these things just don't exist in China). The two lads wanted to go out clubbing, followed by English girl (Irish girl said that she didn't drink, and she was Irish.....?) Nevertheless; this had the makings of a good trip again.

After a too late night in the bar listening to the stories of the other leaders, we had a trip to the Wall. Maybe I'm getting a bit too blasé about this, but I seem to be still drunk every time I go there. Luckily, there was no long hike on that day (I'd read the trip notes; not so stupid to make the same mistake twice), just a 3 hour walk around at their own pace. The pace of the lads left me behind after less than 20 minutes, so I made a disgraceful retreat to a cafe and pretended to do some paperwork. We had a couple of beers in Hou Hai that night and got the first of Jacks great quotes. Pete was talking about spending a night in the cell in Australia after getting too drunk. Jack got involved saying that you wouldn't want to do that here. "You hear of all sorts of things going on in the cells, you wouldn't know whether to sleep on your front or back". There was a quiet moment before Pat said he was off to a club he'd heard about. These blokes were going to have to share a room.

Off to Zhongwei and the desert. I'd never been there and I'd told the group as much, but that didn't stop English girl Natalie asking about the weather and temperatures in the desert, how far away from the town it was if something went wrong, then out came the "Lonely Planet" and she was asking about caves and villages in the vicinity that I'd already told her I didn't have any knowledge of. Then she asked about changing the itinerary, which I also couldn't do and didn't want to do. In the end I was saying that if she wanted to do something in her free time, she should ask the guide. We got picked up at the station by our guide, which fielded most of the stupid questions that I couldn't answer about the place. At one point English girl, Natalie, asked so many questions that Irish girl said "will you ask him what colour the bus is next?" We checked into a hotel in the centre of the small town and it was obvious that the staff didn't see many foreigners as they gawped at us. We had a trip organised down the Yellow River in a goat skin raft on the first day. We took a bus on the worst road I've ever been on to get to the river, just a track between mounds of rock and sand. At one point we even had to get out in order to push another stranded vehicle out of the way. When we got to the Yellow River there were a dozen or so animal skins, blown up and a wooden frame put over them. Three people per raft and an oarsman and off we go. What a wonderful way to see the countryside, unless you're a goat.

That evening our guide showed us to the night market. This is really a 1 horse or rather 1 camel town. You could walk around it, if you really wanted to. There is a central roundabout with a small Ming dynasty tower in the middle of it and four new roads going off at the cardinal points. This is a typical Chinese town, with our hotel a supermarket and two other larger buildings on the central roundabout. Walk down any of the roads for twenty minutes and the street lights run out and the nice buildings become gray concrete hulks on broken roads. It's the sort of place where they have never seen white people. Going to the night market was quite an experience for both us and the Chinese. Finding something that my group would eat was the first challenge. Apart from the fact you're never quite sure what you're getting, it is all prepared in the sort of environment that you would only see on a health and safety video. It's all probably quite fine, but akin to Russian roulette for fragile Westerners' stomachs. We soon found out that the local beer was two Yuan or around 15p a bottle so had a good night and played pool on the outdoor pool tables. These were as even as a crazy golf course, but somehow we survived the local challengers. We also took a look around the rest of town and found a bar. Here, I showed the group how to play the drinking game, with the dice. The rest of the gang got the hang of it and literally, got into the spirit of thing. Jack was definitely in the spirit of things, he just didn't care if he won or lost and had a drink whatever the outcome. As he asked, "you need a game to drink?"

The desert trek saw us pass the remnants of the Great Wall in this area. Not at all the majestic stone fortress cum highway that sweeps across the hillsides to the East. Here, its' pilfered stone leaves it a shabby, sorry mound that divides one wheat field from its neighbour. We met the camels and their drivers, our guide keeping an eye on things and doing the translations. Getting on was an assault course in itself and we were perched astride the wide seats and blankets. It is not the most comfortable of positions, especially as the camel swayed off and you began to roll on your groin. 20 minutes into the camel ride, Irish girl Sandra was feeling uncomfortable and asked if she could get off and walk. The answer was a swift "no" as there was no way that a human on foot could keep up with a camel across the sand. I reckoned we were going to have a problem. The day trip was a six hours of a zig zag route. The desert, evidently, is not that big and on the crest of the larger sand dunes you can see the two concrete factories that dominate either end of the sand. If the concrete factories get their way, there will be more concrete and less desert over the coming years. There is also a project to re-introduce plants into the desert, from which they want to move towards re-establishing fields. According to the history books, a few hundred years ago, this was a fertile region and the desert is a manmade result of over farming. A lunch stop and more zig zags later, we made camp. Our guide had a sled and we could slide down the sand dunes on it. I went completely out of control and ploughed through some shrubs. The Camel drivers were sent back to get more supplies. It seems we were only an hour or so from town. We had to erect our tents and go and find fire wood. The desert is a fragile ecological environment and we can only collect dead wood to burn. We can only go to the toilet in a self-dug pit in the sand, which you then cover whilst the toilet paper has to be burned. I left my small smoking pile and we watched the sunset over the sand-dunes.

The food and beer arrived and all was going well, when I looked around to see the Irish girl Sandra desperately trying to get out of a drinking competition with one of the Camel Drivers.

Unfortunately for her, she'd already consumed half a bottle or rice wine and this stuff is poison for hardened drinkers, let alone the tea total. I gallantly stepped in and she wandered off. An hour later, she was vomiting like no-one has ever vomited before. We used a large proportion of the deserts sand to cover everything that was coming out. Everything did come out. Otherwise we would be looking at some sort of make-shift stomach pump and "camel-vac" to the nearest town.

The following morning, we took the short route back to the road and on to the Town. We spent the afternoon looking at the only other place of interest in Zhongwei, a Taoist Temple. This decorative building of wooden courtyards and pagoda style buildings had a depiction of hell in the catacombs beneath the temple. It was not unlike the Feng Du "Ghost City" on the Yangtze River and both corny and gruesome at the same time. We then had an overnight train to more familiar territory. Next stop, Xi'an, where I've visited nine times previously, then Chengdu.

In Xi'an, we met Philip and after a few drinks out came the musical instruments and we had a banjo/ukulele jamming session in the Bell Tower Hostels. I had not expected to pull off that request. The following day, the Irish girl lost her camera at the Terracotta Warriors. This was one of those moments that I dread, as there is little that I can do and she was a bit of an artist and photographer. She thinks that she left it at the post office counter at the Terracotta Warriors Museum whilst she was posting cards. The local guide rang up, but there was no sign of it. Expensive cameras won't go into the lost property box in China. The local guide said that if we wanted to file a police report then we should go to the police station at the Muslim quarter. Only there would the Chinese police allow a foreigner to say that they had something stolen off them in Xi'an. This doesn't help the Muslim minority at all, giving yet more statistical evidence for the Chinese to treat the Hui minority badly. Anywhere else, and the camera is simply "lost" and nothing can be done about it. The Irish girl needed a police report for the insurance claim. We walked to the police station, which deals with foreigners, but it was closed and we were leaving the following morning for Chengdu. I contacted Chicory, thinking that she might be able to help. If anyone could, she could.

I got a text from Janie a week ahead of me telling me that Tiger Leaping Gorge was closed due to a landslide, this could liven things up. I suppose the great expectation on a trip called Tiger Leaping Gorge is to go to Tiger Leaping Gorge (unless, you are the Irish girl). I decided to keep this one quiet for the time being. In Chengdu I left the group in the more than capable hands of Chicory. Jack had asked what we do in Chengdu. "You go to see the Pandas" said I. Jack looked at me for a while. "Let me get this right, I pay money to go to see a 'bear'? I don't rightly know if I want to do that". Nevertheless, he went. Whilst Chicory helped Irish girl fill in a police report and got Jack to a doctor for a rash as well as all the usual panda and temple stuff, I was being greeted by two fake pandas of my very own.

Amy had gotten in touch with me. She had wanted to go to Chengdu for some time to visit her cousin, who I had met on the boat a few trips earlier and also to go to Floraland. This was a theme park, just outside Chengdu and she asked me if I was interested in going. I had a free day on this Basic style trip, so of course I said yes and got Chicory to book Amy into the same hotel that we were staying at. Amy travelled the three hundred miles or so over from Chongqing to Chengdu. We met up with her cousin and all drove out to Floraland. There was a fake European town as part of the theme-park, which was quite surreal, especially as I was the only Westerner there and the locals probably thought I was part of the entertainment. There were lots of couples in wedding outfits getting their pictures taken. This is a custom in China, to dress up as bride and groom having pre wedding photos taken to put on invitations and to use as backdrops at the wedding ceremony. I got spun around on some rides and felt very sick afterwards. Amy loved it all and we walked through the gardens and fake fairytale castle. All in all a very surreal but wonderful afternoon. This ended with a drive back to Chengdu, Amy's cousin almost falling asleep at the wheel and Amy slapping his face and spraying him with water to keep him awake.

As the group travelled on, we chatted about our lives. Jack had some very interesting stories about life in Yellow Knife. The temperatures dropped to -40 in winter and people still talked about the Dr. Hook concert from 15 years earlier as the highlight of their lives. We asked what people did for entertainment. "Well" said Jack, "Sometimes we'd drive up to the city dump and watch the bears eat diapers. Man, those bears love eating that shit" (laughs). It was a whole different world. As we rode along in the train, looking out of the window we saw a group of workmen watching one of their fellow colleagues swimming naked in a pool. "What are they doing?" Natalie asked, yet another stupid question, but before I could reply "swimming, it's hot" or something equally obvious that it makes the questioner look stupid, Jack said "maybe he's a retard". I think I laughed at that one for the next hour or so.

Next stop was Kunming and the Camellia Hotel. I like this place, a large colonial style building, high ceiling and glass roof with the piano playing. It is somewhat familiar with its decent buffet breakfast and Englishman abroad opulence. The local operator there, Pauline, is one of the most welcoming and friendly people I've met, always on the ball, always happy to help. For me it was a day of paperwork at the end of one trip before having a group meeting to introduce my 5 new passengers to the 6 that were continuing from my last trip. Pat had one last night out with Pete, both of whom got further than they had done previously with the local girls. It turns out that Pat just wasn't going to get a bloke, so decided to have the next best thing. Pete met a girl who took him to the toilets, not a common thing in China and as he was without condoms, did the sensible thing and took the blow job and phone number option.

In the morning we were off to Li Jiang. Pauline had organised baggage carts to transfer luggage to the hotel and also show me the way there. If you remember, I spent over an hour getting lost in Li Jiang last time I was here with Andrea and didn't want to make the same fool of myself with 11 passengers. I'd organised the guides for Tiger Leaping Gorge and Bruce, who was now working in the Office had given me an outline of what research he wanted me to do. This was going to encroach on my much needed break, but you just can't turn these things down. Esmeray had also had her trip changed so meeting up with her on time off had just been blown out of the water. We got to the hotel before the sun went down and I did a quick run around with the group, showing what little I knew of the place and explaining that there was "no local guide" because they are on a "basic style trip", then left them to their own devices. I feel a bit sorry for them every time I have to do this, they mostly cope, but my feedback suffers and they just don't have the experience that they could have. Li Jiang is a fantastic place to explore and get lost in anyway, so I think they had a good time. The winding cobbled streets and wooden houses are very quaint. It's a pity that the Old Town is actually not so old anymore. The local government is actually building new, "old houses" and expanding the original Old Town for tourism. Still, how are my passengers to know that it is largely fake and it's all very pretty anyway. If you want to see the sites, you have to purchase an "Old Town Preservation Ticket". This gets you in free to some temples and sites, others still require a charge. My travel company includes the ticket price and at Y180 it's a fair deal on a basic style trip. They had maps and organised their route through town, to the Black Dragon Pool and the temples on the hills.

My free day was spent trying to find contacts for bike tours around Li Jiang. I was more or less sorted in the first hour, because, there was a place I'd been to last time. Being lost in a town does have its advantages. They had more or less what I needed, but when I mentioned staying with local people in their houses they thought I was joking. When I mentioned cycling over the mountain to TLG they shook their heads, smiling. "No guide will take you", they said. "Some Westerners do this, but we take a taxi", smart cookies these Chinese. As I have said earlier, I may be the most unfit leader working in China. Now I was being asked to ride over a mountain that only the crazy and athletes in training would consider. Did Bruce in the Office have it in for me? I spent the rest of the day wandering around Li Jiang trying to improve upon this tour, but as most Tourist Information places spoke less English than I did Chinese, and none understood the concept of "homestay" or "bicycle ride into the mountains", I gave up. It was very odd walking around this town again. All my memories of the place were also of my time with Andrea. Then, I found an English Pub called Frosty Morning, run by a Yorkshire man. This place had a real village atmosphere where ex-pats of all Western persuasions and their Chinese wives came to gossip and exchange news. I returned there with Pete and Jack later that evening before heading out to the Chinese bars, once again full of the drunken groups chanting and singing at each other across the Jade Dragon Stream. This really is a fun town. I was quite looking forward to coming back here again on the research... apart from the bike ride.

So the next morning, I was a bit worse for wear, but thought I could sleep on the bus to TLG and everything would be fine. I texted my guides, Li and Richard to say what time we'd arrive and they replied with "We can't guide you today". This is not good. Firstly, I'm on a bus with all my passengers and can't let them know that I've been let down. Secondly, I need a guide, it says so in the notes as a health and safety consideration and the Gorge had only been open for 2 days since the last landslide. Thirdly, it was October holiday week, so my guides were probably doubling their money elsewhere and that also meant that I was going to struggle to get anyone else. I did the frantic text thing to everyone I knew. Bruce replied. With Cathy taking time off for maternity leave, Bruce had been elevated to the position of manager. Him replying was still a novelty, but had the same sort of response that I remember having from just about every other manager I've ever had. "Tell them that our travel company (c/w London Met, Guildhall, ULU,) will never use them again." Well that really got me out of a hole (not). In the end I had to call Margo. "I've been let down by my guides, can you help?" There was a sharp intake of breath from the back of the bus and as I went through the to and fro of conversation with Margo, I could hear the sounds of mutiny from the seats behind me

Margo is a bit of a star. By the time we'd got to the Gorge, she'd organised two guides. These happened to be a couple of local farmers who spoke no English, but at least they met with the regulations. Margo fed us, arranged for our bags to be transported to the Tibet Guest House, which was our hostel at the end of the hike and gave us a pep talk about the Gorge. She then rang the bus driver for our pick up in two days' time. All this was done with a running commentary of how bad Li and Richard were, how the locals would try to rip us off, and then running in and out of the cafe each time a Westerner walked past. I'm convinced she's been smoking too much of the local herb at high altitude. Before we set off, I nominated Pete to walk at the front with the guides and wrote down some instructions in Chinese for him. We would be in Mobile contact if anything happened. Then we were off. I really struggled for the first hour, hangover and lack of sleep were taking their toll and a couple of the group seemed to think that it was some sort of challenge to set off at a quick pace. I knew that they all couldn't keep it up for long, but how long? The Irish girl dropped to the back quite soon and then a couple of the others making the 32 bends a little easier as they all stopped for rest. Well, at least Sandra was actually climbing the gorge, a triumph in itself.

We stopped for refreshment at the Naxi Guest House and took photos of us standing next to the biggest marijuana bush I've seen outside of the Amsterdam Hash Museum. This stuff grows freely here. We checked in for the night at Tea Horse Guest House and got a fantastic dinner and breakfast the following morning. The trek was easier than the last time I'd done it, less pressure of time I suppose and before long we were at the Tibet Guest House and another fantastic evening meal. We thanked our guides, taking photos with them and they were so happy to have been involved with our trek. Then we got straight into the beer. By this point, Pete was trying to avoid Natalie. She'd had some designs on him and thought they were going to hook up. He'd sort of gone for it earlier on in the trip, but now regretted it and was giving her the cold shoulder, so we spent time hanging out with the guest house owners. The T.V. programme they were watching was, predictably, about the Second World War and was deamonising the Japanese. I asked the Guest House owners what they thought of it, they hated the Japanese. My poor translation got the gist that, although the government say that they are cousins, we cannot forgive them. The next morning we were on our way again in mini-vans, dodging the landslides to Qiaotou. Mr. Jiangs bus picked us up here and it was a 2 hour drive to the town of Zhongdian, also now called "Shangri-la".

Shangri-la as it is now called is becoming a big tourist destination. It has adopted this mythical name, owing to a book and film about a plane crash in the 1930's which left some Westerners stranded in what they saw as a paradise. Nobody was quite sure where this place was, so the Chinese, always on a look-out for a business opportunity, decided that Shangri-La was not in Tibet, Burma, Bhutan or Nepal as most people had thought, but actually in Yunnan Province China. The town is an ethnic Tibetan village and there are other minority people in the area, but "Shangri-La" the "paradise that will come with the future Buddha?" is a bit farfetched. Especially now that they've started building more and more hotels in mock traditional style all over the town. It's the British equivalent of stone cladding on semi-detached housing, but the Chinese just can't see that and if it works in Li Jiang, it will work in Zhongdian.

I'd been contacted by Eleanor, who was an ex leader and was now working in a charitable school in Zhongdian. She said that she could put together an itinerary with a visit to the school and a local village and farm. More importantly, she would meet me at the bus stop in a city that I've never been to before and get me to the hotel. Priceless when you are leading 11 people by guesswork. She was great. We walked through the Old Town with its wooden houses and cobbled streets, very much like a smaller version of Li Jiang. She told the group where to eat and what to do, then scouted the town with me to find better hotels. I'd been asked to do this by Bruce in the office and Eleanor simply did the work for me. We had also asked about treks in the area, off to the Tibetan villages and temples that surrounded the town. As we explained what we wanted to do, (stay in a local persons house, trek over the hills from village to village) we would get the same puzzled look, then someone would tell us to catch the bus. If we persisted, or tried a different angle on the "trek", we would be told again that there was a new road and a public bus running on it. The villagers had been waiting for decades for this service and it was much better than walking. They just couldn't comprehend what we wanted to do.

Zhongdian looks like Li Jiang would have looked 20 years ago. Winding cobbled streets and wooden houses. It is a very beautiful place. A place to get lost in and I enjoyed the search for new hotels as it gave me a real chance to see some of the Old Town. That evening, we did the tour to the village where the school was, which was exactly what we wanted. Rural life as it has been for centuries. Five meter high wooden racks drying mushrooms. Chickens and cattle running around, people waving as we walked by. We walked out into the fields and fed the yaks from a bucket of salt. Their long tongues smothering our hands. We ate food at a herdsman's' hut, which was no more than a tent on the dirt ground with the room filling with smoke from the dried yak dung fire. It didn't smell anything like as bad as it should have. The school was another experience where we played ping pong and got introduced to the 40 or so 15 - 20 year olds who were studying there. A real first time meeting of 2 peoples for most of us. We were sad to leave. One of Eleanor's colleagues was having a birthday in town, so we went to the Raven Pub. This was a Western style "tavern" for want of a better word, with the converted Tibetan house looking quite the part with the wood and drapes. Drink flowed and the music got quite good so most of us were up dancing. Most of us were still there at 2am, but then slowly drifted off leaving me and the Irish girl. She was actually drinking and didn't seem to mind at all when we both went crashing to the floor at the end of "Come on Eileen" when I tried the "spinning round dance" on her. Well, at least there was one customer enjoying herself I thought, but what a change there had been in her in only three weeks.

We don't spend very long in Zhongdian and were off at mid-day the following day on a seven hour journey to Dali. There was a scary moment when a tire blew. We had to stop to change that and this was impressively done in just over half an hour. However, we were a little late into Dali when Mr. River met us and went through some activities that we could do the following day. All passengers felt too tired and just wanted to eat, so we went off to Georges' Bamboo cafe. Coming here for just 1 day the previous month had made all this so much easier. Most of us stayed out till around 11pm in the Westernised cafe/bar streets of the Old Town centre. Most people prefer Dali to the other 2 places on this trip, but I don't. If anything, there is less character in the houses and although Li Jiang smacks of commercialism, well, so does Dali. I had an easy day the following day and did some catching up. That night we went down to the Dragonfly Bar. This was a group discovery where some western hippies had set up a teepee in a courtyard near the lake (did I mention that marijuana grows freely here?) There wasn't much happening, but Jack brought his banjo and had a jam session. We returned to Dali and had a good night which ended up with us singing songs with the locals in the street until 2am. The Irish girl was one of the last ones again and when we got back to the hotel she was concerned about waking her roommate up, so I let her crash out with me. I didn't think much more about it at the time. I made a bit of a move on her in the morning, but only because I thought I was expected to and I never expected a response.

We were back in Kunming the following afternoon and did the final night dinner. A few people stayed on for a couple of days including Jack, the Irish girl and Pete. He was in hot pursuit of another Chinese girl after the one he'd arranged to meet didn't quite measure up. "It gets a bit boring after a while cos all she knows is 'yes' and 'I love you' and we just drink and play the dice game". She'd also developed some huge zit on her lips. Pete reckoned he wasn't the only bloke she'd taken to the toilets. Things also got very interesting for me too. On the last night, we'd all been drinking then went back to my room and were saying our goodbyes. The Irish girl found herself the last person in my room, and we chatted on the bed. One thing leads to another and then we were in the bed. I had not been expecting this at all or, as she started to remove clothes. She said "I've never done this before" and I think that as she seems to be a nice girl, she probably hasn't done the one night stand thing or jumped into bed with someone she hardly knows. Then, as things progress, it actually becomes apparent that she hasn't done anything like this at all....ever. She was a virgin. I was pretty blown away by the whole thing. It certainly wasn't what I was expecting. Especially when she said "I wonder what my mother would think..?" Then called me a "dirty English Prod".

She left the following morning and it was back to work as usual. I now had my paperwork to do and research a bike ride in Li Jiang. I also booked my train ticket to Guilin. I was definitely going to have some time off, even if it was only 3 days. Back in Li Jiang I had an evening in the Frosty Morning and was a bit useless when I got up for the bike ride that I had arranged earlier. I could give you a blow by blow account of how hard it was cycling up a mountain, but why give myself even more pain? I found a couple of places on route, some of the temples we visited, the village were Dr. He lived and the views overlooking the valley were all pretty amazing for a day out but nothing perfect for the homestay. I couldn't do much more. I was absolutely knackered.

30. You said I was a Chancer 04/10/07 (Camellia, Kunming)

You said I was a chancer
So why did you take a chance with me?
As I held your head in the desert
You didn't seem so pretty
You were just another passenger
Nothing special, not what I could see
How could I ever have guessed
That precious thing that you'd give to me

I've just been blown away by you
Something I never expected to do
A thing I thought had passed me by
Twenty years ago, something I'd never try

Now I just wish we had a little longer
But we both have our own roads to take
And that significant moment in life
Becomes one of ten things in your diary that day
But I can never forget you
And that precious thing you gave
So I am putting my pen to paper now
And a poem for you, I dedicate

31. Strange Synchronicity 07/10/07 (Bus Li Jiang to Kunming)

This strange synchronicity
As I'm walking through a memory
The gods that play look down on me
And place me where I'm going to be
Back where I walked once before
Never thinking I'd be back once more
Flung back through the revolving door
Alone this time, the memory pricks are sore

"Oh, do you remember" I'd like to say
Of the things we saw when we passed this way
What we did, on what day
Getting lost in Li Jiang, getting lost in yesterday
But I am alone with all my thoughts
Looking at emails and texts I've wrote
That haven't been replied to, so I sit and dote
On the strange synchronicity that has left me distraught

Another message sent out on the ether
Wondering if, or when I'll see her
A half-baked day-dream, needing synchronicity
To move time and space to bring her to me.

So, back to Kunming for a night and then the train to Guilin and the bus to Yangshuo. I've done this so many times with a group now that it's becoming second nature. Bar 98 was closed on arrival but I checked in to Monkey Jane's and found Steven in Kelly's bar. Philip arrived soon after. We started early and finished late as usual. I got a text from Pete, from the trip that I had just finished, saying that he was back in China pursuing yet another girl. I picked him up from the station the following morning and bumped into Pierre. He is always good value. I then found out that Zef was also going to be in town. And of course, Esmeray arrived. I can honestly say that the next couple of days were a blur. It was coming to the end of the season and this was probably the last time I would be with a group of friends again like this. These people have become my friends and Yangshuo is now like a second home. It's difficult to pay for a beer at Snows bar 98 or at Monkey Jane's. I bump into people I know walking down the street. I can eat cheesecake every day if I want to. As much as I still consider London to be the place I will return too, well, for the time being, I am loving my time over here and Moo and Lindsay can keep the home fires burning, as long as they don't get too out of control.

Chapter 8

SEASONS END

It is not the strongest of the species that survive, nor the most intelligent, but the one most responsive to change.

Charles Darwin (1809-1882) English Naturalist

"Hi, my name is Mark and I'm going to be your tour leader for the next 21 days. I've been working for this tour company in China now for seven months and this is my sixth Essence of China trip, so I've been to all the places on this trip at least seven times. First of all, I should tell you a little bit about the company and the style of trip and what you should expect to experience over the next three weeks. Has anybody traveled with this travel company before? (Silence). Ok. Well, we are a company formed around twenty years ago by some Australians who loved travel, but wanted to have a way of backpacking, but with all the hassle taken out. We also have a commitment to responsible travel, so this means we take local transport, stay in locally owned guest houses and hotels and we try to travel the way that the local people travel. We eat in local restaurants, I will introduce you to real Chinese food and we will try to limit our impact on the environment as we travel through the country. We also support some charities and will be visiting one on day two. First of all, let me tell you about transport. We take overnight trains, and they are a good standard. There will be a dining car on them, but don't expect to be served if you turn up there. The dining car only served at specific meal times and if we all turn up at once, the staff will not want to cope with all us foreigners and will refuse to serve us. It's better to take snacks and there is constant hot water for drinks and noodles. We also take a couple of public busses on this trip. Don't be surprised with the constant beeping of horns and the erratic driving, triple overtaking on mountain passes and all the passengers smoking. Don't be surprised if we have livestock on the public bus, don't be surprised when half of the Chinese start throwing up, they get travel sick very easily. Accommodation is also of a good standard, similar to this hotel, though when we get to Emei Shan, we will stay in a monastery, and this is by its very nature a little more basic. The toilet and communal showers there are quite an experience. The hotels may have someone on the front desk who speaks English, but many do not and the service standard, although improving, may not be what you're used to. Please remember, in the rural areas, these people were farmers up until recently and may never have seen a Westerner, western food, western toilet or western expectations until a couple of months ago. On the Yangtze River boat, we travel in the best cabins, but they are Chinese tourist boats and often not up to our expectations. I will be on hand to help, but in many cases, we will not be able to alter what is normal for the Chinese. In some hotels you will get phone calls, these are from girls asking if you want a "massage", so just leave the phone off the hook if this happens.

Food is very different to the Chinese food that you eat in our own countries', we will have our first group dinner tonight where we will all share and split the bill. If there is 12 of us, I'll order around that number of dishes, so if you don't like one or two, there is still another ten to choose from. Vegetarians are not catered for in China, I was one once, but on arriving here, I had to return to eating meat. Often, if I ask for a vegetarian dish, it will still arrive with meat on it. To serve someone only vegetables is seen as an insult, as it is peasants food. If you get the runs, it is not food poisoning, it is just the way your body is coping with the new food. Chinese food is cooked at very high temperatures, so there is little chance that you will get poisoned. However, there is something that we call "travelers' diarrhea", which is 24 to 48 hours of diarrhea and vomiting. Nobody knows where it comes from; it is just some peoples' reaction to the food and the environment of being in a foreign country. There is little we can do, but rest and take lots of fluids. Remember, animals have bones in them, they have heads and feet so don't be surprised when they turn up on your plate. The dishes I order for you will be the ones that you can eat, whilst there are a lot of dishes that would just be wasted if I ordered them. When I order, we will expect to pay less than 30 Yuan per person per meal, if you want to find Western food, it can be difficult, it won't necessarily taste like you would expect back home and it will be a lot more expensive than what the locals eat.

My role as a tour leader is as your first point of contact with the tour company. I get you from A to B, I book the hotels and the transport and I'll give you some background information. In all the places that we visit, I will give you an orientation walk, to show you where the ATM, laundry, internet, supermarket and best places to go, but this cannot be guided tour. I am not a local guide and I don't have a local guiding license. My knowledge of China, its history, politics and social aspects is pretty good, but what I can't tell you is the name of every plant we come across, every river we cross or the height of every hill we see. I will usually ask if you want to come to dinner in the evening, I can show you the best local places in each area we visit and I can give you the details of where to go and what to do, but I will not be with you all of the time. I can't go everywhere with everybody, even if I had the time and the money to do so. On our trip, we will have local guides in almost every place that we visit, they are the local experts with the local knowledge so please ask them questions, but also remember that they may know nothing about the customs or practices in the other parts of China and will have little knowledge of the rest of the world. China is the size of Western Europe, so, just as you wouldn't expect a Norwegian to know about Romania, you wouldn't expect one Chinese person from Beijing to know anything about farming around Yunnan. At the end of a guided tour, I will pass around an envelope for tips. I know that most of us being British and Australian are not from big tipping countries, but it has become part of the norm in the travel industry. You don't tip anywhere else, but for your guide, if you can have about Y10 per day per person, this will be a reasonable tip. It is better if you are generous, but please don't put in coins, or small tatty notes, these are seen as an insult and I can get guides asking me what they did wrong.

In China, there are a lot of cultural differences; the first surprise for many of you is the squat toilet and the lack of toilet paper. You carry your own and put it in the bin provided. Chinese people will often stare at you, it is not rude, it is just that they haven't seen a Westerner close up before. If they want to take your photograph, just go along with it, they are not all perverts with ulterior motives. You will have to get used to the spitting, the smoking, the throat clearing, especially in the mornings. If two Chinese are in a room and want to have a conversation, it is much more likely that they will yell at each other from the opposite ends of the room, rather than come together for a quiet conversation. Chinese people are loud and have no concept of personal space, they will sit close to you on the public transport and push past you in the supermarket and the train station, once again, this is not rude, it is normal. Chinese people don't queue. Don't be surprised, if, when you go to the bank, people will jump the queue. Don't be surprised that if you get to the counter, as you are handing over your dollars, a man will walk up, talk to the cashier, whilst smoking a cigarette and push his money under the counter as well. When you take all this into account, you will find it easy to get angry, but getting angry and causing a scene in China gets you nowhere. If the train is stopped on the line for an hour, if the hotel staff can't fix your toilet, if the food you have ordered turns out to be something quite different from what you expected, you have to just roll with it. Service standards here are not the same as back home. A problem is only a problem because you perceive it to be one, the Chinese are too busy getting on with their lives for them to worry about it and if the food was ok for the last 100,000 people, then why should you want anything different? Please remember, we are in somebody else's country, we are the ones that are foreign to every situation. We are the ones that are "different" and respect the people as you find them.

There are three rules, that if you break them, I will have to take you off the trip. No drugs, no prostitution and no violence, that is physical or verbal. We all have to get along together for the next three weeks, some people will be faster, some slower, some will want to stay up late and others will want to get up early. Please be considerate to one another. If things aren't going your way, well, that is part of the experience of Adventure

Travel. Write another page in your diary about this completely "different" country. We are very privileged to be able to come to China. It is a once in a lifetime experience and it is something that you will look back on again and again for the rest of your life. We are going to have one amazing trip. Ok, so we have dinner booked for eight o'clock, does anyone not want to come and has anyone got any questions?"

The group looked at me, I looked at the group. This was not what most of them had expected.

After the back to back trips, the research, Yangshuo and all the rest of the crazy things over the last couple of month, it was really hard to get enthusiastic about my next trip. It was an Essence of China (Southbound) again and I had a full group of 12. They looked on paper like a difficult group again. Three English girls travelling together. Two young English couples, two single female thirty something's, an older Aussie couple and a German, Berti in his 40's. All I would need is a Yank for a full set. Things weren't helped by the Harmony Hotel not having enough rooms. This is becoming a bit of a regular thing and I was racing between the Youth Hostel and the Hotel trying to sort things out when the first un-accommodated passengers arrived. It's difficult enough getting rooms at short notice, but trying to explain to the receptionist at the Hostel, that I wasn't paying but another hotel will foot the bill just makes things worse. However, the upshot was that the passengers all got de-lux rooms in the hostel and a breakfast thrown in by the hotel. I just got off to a bad start. We had the Group meeting, as I just outlined. With a group like this I had to set everything out from the start, but we didn't even start on time. The last English couple being half an hour late for the group meeting (though some of the others weren't much better). The Aussies never even made it. They were still somewhere in the skies above China.

As usual, somebody had asked me about Travellers Checks, which they had discovered they could not change as almost no-body had seen them before. Others asked why they had to bring U.S. dollars, as they couldn't spend them either. Somebody asked if I spoke Chinese, they always do, somebody asked what the weather would be like in Hong Kong in three weeks' time.

The youngest British couple Joe and Jane were completely out of their depth and the culture shock was evident for the first few days. They were doing a round the world trip, with the first stop being China. Not the easiest introduction for teenagers who had not been further than a holiday visiting relatives in Italy. The three English girls fared no better. However, unlike the younger Brits, they saw everything that was different as something that was not to their liking. They had brought suitcases full of beach clothes and high heels and were also late for our first early morning departure as they straightened their hair and got themselves ready. They looked like they were off to a top nightclub, when we were actually going on a ten kilometer hike along the Great Wall. The English couple in their 20's; Dave and Diane were going with the flow a lot more, they were pretty "chilled out". As they were coming to the end of their year travelling, it was easier for them to cope, but it was still a surprise to them that nobody spoke English and that there was no English food. From day one, there were the questions from the whole group of where to get "normal" food and whether they would like what I was ordering for them.

Our visit to Tian An Men Square and the Forbidden City was heavily punctuated as our guide; Kevin would stop to inform the group. They would then run off in every direction, cameras in hand, clicking away until they came to their senses and realise that Kevin and I were not with them. I have never understood why, group after group will do this, taking pictures of things when they have no idea what it is, before coming back and asking random questions rather than first listening to an explanation. As we stood outside Chairman Mao's' Mausoleum, across from the Tian An Men Gate, one of the girls asked "So the dead guy in the tomb is the one on the big picture?" Only once had I heard of a more ill-informed comment. In our company newsletter, there was a section of "the best passengers' quotes". The one

I was thinking about was "So this guy is called Mao? And his first name is Chairman?" We exited the square and had to keep calling out to the wandering ducklings as they were determined to get lost in the crowds. We stopped at the high stone column, with "Hoa" on the top. This is a mythical beast that was the eyes and ears of the Chinese Emperor, who naturally, had supernatural powers and beasts to help him. I told the group that it was a little like a modern day CCTV. It kept the Emperor informed of what was happening outside the palace whilst he was in residence. There was a similar stone pillar, also carved with dragons and topped with "Hoa" inside the Tian An Men Gate, to keep the Emperor informed whilst he was outside the Palace. We crossed one of the five stone bridges, to the Tan An Men Gate, under the watchful eye of Chairman Mao. Kevin told us that he did actually watch; that he was painted in such a way that he always looked like he was watching you, wherever you stood. It was a large crowd and we were not the only ones taking photos as we walked under Mao, with the military, lined on every side, ushering us along and telling us not to stand still. We lost some of the group and were hanging on whilst the English couple, Dave and Diane caught up. Kevin was good; he had seen it all before and took it in his stride. He would wait for them to run around like headless chickens, then have to repeat the information three or four times as half of the group was invariably not listening to him the first time. Much of the Forbidden City was now under wraps, as it was being spruced up for the Beijing Olympics. This seemed to be more about putting gaudy acrylic paint on the ancient weathered timbers rather than a professional re-construction. There were complaints that so much of the Palace was under dust-cloths, but this was eased when they spied the Starbucks Café, in the courtyard behind the Palace of Supreme Harmony. I think this is a travesty and I know that there is a petition to get the coffee shop removed from the largest ancient imperial palace in the world. Dave and Diane were oblivious of the rest of the groups annoyance with their constant lateness, though the three English girls saw this as a green light to always be "fashionably late" whilst they were getting ready. This continued for the next three weeks. They were infuriating dawdlers. At the same time, I had a good few conversations with them.

One of the first things they talked about was "Eco-tours" as they had been on a couple in South America and though that getting out into the countryside was a good thing. But the more they talked about them, the less eco-friendly I thought they were. There was a lot visiting wildlife projects that sounded more like safari parks or even zoos and a lot of holding monkeys and places like the "Tiger Temple" in Thailand. To me it was obvious that the tigers had been drugged, so that you could stroke them, rather than them being happy in the presence of the chanting Buddhist monks (and baying tourists). I said that just because something said it was "Eco-tours" didn't mean that it actually had anything to do with the things that the company that I worked for talked about. We had a commitment to "Responsible Travel". Eco-tourism was "spin" and a selling point and if you dug around a bit you would find that it was more about making money than caring for the environment. I said that the company that I worked for were not perfect, but the company and its employers were serious about these values and I could see that we supported genuine causes and avoided the money making tourist traps that only paid lip service to "Eco-tourism".

After travelling to Central and South America, they kept wanting to make comparisons. One of the first was asking about Communism. They had been impressed with Cuba's' stance and the education and health system, but there was visible poverty and little to buy in the shops that a Westerner would want. China was not like this, with all the department stores and wealthy people in Beijing. So I started to talk about Communism and tried to dispel a few myths and misconceptions. As Westerners, all we had heard about was totalitarian regimes and poverty, it was all part of the Cold War propaganda. It became obvious to Dave and Diane that there was more to communism than what they had been taught, or what they had figured out on their travels. So, I had to start at the beginning. The very beginning of what Communism was supposed to be about. Before the Cold War, before Castro, who initially talked about a "Green Revolution" rather than a "Red, Communist" one, as he only took the final steps to Communism when he realised that he needed backers in the shape of Russian money and arms. Back before the time of Mao and his Long March of peasants fighting against Japanese occupation. Before the Chinese Civil War against the "Nationalists" who were in the pockets of the Western Powers. Before the time when Stalin, in Russia, centralised all power and used the state mechanism as his own personal tool rather than it being a tool of the working classes. I quoted Marx, as best I could from the Communist Manifesto. "Communism is the ownership of the means of production and distribution in the hands of the Proletariat" I developed that, saying that everything that was produced, by factories, or any other workplace, including farms and offices, should be decided upon by the people producing it, rather than it being produced solely for profit. I said that everything from "who gets what" to environmental factors should be taken into consideration when this happens. Next, I tried to quote Lenin. "All power to the Soviets". I explained that the Soviets, were Workers Councils, elected from each workplace and it was their job to determine what was produced, when, how and who it went to. The couple could see that this was not the Communism that they has seen, anywhere and I said that it was a Communism that had only existed for short periods of time before Capitalist nations pressured these infant communes to change and become the monsters that we saw today.

Our regular trip to Beijing Huiling had improved massively on my first visits as Cassie was now in charge. There was a lot more organisation and professionalism. There was a programme of activities and introductions and explanations. It was obvious that the disabled trainees were enjoying their time there too and in some large part, this was due to the involvement of Mr. Wang. He acted as a one man orchestra and had the trainees singing songs and doing dance routines. The small performances were funny because they were meant to be funny and this group had a far better experience than the first groups. However, the hutong tour had been dropped from the day as too many people had complained about the rickshaw pullers trying to extort money from them. I had run into my Hutong tour guide, Emma and she was trying to supplement her income by guiding the Beijing tourist sights. I told her that I would try and use her on my trips.

It was an odd sort of trip, I don't think most of the younger ones knew what to expect. The first couple of days were more like watching the "Big Brother" house as they all jockeyed for position, telling stories of home towns and going to Uni. Of best friends and things that they had done at home that no one gave a damn about. Then talking about the latest developments in Eastenders, then on to talking about what food they missed from home. They were not really having a cultural experience. They would take the occasional photograph from the moving bus, not knowing what they were photographing. Then they played game after card game of "shit head". The ones that really got the most out of the trip were the Aussie couple in their 50's and Berti, the German. They tried everything and asked all the right questions about history, politics and Chinese society. You could see that all this went way over the heads of the rest of the group. For a lot of the time I had to constantly repeat myself that "we are in China" because some of the questions and face pulling disappointment was really unnecessary if anyone had actually read anything about the country they were visiting. 10 days in I was still getting questions like "why can't they have normal toilets and why isn't there any toilet paper again?"

Esmeray made it to Xi'an on her comfort trip at the same time that we were there and we had a good night in the Bell Tower Hostel. Joe, my young British/Italian passenger was a decent guitar player and after a few beers I was singing House of the Rising Sun again, just like my last visit. I'll get a reputation. I also woke up in the five star Prince Hotel and had to sneak past Esmeray and her group in the lobby without them seeing me. I could be recognised as the boy she was with, two weeks earlier on in Yangshuo.

I had George as a guide in the Emei Mountain. For the first time, we were above the clouds and I took a photograph of it. We met Nathan up on the mountain too and George took me aside to tell me that Nathan was cheating the groups. Then he also told me that he suspected that Patrick was also cheating the groups. I mentioned Eugenie and he told me how much a strange and bad girl she was. I also ran into Ollie from the Adventure Co again at Hung Chung Ping Monastery and we had a few drinks at the Hard Wok Café with Betty and Harry, but the group just wasn't getting involved. The only group activity I could get them to do was all scream at once when they saw where they were supposed to shower at Hung Chung Ping Monastery. I have to admit that I got a perverse pleasure from all those English girls shaking in disbelief and screaming at the toilet block, music to my ears. They all came back after the communal shower, saying that there were some local women in there showering as well. They had stared at the westerners, showering in their swimming suits, which was odd enough, but were obviously commenting about the vast difference in the body shapes of the petite Chinese and the bigger, roly poly westerners.

Back in Emei town, I ate at Nathans newly opened restaurant enterprise, where he plied me with beer and told me how much George was cheating the groups. Such a small town mentality. He also told me how he didn't get on with his mother in law, who owned a restaurant on the main road, as she saw him as a competitor. Money was changing the social values and relationships in this small rural town. I could see the similarities with the rumour mill that was Yangshuo. Before we left the monastery, I was taking the advice of the signs and having a "civilized urination" when one of the elderly pilgrims came into the toilet. He was obviously a farmer and was a little confused with the splendor of the facilities. Most rural Chinese would not have anything more than a shed covering a hole and even in the towns a toilet door is such a novelty that people don't actually close the door when they are squatting down, often having a cigarette at the same time, regardless of who can see. This has always been one of the more disgusting things for my groups to experience as most toilets in public places will not have doors, and I suggest to the girls that they may want to take an umbrella with them. However, today it was my turn to experience something that I had not anticipated. The elderly man looked around at the urinals and seeing nothing else similar to a squat toilet, he dropped his trousers and started on a number two.

I met Amy in Chongqing. She was not going to guide us. Instead, we had her friend Tracy. There had been big changes with the way that the boat companies were operating out of Chongqing and Yichang. The companies now wanted the tour guides to hand over a Y1000 bond (around $200) in order to work. This was a very large amount for a guide to hand over and although the pay and tips could replace this in only a couple of trips, if things went bad, you could be working for months for nothing. Amy was one of many who didn't like the new regulation and many of the other guides just quit. Amy was still on the books, but had taken time off to take a translation course. What she had not told her boss, Mr. Qin, was that she was going to apply to the tour company that I was working for. Whilst I was there I gave her all the information that I could. Trip notes, accounts sheets, background company information. She also told me that she had finalised a deal on buying an apartment. I asked her where she had got the money from, but wouldn't tell me any more than she had called in a few debts and her mum was helping out a lot. It seemed to me like one heck of a risk. Then we were off on the boat again.

I'd tried everything I could to enthuse some of the group into what a wonderful country China is, but all I was getting was talk of food back home, T.V. and the beaches in Thailand and Australia that they were going to visit. They had played a hell of a lot of games of "shit-head" too. So the group certainly bonded well and I suppose they got more out of the trip than what they were expecting, but some of them just didn't want to be there. Then, after trying my upmost for two weeks, I finally stumbled upon what the group actually needed. We were on the boat with our unfortunate guide, Tracey, who couldn't get anyone to do the activities. She was at her wits end, wondering what she had done wrong and why no-body was interested in "The Romance of the Three Kingdom" saga or the "Ghost City". Then we went into the bar and found the group, not long settled with a bottle of vodka and eight cans of Red Bull. This was washed down with some beer. After dinner the boat crew began a performance that ended in a game show. Everyone got up to throw the giant inflatable dice across the dance floor and everyone drank some more. At midnight we were all singing Karaoke and having a great time. The conversations were in full flow and The English couple Dave and Diane started to tell us more about what they did back home. We knew that they were film graduates and has just broken into some live television work, but only now did Diane say that some of it had been filming for the Playboy Channel. This had earned them the money to fund the trip, you would never have guessed to look at them. Joe then did a turn on a microphone with me backing, another great laugh. Once the boat crew had closed the bar and chucked us out of there, we went back to my cabin, where it all got messy. I exposed myself (all be it unwittingly) when I was staggering around and Dave made a grab for my shorts, pulling them down over my arse. That sort of brought the night to a close.

In Yangshuo I showed the group around the bars as usual and we all did the cooking school. Pam was going back to Australia for the winter, it seemed like everyone was leaving. When I looked at the schedules, which were sent out every week, it showed Tour leaders as being on a final trip for the season. There had been a lot of people who had originally said that they wanted to continue leading over the winter, but one by one they were dropping out. As I had agreed to work through winter, I had also agreed to work trips to and from Vietnam, as these were the only ones that ran throughout the whole year. China gets very cold in winter. Yangshuo was one of the few places that I'd be returning to in China on my next trips as my employers had rota'd me for a couple of trips between Hanoi and Hong Kong, coming through Yangshuo.

As we were talking and playing with Pams "cooking school dog" she told me that when she returned after New Year, she hoped that the dog would still be there. I asked why, so she told me the story. The previous year, she had gone back to Australia for Christmas and New Year, which also co-insides with Chinese New Year. Unfortunately for Pam and her other dog, this is a big celebration where dog is a specialty. When Pam returned, the dog was not there, the neighbours had eaten it. They had decided that as the dog lived in the cooking school, it was well fed and should be tasty. They also didn't see the dog as being owned by Pam, it was just another dog, like it could be a stray chicken scavenging at the school yard. Pam was obviously upset when she got back and found out, but her neighbours just couldn't understand. As way of making up to her, they offered her an invite to eat with them the following New Year. Pam declined, as she knew that dog would be on the menu. Whilst I was in Yangshuo I got on with planning my Vietnam trip. I had a week off at the end of this trip, so I decided it would be a valuable use of my time to go there and suss the place out. It is 3 years since I was last in Hanoi or Ha Long Bay and I thought that leading an entire trip blind would just be tempting fate. It just so happened that Esmeray was finishing her last ever trip for the company in Beijing. This was just before I finished in HK. She had to start her "Amazing Race" trip in Ho Chi Minh City just after I would have to return from my time off. Perfect, we decided to spend a week in and around Hanoi. Now all I needed was a visa. Bruce in the office said that the company could sort this out, so rather than me running around H.K. for two days, then trying to get a cheap flight, I decided to go with Bruce's suggestion and booked a flight there and then for the day after my trip finished.

32. Back in Chunking Mansions,
1/11/07 (Chunking Curry House, H.K.)

Back in Chunking Mansions
And a dormitory bunk
Walking the roads of neon
Avoiding getting drunk
A little bit too much time to kill
On the hunt for something new
Wrestling myself control from seeking the thrill
Of the big city seedy life I belong to

A kebab and a curry
For not much money
In the emporium city
With all the nations around me.

In Hong Kong again and I sent off a reminder to Bruce about my visa before going out with the group to watch the end of trip "light show" on Hong Kong Harbour. True to form, the three English girls could not make the appointed meeting time and Berti, who had been simmering away now for three weeks finally said what we all knew. "You English girls, I have waited for you every day, again and again and now I will miss the light show because of you". He was the only one of the group leaving in the morning. I decided to spend the following day in Hong Kong as well, rather than going to and from Shekou, wasting time just travelling over the next 24 hours. The Shekou apartment had been badly managed and the facilities, computers, T.V. etc. had not been looked after and I had been told that they were in need of repair. I thought that there would probably not be a working printer for my Visa confirmation, so I stayed in Chungking Mansions again and got all my paperwork done between there and the West Hotel. I had a chance meeting with some guys who were producing an alternative "What's on" magazine for Chengdu, called "Chengdoo" something definitely worth checking out for later. I picked up my flight tickets and emailed Bruce again. He replied, telling me not to panic and that if the worse came to the worse I could get a visa on arrival at the airport. I texted Esmeray in Beijing and she replied later that day saying that Bruce had told her the same thing. I went out with my last group again that night and had a really good last goodbye with them. Lots of happy hour drinks at the Eight Fine Irishmen and turning little Diane on her head for good measure. To Bruce's credit, I did see the emails that he'd sent to the Vietnam contact a few days before stating that I needed a visa a.s.a.p. because I had booked a flight. This still didn't help me when no visa arrived and it was time for me to board the plane. Nevertheless, customs waved my British passport through and I was soon on my way to Vietnam, without a visa

It's not that easy getting into a Communist country without a visa. Esmeray was waiting at passport control as I explained that I didn't have a visa and was waved back. The conversation went a bit like this:-

Me: "My company said that there would be a visa on arrival for me, I work for..." (hastily show work card and passport)

Customs: "Where is your letter?"

Me: "I don't have one, my company said......"

Customs: "No letter, no visa, you can't come in without a visa"

I tried to ring the contact in Hanoi, but no reply. There was a lot of standing around for me whist the customs officials dealt with other people. It looked like they weren't bothering with me because I was a cut and dried case. As the man said, "no letter, no visa, no entry". I rang Esmeray and asked if she could find the internet and try to print off the letter (if indeed it had arrived). I went to the customs again and tried to explain this. I was given a choice. "$150 for visa". Well, no point in trying to argue the point. Out came $150 and a short while later, still panicking that I'd unknowingly bribed the wrong official, my passport was returned, with a visa inside. A short time later we were getting ripped off by taxi drivers who were getting lost trying to find our hotel in a big city. Back to normal then.

I have to inform everybody about the name of the Vietnamese currency. It is called the "Dong". There are about 31,000 Dong to the British Pound. Or to put it another way, my British pound is the equivalent to 31,000 Vietnamese Dong. This is very impressive. I re-iterated this fact many times to Esmeray, letting her know exactly how much Vietnamese Dong would be needed to equate just one pound of mine. Esmeray had been to Hanoi a couple of months earlier, so her memory of the place was much fresher than mine from 3 years previously. We had a wander around the Old Town, narrow crowded streets filled by motorcycles coming from every direction. There is an art form to crossing the road, you just walk into the mass of on-coming traffic and have faith that it will weave around you. The nearest thing that I can compare it to is swimming into a school of fish, or possibly flying with birds as they all move with a collective consciousness around you. We headed off to a night market for something to eat and drink and felt very content with the warm weather and feeling that we were sort of "on holiday". The next day we went off around the city. I introduced myself to the Victory Hotel, where my Vietnam to Hong Kong trips would be based, then found a deal on a two day excursion to Cat Ba Island. My trips were going there as well and I needed to take a look at the place. I also had a contact there, Mr. Hai, who I thought I should introduce myself to. That night we headed off to Beer Hoi Corner, where you drink glasses of beer on the street for 7p, yes, 7p. There is even a kebab stall opposite. I'd just hit the jackpot. Esmeray drinks as much, if not more than I do and we extended the night by going to an underground reggae bar. In Hanoi, there is a curfew around midnight, but all that happens is that the bars pull down the shutters whilst everyone inside continues with the drinking and dancing. For those in the know, there is a lot happening behind seemingly closed doors. Things were working out just fine.

Our journey to Cat Ba Island started with a four hour, tour bus drive to Ha Long Bay where we boarded a "Junk boat" for our 1 night stop-over on the boat. The boats have a lot of character, wooden vessels in a traditional "Chinese Junk" style, some with sails and all with high prows and sterns. They have all been enlarged and the design adapted to fill them with tourists, but the charm is still there. The scenery was fantastic with many little boats anchored in the bay between the Karst Islands. Girls paddled up selling market goods (and beer) between the boats, all conical hats and facemasks, shouting and laughing. That evening, the sun went down over the islands and bays, the stars shone reflecting in the water and the lights from the other bobbing boats made this a night to remember. There were around thirty others on the vessel, mostly young and up for a party. This involved a lot of drinking and staying up late and even singing karaoke. The following day we arrived on Cat Ba Island, and unlike the others on the trip who wanted to go hiking (seemed too much like work), we just lazed around. In the afternoon there was a trip to Monkey Island. It must be a good couple of years since I sat on a beach, or swam in the sea. It was near 30 degrees, and the water was warm once you'd got over the initial shock of getting in. I didn't realise how much I'd needed to do this. Just sitting around, doing nothing, not a care in the world.

In the evening we got motor cycle taxis and went to another beach. There is something magical about racing along an esplanade in summer, the wind racing through your hair, on the back of a bike. Here we walked along the wooden board walk that skirted the cliff from bay to secluded bay. I'm told it's busier in high season, but at that time, there was just the two of us and the odd random tourist. The sunset was spectacular over the bay. We had already decided that we wanted to stay longer when Mr. Hai replied to our text message. We could meet him for beer Hoi later. Jim, an American tour leader who I trained with in Beijing was also in town, and joined us. I'd not seen him since that first week. Mr. Hai said we could stay at his hotel the following night, so the beer flowed and we snacked on warm quail eggs that we dipped in a home style condiment made from mixing salt, pepper, chilly, and lime juice.

Day two on Cat Ba was another beach day. Once we'd arranged with our tour company that we were staying longer and moved our bags to Mr. Hai's hotel. Afterwards, we walked along the wooden board walks again between the bays. Jim joined us in the afternoon and we returned to his hotel for the most impressive sunset over the bay. The light on the anchored boats turning on as the golden sun dropped behind the karst islands. The stars slowly appearing and the many more stars, on the boats, floating in the bay. It was just about perfect. It was almost too good to be true. Then we had another night out in the couple of bars dotted along the sea front.

33. Inspiration 05-08-09/11/07, (Cat Ba & Hanoi)

Inspiration, like a cool morning breeze
Comes to me in this too perfect place
Suddenly, I'm in summer and paradise
Forgetting who I am as I caress your face

Bobbing, red flagged, wooden boats
Yellow stars blowing atop the masts
Girls in boats, selling drinks
From underneath a conical hat and facemask

We talked of yearning for the riches of the poor
Romanticising though we have much more
I, a child that dropped through the safety net
Bodies come to the surface of the water that I'd rather forget

I nearly spoil it all, nearly rant
Nearly dragged back to teenage Blackburn jealousy
I didn't want to become
A Monty-python sketch parody

But it jerks me back to reality once more
It's getting cold, the dream turns sour
And I know you're never going to be the girl for me
Though you inspire me with poetry

34. Untitled 06-09/11/07 (Cat Ba & Hanoi)

Waking up to a window
Filled with a blue sky
Like a painted picture
Of some island paradise
Some place you only dream of
A tropical fantasy
The beach that no one knows about
Where we all want to be

Through the hills of Cat Ba
Speeding our way there
Motorcycle Emptiness
Blowing through my hair
And an almost deserted beach
Then swimming out to sea
In the warm ocean til sunset
And the balcony view, never to forget

Watching the saffron sun
Dropping through the azure sky
And the clear reflection
A shining pathway across the bay
Like a golden road to journey on
A paradise road to the horizon
Then as it sets, kissing the island
A wish on the last glimpse of the diamond

Dragging the colours down the sky
Like a washed out rainbow
Changing from blue through to pinks

And mirrored in the glass bay below
With the floating village on changing colours
The jumble of wooden houses on water
An ever changing home setting
The floating village of wood and netting

The sky darkens and darkens
Around the karst - islands
Then in silhouette, then darkness all around
Til the nighttime fills the sky to the ground
And the lights come on in Cat Ba Bay
The floating houses and the family
Keeping a home light on
One home, one heart, one light, I look on

I can see one star in the sky
And a hundred stars in the bay.

It was very difficult to leave. But leave we had to, and were back in Hanoi looking for Hotels by midafternoon. We found a cheap place in the Old Town and I got in touch with Steven, and Bruce, because I heard they were also in town now. We arranged to meet at Le Pub. Steven is one of the best people I've met in China, Bruce is my boss and I knew this would be a bit of a strange night out. Bruce asked me how I'd gone on with my Visa on entry. I related the story, to which he said "You can't do that...they shouldn't even have let you leave Hong Kong". Well, that was nice to know, and only 4 days and 1000 miles too late. Nevertheless, we all like a drink and went to a couple of bars before Bruce left us in KOTO. If you ever get a chance, go there because the bar/restaurant is staffed by "trainees" who used to be "street children" who get skills and qualifications through working at KOTO. The initials stand for Know One Teach One and I'd visited the place five years previously on a trip with a tour group. Bruce didn't stay too long, so the three of us found more places to drink in and ended up drinking the last bottles by a street vendor at around

2am. Esmeray and I got a taxi back to the hotel to find that it was shut up for the night. This is pretty usual and a bit of hammering on the door usually rouses the bloke who sleeps on guard. Every hotel has a sleeping guard and a couple of motorbikes in the reception. Unfortunately, there was no bloke on guard; there was nobody around at all.

After a good half an hour, banging, shouting, trying to scale the outside of the building and contemplating sleeping by the lake, I decided that I could possibly break in. I was quite pissed and don't know how I came up with the idea, but somehow I lifted the metal shutter and squeezed underneath. Then, I wriggled myself feet first through a gap between the glass doors. They were only tied together with a loose chain. I'm a lot skinnier than I was this time last year and also a lot fitter. I made it, feet first and wriggling and I was inside. I was trying to figure out how to open the doors when Esmeray also got herself under the now buckled metal shutter. Ok, so far, so good. Then it all went wrong. There was nowhere else for her to go and as she tried to move, there was a "crack!" and yes, there was a crack, splitting the glass door. I don't think the 3 meals a day on the comfort trip had helped. Getting in was a lot easier for her now, but how the hell were we supposed to explain this. Time to sleep on it.

The following morning we woke to find the hotel and associated trip booking office and internet cafe closed. The glass door was cordoned off. It didn't look good. I'd decided that if they asked that the only honorable thing was to come clean and pay for the damage. Accidents happen. Surprisingly, nothing was said as we went for breakfast. We checked out an hour later, the hotel and business still closed, feeling very guilty. We walked down to the Vietnam Airlines shuttle bus and Esmeray paid her $2 to the airport and we said goodbye, wondering if or when we would ever meet again. This is a strange lifestyle to lead. I went on to the Victory Hotel and checked in for the night and booked a taxi to the airport for the following day.

I ran into Bruce again that evening and he suggested that I could share his taxi to the airport the following morning. It was all booked through the Victory, so it seemed a good idea. At 7am we were on our way to the airport. At check in, I couldn't see my flight number. Bruce said something about the date and I said it was the 10th. He looked at me quizzically; his flight was for the 9th. You have to remember that he is my boss, in a travel company, where it is my job to get people around on transport from destination to destination. Yes, I'd got the wrong day. I was 24 hours early for my flight. Very embarrassing. I got a minibus back to the Victory and checked in again for another night. I think they were also wondering what type of fool the new tour leader was too.

The next day was a hectic flight back to Hong Kong, a boat to Shekou to pick up my cold weather stuff that I'd stashed there in May and then back the following day to start another trip. This was going to be the smallest group I'd ever had. Only five people. A brother and sister in their early 20's with Malaysian/Chinese parentage was going to be my challenge this time. I also had a girl whose mum was Filipino, a Scottish girl just finishing her Round the World trip and an English girl just starting hers. That's a high percentage of girls, and I knew that the weather was getting worse by the day. Being an Essence of China trip, things should go smoothly. For those with the Asian background, I was worried that they'd judge me as a foreigner, not knowing enough or being able to give them the authentic China experience. Their parents had filled with them with stories of the bad old days, understandable, but I thought I could show them a new China, while still talking about the politics and the social aspect of the country as only a foreigner who lives here can do. We met my Chinese friends in Yangshuo, and I even took them for dinner in Yangshuo Park at Megs place. I had made a good start.

Whilst I was in Yangshuo, I ran into Eugenie for the first time in months. As we chatted at bar 98, she told me that she was thinking of going to England to study and asked my advice as to what University to recommend and the pros and cons of living in London or elsewhere in the U.K. Whilst there, Amy also called me, she was completing her job application form and needed a little information. Tang had also been helping her too and I told her what I could, saying that she would have no problem getting the job. That was definitely something to look forward to for the next season. I also completed the booking form for my next trip. My first one from Hanoi to Hong Kong. The Irish girl from a couple of trips ago had continued to text me whilst she was in Nanjing and we'd been getting along fine. Her acupuncture course had not been going so well. She had come to the conclusion that she had a phobia of putting needles into people, not a good start if you want to peruse a career in acupuncture. She had passed the first part of the course, but was now mostly hanging around waiting for the second part to be over in an ever colder Nanjing. I'd told her which my future trip plans were and had previously suggested to her to join up on the Vietnam trip, just to give her a bit of a break. This is when she told me that she'd also booked onto my next trip, as a passenger, and lo and behold, there her name was on the booking sheet.

Jane left town that day so we had a 10 min catch up. Zef, Jim (who gave me the low down on my Vietnam trip) and Steven "Rockhard" another experienced Australian tour leader were also in town so we all caught up for a drink. I also asked Farmer Tang to guide us on the bikes. He did a fantastic job, visiting a Bai Jiu distillery and brick works on the way before we ate in his house. At the bai jiu distillery we saw how rice wine was made, the traditional farmers' way. For want of a better word, it is "moonshine". The rice is cooked and left to ferment. The mash is then put into a big jar, around four feet high. From this, the alcohol is slowly boiled off and it drips, as it condenses, into a jar of rice wine. Farmer Tang has now got his own Facebook page and is officially the most popular person in Yangshuo, though he doesn't know how to get on to Facebook and hasn't seen the page. I promised that I would check it out and show it to him and I booked him there and then for my next trip from Vietnam going through the Long Ji rice terraces.

After an uneventful Three gorges trip, I had another night out in Chongqing with Amy and her friend Kimi. Amy had bought her apartment and had started to decorate it. She had sent me the pictures, walls covered in flowery wallpaper. She said I could come and visit, and stay with her but it was beyond me when this could ever be possible. She asked me if I could come for the Chinese New Year, but all I could say was that as a Westerner, I had to work Chinese New Year because all the Chinese tour leaders had booked this time off. We got to talking about names, hers is Ren (her family name) Li Juan, which roughly translates into beautiful, girl with beauty like the moon. Most girls' names in China are of this ilk. Often, a girl will be nicknamed Xiao "..*something*...." this means little "..*something*....", so I asked if I should call her Xiao Ren. Unfortunately, this translates as a small, or bad person and Xiao Li Juan doesn't work either. She said a lot of her friends called her Lao Ren, the Lao being a sign of respect, but usually reserved for older people or teachers. That didn't work for me either, so we kept to Amy. She asked me if this name had any meaning in English and I said I thought it meant "to be loved". She was a bit put out at this, saying "to be... you mean at some time I will be loved, but not now?" I tried to correct this "lost in translation" moment, before giving up as we just kept laughing about it. Other things had moved fast and Amy was going to be interviewed to be a tour leader for the next year, we had a lot to talk about and once again it ended around 2am, this time sharing noodles at the street stalls.

We moved on to Chengdu and then to Emei Shan again. As for my passengers, the group got involved in everything at the start, although the Brits found the food and cultural differences a bit much. There were goodbyes to Patrick, Nathan, George, Betty and Harry in Emei Shan. There were final text messages from Lyn and Jane and emails from other leaders as they left China for the winter. Most people had decided to go home for Christmas and New Year. The Chinese winter had little appeal for them and less than a dozen Leaders would be needed to lead the trips. Esmeray updated me with her adventures as she got stuck with passengers without visas on her final "Amazing Race" trip, so they never completed it. Then she sprained an ankle when she was supposed to start her Dive Masters diving course in Thailand. It was all coming to an end. Lyn had also been in touch and we were in Xi'an for a couple of hours as I arrived and she departed. It all felt so strange, people moving on, going home and I was still running a trip and off to do more trips in Southern China and Vietnam. There was a definite change in the air. The weather was also turning colder and there were less people than usual at the South Gate for the singing and dancing in Xi'an. Then in Beijing, it was actually cold as we ended the trip, walking around Hou Hai Lake.

35. Seasons End

(A) 08/10/07 Train Kunming - Guilin

I am far, far away from my country
Far from the land of hope and glory
Where those feet in ancient times
Over the green and pleasant land climbed
Where the unicorn walks with the lion
Through the English meadow and secret garden
Where I can pick the red, red rose
My homeland, my heartland, it feels so close

Oh I wish that I was with my friends
Now it's come to seasons end
But I'm on my own, on a train again
At seasons end

Continents adrift. I have traveled
Crossed mountains and deserts. Oceans I've sailed
Now I'm thinking of home from across the world
Wishing on a star, when all I have is email
But if we are looking at the same star in the sky
Then maybe some part of me might fly

And somehow I can be back home again
Back home amongst friends at seasons end

Let the wave wash over me again
I find myself crying at seasons end
Thinking of home, thinking of friends
I have come to seasons end

It makes my breath shake in my body
Small heart attacks in a swirling melody
Six senses crashing down through the ether
In the colliding universe in my head that's on fire
And running away, so out of control
I can do nothing about it all
At the mercy of all these feelings again
That have built like a wave to crash at seasons end

Let the wave crash over me again
I find myself crying at seasons end
Thinking of home, thinking of friends
I have come to seasons end

I have written my diary
I have written some poetry
And I just want to talk to somebody
Who knows me

(B) 17/10/07 City Hotel, Xi'an

Saying my first goodbyes to my first new friends
How I held you and talked of the good times
In a few moments we said hello, and goodbye and then
Walked out of each other's lives like it never happened

Just wanting to bump into somebody around the bend
As I walk from the Bell Tower with emails to send
And last month to write about, the good times I spent
Wouldn't it be good to share all those good times again

(C) 18/10/07 Train from Xi'an to Chengdu

We had one last night in Xi'an
Back in the place where it all began
Talking til close outside Music Man
Then noodles on the street til five a.m.
Watching as the rainstorm blew in
You stayed with me, just best friends then
And now we have yet another parting
Another goodbye at this seasons end

Then all too soon I'm on a train
With another piped music piano playing
Another Chinese love song about leaving
And music fills the empty compartment I'm staying in
Fills my head with melody, my eyes star filling
And all too soon I'm being taken
Over the mountains and the far distance
Closer to the ending of the season

(D) 24/10/07 Yangtze River Boat

A smile as I leave a well-worn bedroom,
And imagining a hand in hand on the street
A nod to the buildings that have been my home
Where I have left a little piece of me in the concrete
This will always be something to return to
Whoever I become in the years in the future
And although no-one else will understand what I've been
through
There will always be this Middle Kingdom, like a book to re-
visit when I'm older

(E) 21/11/07 Emei

Then there was my last two trips
Moments like Buddha in the swirling mist
The people that came and quickly went
Blurred at the edges of the 6 months I spent
In 100 hotel rooms that I passed through
And people I got to know, but never really knew

All jumbled and jostling with the thoughts of home
And the dreams that play in my moviedrome
To the soundtrack that brings me memories
And makes me think about how it is
And wondering how everything is going to be
Pricked by the daydream of how it could be
Worrying if all my mistakes would come
Back to haunt me, weigh up what I've done
These little dreams, that come out of the mist
The words I've written, the girls I've kissed

Then today, I was above the mist
And the sea of clouds, the mountain in frost
Contemplating exactly where I am
In the incense and chanting of Emei Shan
My worries somewhere down below
What the future brings now, I can't control or know
But I'm here, here now, whatever the gods send
Here and now is where I'd rather be in the end

At this seasons end
This is seasons end.

In Beijing I was surprised to find anybody else in the office as so many other leaders had left for the winter. Over the previous month I had run into a number of them, others I had heard about through the "grape vine". When I had seen Eugiene in Yangshuo, she told me that almost all of the Chinese leaders from her intake were now finishing. Only her, Senior Leader Suzy Li, John He, Ying and Nicole Tan would come back after the winter and "Chinese New Year" break. Of the westerners from the previous intake, there was just Sharon Black, Big Nigel, Mill, Stephen "Rockhard" and Zef returning. There had been new leaders brought in over the year, and I had met Eugiene's trainee "Yolanda". I had also met Baidi Li, as she trained with Sheila and had tried to get her to Monkey Jane's to play beer pong. Merrick was another new leader and was from a poor family in Gansu Province, there were already rumours of him not taking the local guides and pocketing the money for himself.

Of the Three Mongolians from training, I had not seen anything all year. Janie, my co-trainee was returning to the States for Christmas and New Year. Her first solo trip had been a nightmare, with an American police woman as the main problem passenger, but had also to contend with all the young opinionated English "gap-year" students as well. No one had taken her seriously. They were testing her all of the way and the police woman was saying from the very beginning that she wanted a more experienced leader, preferably a Chinese one. She had got very bad feedback from that trip and had considered quitting there and then. The way that the company works, is that you need to get a certain number of points on your feedback and with her having such a bad start, it was always going to be difficult for her to make the grade and keep her position. Since her fist trip, things had improved, though she was lucky that the management had understood how badly her first trip had affected her scores and would let her back for a second season. On the few times that I had run into Steven, he was usually telling me a story about bedding one of his passengers, he didn't seem to be too fussy, as I'd seen a couple of them and would never have considered it myself. He also told me about his one and only encounter with Chinese leader Ying. He had agreed to share a room with her in Hong Kong and had come back after his last night with his group and gone straight to bed, In the morning, he was wakened when Ying, came out of the shower, said "hi" and jumped into bed with him. Ying was unlike most Chinese girls and Steven was glad for it for the next 24 hours until she left to start a trip. He was still on probation, as his drinking was still being monitored. Jane was also still on probation. She had done her first trip, completely "blind" as she had left her trip notes somewhere in Xi'an. She had put up with English girls, who would refuse to go to the toilet for days, and demand people to move their bags. Jane saw this as more to do with them being jealous spoilt bitches than anything else. Over the year she had been flying by the seat of her pants and just about pulling it off with minimum preparation. Her romance with the Australian businessman had come to nothing. This had actually been an inspiration to Lyn, who saw Jane as a role model, a "force of nature" as she put it. Lyn had also had a run in with management, namely, for sleeping with her passengers. She had slept with two on the same trip and this had got back in the feedback and she was being told that she had to keep her mind more focused on the whole group, not just the handsome young men.

I had seen Tang a few times, especially as she would return to Yangshuo in her time between trips and come to Bar 98 to meet the other leaders. I hadn't seen Yu since her first disastrous training trip, but had heard that her leading life was not going well and would have to undertake a second training trip if she was to continue in the next season. Thai Chili was having a break from the cold in her native Thailand. Beata was going back to Hungary for the winter as there were no Tibet trips until the Spring, the climate is far too harsh to run them. Pierre was almost a native Chinese, having lived in the country for six years and was only going back to Quebec to see family for Christmas, then would be back "home" again. When I talked to him, he was full of plans. He wanted to run his own trips, set up his own company, open a guest house and had even gone so far as looking at opening a paint ball park in Yangshuo. Ada was signing up for another year, though it was putting her relationship with her boyfriend under a lot of strain.

All these people had said that they intended to return the following year, there was a growing number who had said that they would not. Firstly, Gary, had got a job working with our companies new U.S. arm in Colorado. I had been told that Tibet expert Bella had gone to work as the senior leader for our competitor G.A.P. Adventures. When I had last seen Jim in Hanoi and then Yangshuo, he was telling me about his plans to open a cafe-bar with his Vietnamese girlfriend in Sapa. Then, I talked to Sheila and she said that she was leaving "because it was too hard". As a leader of many years and countries, I needed to know why she thought this. She told me that everything, from the Chinese language, to not being able to communicate the simplest thing to the Chinese as you would a westerner was the biggest problem and not only for her, but for the groups she was leading. The groups were having problems to adapting to the culture shock of China and Sheila couldn't help. Sarah had decided that she wanted to go back to her life in Shanghai, she had left a job in tourism there in order to become a leader. Philip had done a complete turn around and was the biggest surprise. He had decided that he wanted to go back to Australia and complete a University course.

I had run into Ting Ting a couple of times since she had helped me buy my phone at the beginning of the season. On our last meeting, she had jumped from her bike in the middle of Yangshuo West Street and run over to hug me. She was always asking me, and others for help and meeting me meant an opportunity for asking about bars in Hong Kong, as she didn't drink and her groups did. I had also heard the story of her taking both her mum and her boyfriend on a trip. Her passengers had rightfully complained about this. She was still hoping that her boyfriend would "do the right thing for a Chinese girl" and marry her. I had also bumped into Jay on a bus to Yangshuo. He had been given some time off from working with our company in order to go back to some of the guiding that he was doing before. He was working with US college kids and he actually got them to spend a day working in a rice paddy during harvest time. They had never worked so hard in their life. On the surface of it, he looked like a real "right-on" tour guide, but then, we had also heard of his pursuit of Ting Ting and any other girl. His afore-mentioned intent to get in touch with his Chinese roots seemed a lot to do with getting in touch with Chinese girls.

There were also changes in the office. Bruce was acting manager, but only until there was a replacement and a complete re-structuring. We could only guess what the new season would bring

Unfortunately, no-one had any idea where my flight tickets to Hanoi were. I was supposed to be flying in 48 hours and starting my first trip in Vietnam. The group did the trip to the Wall and we had a minor accident en route. This is where Chinese bureaucracy takes over. We are not supposed to move vehicles after an accident until the police come to investigate. We waited half an hour and then actually both us and the car we hit drove to the police station. There we waited for another 2 hours, me texting and trying to get a replacement bus. One finally arrived, getting us to the wall at 2pm. This meant that we would have to walk the 10k in under 4 hours. Not the experience that people who'd waited so long to walk the wall had paid for. Still, I put the spin on it that we'd be the first group to see the sunset and that we did, only descending when it was getting dark, on the verge of it being dangerous. The temperatures plummeting to freezing, making the climb treacherous and there is only starlight to see by. Still, that is adventure travel and this adventure was about to take me to Vietnam, then, who knows where?

Cast of Main Characters in order of appearance.

Me – A new trainee tour-leader in China

Jack – An ex-flat mate in London

Lindsay and Mike (AKA Moo) – Flatmates renting my place in London

Hannah – Asia Regional Manager at Adventure Travel

Cathy – Manager for China at Adventure Travel

Julia – Manager for Russia at Adventure Travel

Bruce "Bear" – Senior Tour Leader at Adventure Travel

Li – Office assistant at Adventure Travel. Chinese girl

Steve – Trainee leader from Australia

Sheila – Experienced leader doing training for China, from Australia

Jane – Trainee leader from England

Philip – Trainee leader from Australia

Ting Ting – Trainee leader from China

Yu – Trainee leader from China

Thai-chili – Experienced leader doing training for China, from Thailand

Pierre – Trainee leader from Canada who had been living in China

Beata – Trainee leader with experience of tours in Tibet, from Hungary

Bella – Trainee leader with experience of tours in Tibet, from Europe

Ada – Trainee leader from Germany

Jay – Trainee leader from Singapore

Janet – Trainee leader from U.S.

Jim – Trainee leader from the U.S. interested in "active trips"

Lyn – Trainee leader from U.S.

Sarah – Trainee leader from U.S.

Gary – Trainee leader from U.S. who had been living in China

Pam – Owner of the Yangshuo Cooking School and ex leader from Australia

Snow – Experienced Chinese leader and owner of bar 98 in Yangshuo

Bataar – Trainee leader from Mongolia, who was operating Mongolian trips

Bolo – Trainee leader from Mongolia who worked for Bataar

Bola – Trainee leader from Mongolia who worked for Bataar

Esmeray – Experienced leader from Turkey, beginning training in China

Eugenie – Experienced Chinese leader and trainer

Annie and Adrian – Mother and son, passengers on my training trip

Joe – Passenger on my training trip

Steve and Sarah – Passengers on my training trip

Jake and Jill – Passengers on my training trip

Mike and Michele – Passengers on my training trip

Emma – Chinese tour guide for the Hutongs in Beijing

Ren Ming – Tour operator and businessman in Xi'an

Jim – Tour guide for the Terracotta Warriors in Xi'an

Chicory – Tour guide and tour operator for Chengdu

Patrick – Tour operator for Emei Shan

George – Tour guide for Emei Shan

Nathan – Tour guide for Emei Shan

Betty and Harry – Owners of the Hard Wok Café on Emei Shan

Ollie – Tour leader with the Adventure Company

Amy – Tour guide on the Yangtze River Boat

Emily – Tour guide for the Yangtze River Dam or the Boat

Suzy Li – Experienced Chinese leader

George Chan – Tour guide in Yangshuo

Monkey Jane – Owner of the guest house and roof top bar in Yangshuo

Henry and Henrietta – Passengers on my first solo trip

Graham and Geraldine – Passengers on my first solo trip

Gerry and Georgina – Passengers on my first solo trip

Alison – Passenger on my first solo trip

Melody Wang – Tour operator in Beijing

Xiao Feng – Tour operator in Beijing

Eva – Experienced Chinese leader

Meg – Tour guide in Yangshuo

Rosemary – Tour operator in Yangshuo

Abigail – Passenger on my second trip

Martin and Maureen - Passengers on my second trip

Bob and Rachel - Passengers on my second trip

Dave - Passenger on my second trip

Joan - Passenger on my second trip

Andrea - Passenger on my second trip

Dr. Lillyi – Doctor of medicine and massage in Yangshuo

Colleen – Passenger on my third trip

Jim and Janet – Father and daughter passengers on my third trip

Farmer Tang – Tour guide for Yangshuo and Long Ji rice terraces

Sonny – Passenger on my fourth trip

Drujia – Tour guide for Amdo Tibet

Margo – Tour guide in Tiger Leaping Gorge

Helen – Passenger on my fifth trip

Jack – Passenger on my sixth trip

Pete – Passenger on my sixth trip

Pat – Passenger on my sixth trip

Natalie – Passenger on my sixth trip

Sandra – Passenger on my sixth trip

Pauline – Tour operator in Kunming

Berti – Passenger on my seventh trip

Joe and Jane – Passengers on my seventh trip

Dave and Diane – Passengers on my seventh trip

Kevin – Tour guide for the Forbidden City and Beijing

Mr Hai – Tour operator on Cat Ba Island